EVERY ONE THAT BELIEVETH

Every One That Believeth

*Expository Addresses on St. Paul's
Epistle to the Romans*

By
HAROLD J. OCKENGA, Ph.D.
Minister, Park Street Church, Boston

WIPF & STOCK · Eugene, Oregon

Wipf and Stock Publishers
199 W 8th Ave, Suite 3
Eugene, OR 97401

Every One That Believeth
Expository Addresses on St. Paul's Epistle to the Romans
By Ockenga, Harold John and Rosell, Garth M.
Copyright©1942 by Ockenga, Harold John
ISBN 13: 978-1-5326-1737-9
Publication date 1/25/2017
Previously published by Fleming H. Revell Company, 1942

DEDICATED
TO
MY BELOVED FATHER,
HERMAN OCKENGA

FOREWORD

THESE sermons are printed exactly as they were dictated for preaching at Park Street Church. I always gradually prepare my sermons during the week and on Saturday morning sit down to dictate them to my secretary who types them as they are dictated. The preaching of them on the next morning is without reference to the manuscript, but generally follows it very closely, although in preaching there are often extemporaneous interjections which come through the inspiration of the moment. These, of course, lift the level of preaching above anything which can be prepared beforehand and give it its direct sense of authority from God.

I do not present these as any scholarly attainment, but merely as an example of preaching in the book of Romans. I have freely used every source upon which I could lay my hands. The incessant demands made upon the time of a city pastor prevent him being what might be called a scholar, but by the utilization of every source of information, he may preach close to life and true to the Bible. I am willing to have any one else use this as a source in his own preaching, as I have used many other books.

My own conviction is that we must get back to expository preaching, beginning, as did Zwingli the Swiss reformer, in the first verse of the book of Matthew and preaching right through the New Testament, so that our congregations may be truly conversant with the doctrines, precepts and practices of New Testament Christianity. I have so preached through various books of the Bible and now submit this book of Romans as an example.

The most helpful books in the form of commentaries on the book of Romans which I found were as follows:

"The New Testament," by Henry Alford
"Romans Verse By Verse," by William R. Newell
"The Epistle to the Romans," by H. P. Liddon
"The Commentary on the Romans," by F. Godet
"The Biblical Commentary on The New Testament," by Hermann Olshausen
"The Commentary on The Epistle to the Romans," by Charles Hodge
"The Commentary on St. Paul's Epistle to the Romans," by Friedrich Adolph Philippi

FOREWORD

"Critical and Doctrinal Commentary," by William G. T. Shedd
"Lectures on the Epistle to the Romans," by H. A. Ironside
"Exposition of the Romans," by J. N. Darby
"Notes on The Epistle to the Romans," by W. Kelly
"Lectures on the Epistle of Paul to the Romans," by Thomas Chalmers
"Commentary on the Epistle to the Romans," by Moses Stuart

Numerous other works were referred to, such as those of Joseph A. Beet, Handley C. G. Moule, John Albert Bengel, Wm. S. Plumer, James Denney, John Calvin, John Taylor, E. H. Gifford, F. A. G. Tholuck, and William Sanday and Arthur Headlam.

Every sermon in this series was preached over the radio to a large New England audience. It is really the response from this radio congregation which led me to put the sermons in print. I send them forth with the prayer that the reading of them will seal the redemption of many lives by this Gospel of God.

H.J.O.

Boston, Mass.

CONTENTS

	PAGE
I. THE GOSPEL OF WHICH TO BE PROUD (Rom. 1:1-17)	11
II. THE WRATH OF GOD (Rom. 1:18-32)	20
III. THE FALSE SECURITY OF THE SELF-RIGHTEOUS (Rom. 2:1-16)	30
IV. RELIGION VERSUS SALVATION (Rom. 2:17-29; 3:1-8)	40
V. THE SINNER'S PICTURE PAINTED BY GOD (Rom. 3:9-23)	50
VI. THE RIGHTEOUSNESS OF GOD (Rom. 3:24-27)	58
VII. THE RIGHTEOUS SHALL LIVE BY FAITH (Rom. 3:28-4:25)	68
VIII. THE GLORIOUS BENEFITS OF BEING RIGHT WITH GOD (Rom. 5:1-11)	78
IX. THE REIGN OF GRACE THROUGH CHRIST (Rom. 5:12-21)	88
X. THE QUALITY OF LIFE A CHRISTIAN SHOULD POSSESS (Rom. 6:1-23)	98
XI. THE RULE BY WHICH CHRISTIANS LIVE (Rom. 6:14, and 7:1-25)	110
XII. THE INDUBITABLE PROOF OF THE BELIEVER'S SALVATION, DELIVERANCE AND VICTORY (Rom. 8:1-27)	118
XIII. THE HIGHEST, BEST AND MOST WONDERFUL REACHES OF CHRISTIAN DOCTRINE (Rom. 8:28-39)	128
XIV. THE POTTER AND THE CLAY OR GOD'S REJECTION OF THE JEW (Rom. 9:1-33)	139
XV. THE PREACHER AND THE WORD OR THE INTERIM RELATION OF THE JEW TO GOD (Rom. 10:1-21)	151

CONTENTS

		PAGE
XVI.	THE OLIVE TREE AND THE BRANCHES OR GOD'S PLAN THROUGH THE JEW (Rom. 11:1-36)	164
XVII.	A REASONABLE PLEA FOR CHRISTIAN CONDUCT BASED ON DIVINE MERCIES (Rom. 12:1, 2)	175
XVIII.	GOD'S PLAN FOR THE UNITY AND LIFE OF THE CHURCH (Rom. 12:2-21)	185
XIX.	THE CHRISTIAN AS A MEMBER OF THE STATE (Rom. 13:1-14)	196
XX.	SOME PRINCIPLES OF CHRISTIAN CONDUCT (Rom. 14:1-23 and 15:1-7)	208
XXI.	JOY AND PEACE IN BELIEVING (Rom. 15:8-13)	217
XXII.	THE FULLNESS OF THE BLESSING OF THE GOSPEL OF CHRIST (Rom. 15:14-33)	226
XXIII.	THE RECOGNITION OF THE MINISTRY OF WOMEN (Rom. 16:1-16)	236
XXIV.	ESTABLISHED IN CHRIST (Rom. 16:17-27)	246

I

THE GOSPEL OF WHICH TO BE PROUD

TEXT: *"For I am not ashamed of the gospel of Christ; for it is the power of God unto salvation to every one that believeth; to the Jew first, and also to the Greek."*—ROM. 1:1-17.

A NEGATIVE statement is often the most effective way to present a positive fact. In this text, Paul declared he glorified in and was proud of the gospel, although he put it in the words, "I am not ashamed of the gospel of Christ." The gospel of God or as it is called, the gospel of Christ, is a gospel of which to be proud.

The theme of the Epistle to the Romans is "the gospel of God." This means that the gospel is a revelation of God, not of man. It is no system of philosophy, but is God's message to man. Paul said, "For I neither received it of man, neither was I taught it, but by the revelation of Jesus Christ." The origin, truth and authority of the Gospel are God's (alone).

Paul was separated to this gospel from all friends and countrymen and relatives. The means of his separation was a divine call, established before his birth and revealed through Jesus Christ on the Damascus Road, in order that Paul might be a minister unto the Gentiles. I warn you that this gospel of God will make a difference in your life if you listen to it. It will be a divine call that will separate you from everything else as a chosen vessel of God for His service. After you have heard it you will never be the same. You can not be. You will either obey it or disobey it. Happy are you if you choose the former course. Woe unto you if you do not obey its demands upon you. It will be better for you if you do not listen to this gospel than that you should listen and disobey, for your responsibilities will then be less. By the gospel Paul became a bondslave of Jesus Christ.

This gospel was promised before through the prophets in the holy Scriptures. The gospel is not the proclamation of salvation, but it is the good news itself, that is, the fullness of grace and truth given to the world in Christ. The source of the gospel is God. The substance of the gospel is Christ in His redeeming work, and for this reason there is a synonymous use in this chapter in verses one and nine of the gospel of God and the gospel of Christ. The entire New Testament agrees that this gospel was preached before by the prophets of the Old Testament, who told of His sufferings, death and resurrection. "Those things which God before had showed by the mouth of all his prophets, that Christ should suffer, he hath so fulfilled." "To him give all the prophets witness, that through his name whosoever believeth in him shall receive remission of sins." "Christ died for our sins, according to the Scriptures, and that he was buried and that he rose the third day, according to the Scriptures." Thus we have full New Testament authority for the belief that the prophets before announced this gospel of God, which is now declared in the book of Romans. Throughout the ages men looked for the reality of that promise, the substance of which we are to study.

This gospel is defined at the beginning as "concerning his son Jesus Christ our Lord, which was made of the seed of David according to the flesh, and declared to be the son of God with power, according to the spirit of holiness, by resurrection from the dead." Here Christ is announced as the object of the gospel, not as the one who preached the gospel. This gospel concerns Christ. He is the center of our message. "Made of the seed of David, according to the flesh" manifests Him to be the Son of Man, definitely human with a body of flesh, not sinful but capable of temptation. "Declared to be the Son of God, according to the spirit" presents Him as the unique and only begotten of the Father, anointed with the power of God and partaking of Deity. Thus the powerful attestation of the unique resurrection of the Lord Jesus Christ reveals the supernatural in Him, that He is the Son of God. This glory was made plain before all who will believe. Had Christ not risen from the dead, He would not have been the Messiah and the Saviour and our preaching would have been in vain. We would yet be in our sins. But this Son of Man and Son of God is the Lord, our Lord, which places Him in the position of living Master and King of all believers. That Christ should be given such a place is the objective toward which we are aiming in our preaching of the gospel.

By the preaching of this gospel, namely, the presentation of the Person and work of Christ, God's gifts of grace are received by believers, such as, illumination, conviction, conversion, regeneration, guidance, perseverance—all for the purpose of obedience to God, which obedience faith produces among even heathen nations, of which the saints in Rome were excellent examples. Certainly this gospel of God should be mastered by all believers.

THE GOSPEL OF WHICH TO BE PROUD

Paul wrote to "all that be in Rome, beloved of God, called to be saints," that is, to the believers. That there should be saints in Rome in such an environment of heathen corruption makes the excuses of today weak and unsubstantial. If people desire to be saints, they may be saints, for God has provided the means. Would-be believers should be ashamed for conforming to the world. Paul called them "beloved of God," emphasizing the relationship in which Christians stand to God through the redemptive work of Christ. They were "called to be saints," which implies their own consecration to God. In this prelude or introduction as well as in the conclusion to this great Epistle, Paul acknowledged with praise the noteworthy faith of these people. The thankfulness of Paul marked the beginning of most of his epistles and blazes a pathway for any letter or any life.

For a long time he had prepared to preach the gospel among them. If this long standing interest in the Roman Church were surprising to them, Paul calls God as his witness that it was truly deep seated in his heart. Here we get something of an insight into Paul's own spiritual life. He speaks first of his service, rendered in his spirit in the gospel of Christ. How different from a dull sense of duty which motivates so many! Here was an inner desire and interest ever leading Paul on, almost driving him to undertake things which he ought not to have attempted because of his limited physical power. Then Paul mentions his unceasing prayer for them. How energetic Paul was toward God in behalf of Christians whom he had never seen! Most Christians are not even interested in those whom they have seen sufficiently to pray unceasingly to God for them, but whenever one's spiritual interest precedes his personal interest he may be sure that this is of God. Finally, Paul spoke of his desire to be in the will of God. He only wanted to come to Rome if it were God's will. Paul never moved outside of the will of God. He was soon to learn that it was God's will for him to go to Rome, and that he was to come in a way in which he never expected, a prisoner in bonds, afflicted by many sufferings.

Do not forget that the place to which he desired to go was Rome. This was the most challenging place in the world in Paul's day. He had been called to be an apostle to the Gentiles and this was the center of Gentile government and culture. It was only logical that Paul ultimately should desire to minister at Rome. In the history of his career it was the climax of his service. Thus he said, "I long to see you, that I may impart unto you some spiritual gift, to the end that ye may be established; that is, that I may be comforted together with you by the mutual faith of you and me." Paul's ministry would confirm them or establish them in the faith. He, in turn, would be strengthened by them. Notable is it that when he did arrive and saw the Christians at The Appii Forum he thanked God and took courage. Above all there was the hope that he might have some spiritual fruit among them. This fruit-bearing was the passion of Paul's ministry. He was forever reaching out for souls for Christ. Why is this passion so lacking in our ministry today? Perhaps if we can understand this gospel of God, it will communicate to us the passion for soul winning.

I. THE GOSPEL OF GOD MAKES US DEBTORS.

The first admission made by Paul on which we wish to lay emphasis is, "I am a debtor." Paul's debt was owed to all nations to make the faith known. Because of this he was ready to preach the gospel to them who were in Rome. We suggest that this debt is owed to God, that it is discharged to our fellow men and that it is liquidated only by preaching the gospel.

If God has saved you, you are a debtor. The book of Romans makes it clear that it is God Who seeks to save men. This is the Gospel. Men are fallen, are in sin and do not seek God, whether they are heathen, moral or religious individuals. They have turned their back upon God, but God revealed Himself to such hopeless creatures and sent His only begotten Son to seek and to save them while they were in this lost condition. It is due to no merit of an individual that he is saved, for there is no possible way in which he may save himself. The entire history of the human race proves that man, when left to himself, degenerates instead of evolves toward Divine life.

The very case of Paul's own conversion and call illustrates God's seeking of man. It was by no act of his own that Paul was what he was, that is, saved, called to be an apostle and separated unto the gospel. Paul had been a persecutor of God's people, a hater of Christ and an opponent of the gospel, but in spite of this, God chose him, God revealed himself to him in a miraculous way, God taught him the gospel by revelation and God sent him forth with the Divine authority which was not of man. This teaching that God chose him is the underlying foundation of Paul's authority and strength. He did not chose God.

The very burden, then, of the book of Romans is that we are all saved by the work of God, the work of Christ and the work of others in seeking us out. Churches in their preaching, public evangelistic campaigns, missionary works, street corner preaching, passing of tracts, and private testimony are illustrations of the way in which God is seeking out sinners today. Hence, if we are saved, we stand as recipients of grace and as debtors in need of discharging this debt, which we owe to God for giving us salvation.

This debt simply cannot be discharged toward God. It must be discharged toward our fellow men in fulfilling God's purposes for them. When we, as lost sheep, are found of God and redeemed by Him and given eternal life through His Son, we are obligated to spend ourselves in seeking out others. This is the necessary soul passion on the part of every Christian. If a man is a Christian he must immediately become a missionary. As soon as we fully realize what God has done for us, gratitude and love motivate us in wanting to impart this same blessing to others, in desiring to be channels used of God in seeking out other souls. As long as there is a nation without Christ, or an island which has never heard, or a community which is churchless, we must go on and on paying our debt in blood and sacrifice. There simply can be no ease in Zion, no satisfaction in what we have accomplished, while so much remains to be done.

This debt which we owe to God can be liquidated only by preaching the gospel. Thus Paul said, "I am ready to preach the gospel to you that are at Rome also." Paul's sense of duty to Rome was a consequence of the debt which he owed to the whole of heathenism. He was ready to preach. He was eager to preach. He was earnestly inclined to preach. In fact, on another occasion he said, "Necessity is laid upon me; yea, woe is unto me, if I preach not the gospel!" Christ is this gospel. He is made unto us righteousness, wisdom, sanctification and redemption. Hence we are to preach Christ unto all. Nothing can substitute for the preaching of Christ. There is no other name given under heaven whereby men may be saved. There is no other program which is acknowledged of God. We still have the great commission, "Go ye therefore, and teach all nations, baptizing them in the name of the Father, and of the Son, and of the Holy Ghost: teaching them to observe all things whatsoever I have commanded you." Remember that it is better not to have heard this message at all than to have heard it and failed to obey the gospel of God, to discharge our debt unto the heathen of the world.

II. THE GOSPEL MAKES US BOLD AND DARING.

The Apostle declared, "For I am not ashamed of the gospel of Christ." There were mighty obstacles to the preaching of this gospel at Rome. Think for a moment of the citadel which Paul planned to attack. It was the mighty city of the Caesars with its glory at its height. The hills of Rome were crowned with buildings which have been the envy of the centuries. Great orators graced the senate chambers. Poets and literary men walked the streets of the city. Legal knowledge reached its height with the flower of heathenism. The meeting place of the nations in commerce, creed, culture and character! In this city there was a powerful Jewish element who, just as they had obstructed his teaching and persecuted him in Thessaly, Corinth and Ephesus, would oppose him here. Paul knew that his coming would have been heralded long before he arrived and the leaders of Israel would be ready to refute his arguments concerning the Christ. Moreover, Paul knew that this church had been founded by other teachers unnamed in history, upon whose foundation Paul would seem to build and who would have precedence before him. Hence when he wrote his letter he assumed nothing and laid a foundation in doctrine from the very bottom, telling of the truth which he would present when he came.

The text reveals that Paul took a great pride in this gospel. Whatever had hindered Paul from going to Rome for so long a time, when it had been his purpose, certainly was not fear or shame. Paul was aware of how the wise men of the world considered the gospel of the cross foolishness, how to the Jews it was a stumbling-block, how some had disputed it and others had ridiculed it and some had grown angry and persecuted him, but he still was unashamed. The preaching of the Cross and of the resurrection of Christ caused Paul's own suffering in many places. In Philippi he was scourged and at Athens he was so ridiculed that his spirits were terribly depressed; but though this sect was everywhere spoken against and was thoroughly unpopular, Paul was proud to be a Christian.

There are reasons why he was unashamed of the gospel. Though his project of going to Rome to preach was no jaunty, light-hearted adventure, though he knew all the obstacles, Paul was aware that the very power of God was in this gospel. Not only the omnipotent power of God, but power directed toward salvation for every one who believed, whether he was a Jew or a Gentile! Paul also knew that this Christianity or this gospel had proof. His religion had a systematic foundation more tenable intellectually than any other religion of history. Being educated in the cultural center of Tarsus, Paul was acquainted with the other systems of religion and could dispute with the world wisdom. Moreover, Paul was unashamed of the gospel because it worked. Wherever it was preached, there ensued practical demonstrations of life giving power and an inner satisfaction of fellowship with God. Even at Athens there were Damaris and Dionysius who believed and attached themselves to Christ. In most of the other towns where Paul preached we have the record of churches being formed. God demonstrated the power of the gospel unto salvation. Rather than being ashamed, Paul was proud and boastful of the gospel. He never boasted of himself but he boasted of his Christ and of his message. This was a justifiable pride.

The Bible declares that power belongeth unto God. Here we read that the gospel is the power of God. C. R. Erdman has suggested that the gospel can do something. It is a power. It is not simply a pleasing story or an interesting system of philosophy. It can actually accomplish something. Second, the gospel is the power of God. Therefore, it can do anything, for omnipotence rests within it. Third, it is the power of God unto salvation. It can do anything the soul needs for time and eternity. Let the soul turn unto this power and it will find satisfaction. Fourth, it is the power of God to every one that believeth. The gospel can do everything which is needed for every one. What a gospel this is!

III. The Gospel of God Brings Salvation.

The word "salvation" is one of the greatest words in the Scripture. It means the rescue of the soul from sin, unrighteousness, the wrath of God, death and eternal punishment, unto grace, righteousness, forgiveness, eternal life and fellowship with God. The heart of salvation is the righteousness of God revealed in Christ. Salvation is the revelation of the righteousness which is "by faith." Liddon says, "Righteousness is the right relation to the requirements of Divine law, which God provides for those who trust in Christ. It signifies an acceptance granted to sinful man by a holy God." Through Christ, the Divine apparatus of redemption, God is just and the justifier of a believing sinner. God takes a wicked and corrupt man and before the universe declares that he is righteous, that he is saved. This could never be achieved by man, but could only be achieved by God Himself. Thus Paul emphasized the word "believe." It is by grace to every one who believeth. This righteousness is received by faith and the righteous person lives by faith. Justification and life itself are through faith. Faith itself becomes the key.

Salvation in its large sense includes all the redemptive acts and processes of grace such as calling, justification, propitiation, imputation, sanctification, transformation and glorification. Each one of these magnificent subjects is explained in detail in this epistle. Romans is a theological treatise second to none. Its concepts are clear. Its principles are progressive and its arguments are logical. We shall follow man from the depth of degradation to the very height of a transformed life culminating in the image of the Son of God.

Salvation commonly is said to have three senses or aspects. The first aspect of salvation is that from the guilt and the penalty of sin. This is the object of discussion in the first division of the epistle, from chapter 1:18 to chapter 5:11. The second aspect of salvation is from the habit and power of sin which is discussed from chapter 5:12 to chapter 8:39. The third aspect of salvation is from the results of sin or worldliness and this is discussed in the last section of the epistle from chapter 12:1 to chapter 15:13. These great problems, of guilt for what we have done, of a corrupt nature, and of the environmental results of sin in the world, are great hurdles over which the soul must leap before it may be conformed to the image of the Son of God. In this magnificent book we are shown how each one of these obstacles may be overcome by the gospel which is centered in the Person and work of the Lord Jesus Christ.

This salvation announced here is a universal salvation. It is addressed, "to every one that believeth." Faith becomes the only limiting circumstance or condition in reference to salvation. The responsibility of faith is placed upon the individual. He has the power to convert or to turn and if he will convert or turn and believe he shall be saved. Race and class divisions do not exist in this epistle. Paul distinctly tells us that outside of Christ there is no difference, for all have sinned, and in Christ there is no difference for all become children of God. There is no Jew and Gentile outside of Christ. There is no Jew or Gentile in Christ in this present way of God's dealing with men. It is true that salvation goes to "the Jew first" because the Jew has had preeminence. The section concerning the Jew, chapters nine to eleven, reveals that the Jew had the adoption, the glory, the covenants, the giving of the law, the service of God, the promises, the fathers and even Jesus Christ, or that salvation came to the Jew first, but the Jew today has no preeminence over the Gentile in receiving the gospel of Christ. As soon as the Jew as such showed that he rejected the gospel it was extended unto the Gentile, who was included in God's plan from the beginning. There is no contrast between Jew or Gentile, for God is no respecter of persons and the middle wall of partition which formerly existed between Jew and Gentile has now been abolished in Christ's flesh, for those who were afar off have been made nigh by the blood of Christ.

Salvation rests in this gospel which is the power of God. God's might and God's wisdom are displayed to the world in the Incarnation of Christ, in the exhibition of His justice upon the Cross of Christ and in the manifestation of His power in the resurrection of Christ. This makes the Cross of Christ the center of history, from which a Divine power has emanated from God into the human world. By the gospel, God will save from the uttermost to the uttermost all who call upon Him now. This power is just as effective at present as it was in the days of Paul. The results of salvation by the gospel may be seen upon the character and the life of men. Since the gospel is preached today God still makes an offer of salvation, a salvation which is not social or political, but which is personal, which involves the eternal happiness of the individual soul in connection with the Messiah of God, the Saviour.

II

THE WRATH OF GOD

TEXT: *"For the wrath of God is revealed from heaven against all ungodliness and unrighteousness of men, who hold the truth in unrighteousness."*—ROMANS 1:18-32.

OUR text tells us something about the nature of God. The Bible makes four declarative statements about the nature of God. First, it says, "God is a Spirit." This definition of God was given by the Lord Jesus Christ to the Samaritan woman by the well of Sychar. She had a rather localized conception of Deity and Jesus lifted it to the realm of spirit. It was not necessary to prove this declaration to the woman for she did not attempt to refute it. According to students of religion wherever any one believes in God it is as a Spirit. Fetishism and animism sometimes say that the particular totem or fetish or idol is the object of worship, but in reality mean that it represents the object of worship and that it is indwelt by a spirit. Hence, some worship the spirit of the sun or the spirit in the growing trees or the spirit in the events of life. The difference, of course, between the Biblical view of God as a Spirit and these heathen conceptions of God as a spirit is the kind of spirit which God is. The Bible presents Him as a Spirit, infinite, eternal and unchangeable in His Being, wisdom, holiness, power, justice, goodness and truth. No such conception is ever found among the heathen.

The second declarative statement is "God is light." John said, "This then is the message which we have heard of him, and declare unto you, that God is light, and in him is no darkness at all." Jesus was proclaimed as the light of men. He even said, "I am the light of the world: he that followeth me shall not walk in darkness, but shall have the light of life." Thus it was that when Christ was transformed on the mountain, He Himself became the source of light which permeated His clothes and the cloud that enveloped Him. His metamorphosis was into a source of light. Thus it was also that John the beloved saw him upon the isle of Patmos as the Christ of splendor, the source of such light that he fell as dead at His feet. We are told that in heaven there shall be no sun or moon, for the Lamb of

THE WRATH OF GOD

God shall be the light of it. This light is always contrasted with darkness. When men are converted they are changed from the kingdom of darkness to the kingdom of light and their condemnation is that they love darkness rather than light because their deeds are evil. God, then, is light and all that it represents.

"God is love," is the third declarative statement concerning God. This perhaps is the most stressed attribute of Deity and well may be, although it is not the foundation attribute of Deity as we shall see in a moment. One of the tests of our salvation is that we are children of love. If we love we are born of God, John tells us, because God is love and every one who loveth is of God. To love God and our neighbor as oneself is said by Jesus to be the greatest of all commandments. Love is proclaimed by Paul as the greatest thing in life. We have learned to know God as a God of love because He became incarnate in Christ and Christ was love personified. His life was an object lesson in love. The forgiveness of sin, our redemption, was wrought out because of the love of God. It is no wonder, then, that men lay emphasis upon this attribute of Deity.

The Bible, however, says also, "God is a consuming fire." Fire means a punitive, purging, chastening force. It is a symbol of hell and is a symbol of destruction. We are told that the Devil, the false prophet, and the beast shall be cast into the lake of fire. The judgment of Sodom and Gomorrah came with fire. Whenever idols were to be destroyed, they were burned by fire. Even when sin was to be cleansed out of the camp of the ancient Israelites it was done by fire. Thus it was, that when the Holy Ghost came upon the early New Testament Church it was with a manifestation of tongues of fire because sin and evil were consumed, cleansed away and cast out. The place of fire in connection with the Holy Spirit is that of true purification and cleansing. It is not without meaning that God is described as possessed of fiery indignation and wrath against sin and the sinner.

Underlying all of the attributes of God is the primary characteristic of righteousness. The verse preceding our text says that the righteousness of God is revealed from faith to faith. This righteousness of the infinite Deity is the theme of the book of Romans and it is made evident by the gospel of God, namely, His dealing with the sinner. Although the gospel is in the most marvelous way the unfolding of the mercy of God and exalts His grace as nothing else can, yet it is because it rests on a firm foundation of righteousness that it gives such a settled peace to the soul who believes it. Because

Christ died, God could not be faithful to Him or just to the believing sinner if He still condemned any one who trusted in the Christ who bore our sins in His own body on that tree. It is for this reason that the righteousness of God is exalted in the epistle to the Romans. Socrates is supposed to have said to Plato, "It may be that the Deity can forgive sin, but I do not see how." It is an answer to this problem which the book of Romans gives. Hence, the righteousness of God is an inner characteristic of God which expresses His consistency with His own nature. This is His fundamental and inviolable attribute. Some people may insist on recognizing no attribute but love and in ascribing all other physical attributes to love, but this can not be so with God. Righteousness has an independent place as an attribute of God that can not be set aside. It has reference to distinctions of right and wrong—to moral norms, which even love must respect. It is out of the righteousness and love in the character of God that wrath issues. If God were not righteous, He could freely and complacently forgive sin without any retribution and without any satisfaction of law, but since He is righteous this is impossible. Romans is a declaration of the satisfaction made to the righteousness of God in order that He might forgive sinners and still remain just.

We are not to think of God getting angry as man gets angry, even though wrath is an affection in the nature of God. By wrath is meant the intense moral displeasure with which God regards sin—His holy abhorrence of it—and the punitive energy of His nature which He puts forth against it. As defined by Thayer it is, "That in God which stands opposed to man's disobedience, obduracy, (especially in resisting the gospel) and sin, and manifests itself in punishing the same." Whenever it is used of God it is opposed to mercy and means wrath, the effect of which is to exclude from redemption. So regarded, wrath is not opposed to love, but, on the contrary, derives its chief intensity from the presence of love and is a necessary element in the character of an ethically perfect being. Wrath is the reverse side of God's love. Thus the wrath of God is grounded on the righteousness of God and far from being a passing burst or flush of anger, it is an abiding attribute of justice and righteousness which may well be expressed under the symbol of the avenging sword. As the first man fell under this moral displeasure of God, so all men because of their disobedience have remained under the moral displeasure of God. "There is none good but one, that is,

THE WRATH OF GOD

God." In this Scriptural passage we have an example of the Divine wrath on the sons of man.

I. Wrath Manifested Against Men.

This wrath is revealed from heaven, not by the gospel as the righteousness of God is revealed, for the glad tidings do not speak of wrath, but as the result of the rejection of the gospel and of God's righteousness. It is this wrath from which the gospel is a means of escape. It is manifested against those persons who are not only full of ungodliness and unrighteousness but also who know the truth and remain unrighteous.

The ungodly are people who are not like God, that is, they are not righteous. They do not maintain in their conduct what ought to be, that is, what they owe toward others and toward God, namely, the consistency of their ways with the duties of their relative positions. Instead, they are irreverent, impious, without a sense of value. They are sinners. Esau may well be chosen as a type of such. Esau lived for the pleasures of this world, for hunting, for lusting with the daughters of Heth, and for filling his stomach with the satisfying foods of life. He had little sense of the duty which he owed to God and to his fellow men. Therefore, the Scripture says that God hated Esau. God's moral abhorrence of the type of man Esau represented reached its height in this case, so that it might be described by the word, "hate." For such who are unlike God, wickedness is their lot, self is their god and hell is their home. Yet the Bible tells us that Christ died for the ungodly. Hence, no matter how far a man has fallen, no matter how impious his deeds, no matter how far away from God he is, no matter how much under the wrath of God he abides, Christ is able to save him. It is written, "He is able also to save them to the uttermost that come unto God by him."

The unrighteous are those without a perfect obedience to the law of God and to the requirements of God. The only means of righteousness in God's sight is to have the imputed righteousness of Christ, which is a new standing before God. Without this righteousness, the soul is condemned in the presence of God. The word "unrighteousness" does not describe necessarily a murderer, a perjurer or an adulterer, but a man who is without God's righteousness, who has not yielded to him a perfect obedience. The man is under the wrath of God. "He that believeth not . . . the wrath of God abideth on him."

The wrath of God is manifested against those who hold the truth in unrighteousness, who know the way, to whom the truth is clear, but who suppress that truth by deliberately rejecting it. We are quite aware that this passage of the Scripture originally applied to those who are heathen and to the degradation of heathen through their rejection of God but we believe it also applies to every individual soul who has the truth and who rejects that truth in unrighteousness. There are some people who know the truth and who some day may expect to surrender to it, to obtain God's righteousness through salvation but at present they have not yielded. They are suppressing the truth in their life and the wrath of God abides on them. Woe to such a person if he is cut off before the time of his reconciliation. Woe to him also because he has begun in his life the downward steps to utter heathenism. Woe also to them who know the truth and do not preach it. We must speak it forth. We must, in accordance with the truth, restrain, rebuke and reprove with all long-suffering and doctrine. It is necessary to be in earnest with God. Otherwise, we invite the judgment of having our whole inner being, our heart darkened, so that it is incapable of discerning the truth in the future.

II. WRATH JUSTIFIED BY THE ACTIONS OF MEN.

This wrath of God against the heathen world is justified "because that which may be known of God is manifest in them; for God hath showed it unto them. For the invisible things of him from the creation of the world are clearly seen, being understood by the things that are made, even his eternal power and Godhead; so that they are without excuse." These words, "They are without excuse," reveal that the power of God as creator and the Deity of that Creator are clear through two avenues, the person of man and the realm of nature. Paul says, "That which may be known of God is manifest in them." The doctrine of God can be proved from the very being of man himself, as a thinking being, as a moral being, as a personality and as a social creature. Thus it is that man knows that there is a God Who is a lawgiver and to Whom he is responsible. Paul says, "When the Gentiles, which have not the law, do by nature the things contained in the law, these, having not the law, are a law unto themselves; which show the work of the law written in their hearts, their conscience also bearing witness, and their thoughts the mean while accusing or else excusing one another." This is very important because it means that all men everywhere are personally responsible to God for a knowledge of Him. This declares that the heathen originally possessed such knowledge of God as could be derived from conscience and nature, but like all religious truth it could only be retained on the condition of being acted upon. The heathen undoubtedly possess a much higher knowledge of God than we sometimes accredit them. Undoubtedly every man throughout the world will be judged by an infinite and omniscient God according to the limit of the revelation which he has, but this passage of Scripture makes it very clear that men do not live up to the knowledge of God which they have in themselves.

The second part says that it was manifested unto them. This, of course, is through natural theology. General revelation includes both our conscience and nature. The Scripture alone is special Revelation. Conscience may be called the internal revelation, nature the external revelation and Scripture the special revelation. The existence of God may be demonstrated from purpose in nature, from cause in nature, and from order in nature, but we can not review these arguments here. As a matter of history, heathen philosophy failed to know Him Who had revealed himself in part through conscience and through nature, but Paul says that this leaves man without excuse.

If, in the eyes of God, man is utterly without excuse, because he would not retain God in his knowledge and would not give unto God the correct worship and service, our only conclusion is that wrath is justified against man. If man could have seen and could have understood and could have apprehended through the mind the things of God, manifested in him and in nature, then because he did not do so he deserved the wrath of God.

III. Wrath Instigated.

Paul shows the course of godlessness and unrighteousness in the history of the race and of the individual. Concerning the race, this may be called the philosophy of religion. It defined the steps in man's descent, from knowledge of God to utter heathenism. Because man in the beginning turned aside from his primitive knowledge of the one God, he came to worship many gods. His love of sin caused him to be uncomfortable in relationship to one God, so he imagined and invented mediators, lesser deities, to stand between him and the infinite and righteous God. The process of this is given here in these three verses.

First, "when they knew God, they glorified him not as God." This shows what happened in the beginning when men knew God.

They had a knowledge of His infinite perfection, of His power as the creator of the world and of His moral justice, yet they did not glorify Him as God, that is, worship Him, which is the moral correlative of their knowledge. They did not permit Him to be the God of their lives and hence they took the first step downward. Whenever any individual who knows about God and knows the truth withholds his worship and adoration of God and his obedience to God through the gospel, he takes the first step away from God, down into sin and heathenism and ultimately to wrath. Mankind, originally having the internal, external and special revelation of the true God, let other gods rule their lives and they became hardened.

The second step says, "neither were thankful." Although men knew that all that they were and all that they had was given to them by God, yet they did not thank Him for it. The grace of thankfulness shows our humility. We realize that we are dependent upon God and that we owe Him all and as a result we praise and adore and thank Him. Whenever we see a thankless person, or a thankless generation, we see a mark of degeneracy. Just as the Bible describes thanklessness as a sign of the utter degeneration of the age just before the coming judgment, so it is a sign of the degeneration of the individual. Though it may be one of the first sins, it marks the downward trend.

The third step is, they "became vain in their imaginations." When human beings are practically indifferent to known truth, they then begin to indulge in worthless speculation about God. The heathen became mere triflers in their thoughts about God. Even though men do not thank and praise the true God they can not help but think about Him, and when they think about Him without the practical safeguards of devotion and adoration their thoughts become empty and fruitless or vain. Once we abandon obedience to the true God we begin to substitute ourselves for God. The history of philosophy is that man became the measure of things rather than God the measure of things. Today man judges God on the basis of his own concepts rather than judging himself according to the revealed concepts. With the increase of our knowledge men today say that they can have nothing to do with the justice of the God of the Old Testament, with a miracle working God of the New or with the atoning God of the Lord Jesus Christ. They, in turn, create their own conception of God and fall down and worship him, which is nothing else than idolatry.

The fourth step is, "their foolish heart was darkened." The heart is the center of the soul's life, of the will, of thought and of emotion. Whenever this becomes darkened because of empty speculations, the life becomes incapable of understanding what is true and right. If God is light, when God is rejected, darkness will reign according to cause and effect. Hence, it was, that the idea of God disappeared from the human mind. Paul was commissioned by God to turn men from darkness unto light and from the power of Satan unto God. It is also possible to turn from the light of God unto darkness. The history of the race is not the turning from darkness to light but from the light to darkness. It was this turning away from God which necessitated man's being expelled from the garden and the coming of the flood for judgment. As we look out upon some of the appalling darkness of the intellectual centers and the student world today because of its rejection of God, we can not help but believe that a similar judgment will come upon us.

Fifth, it says, "professing themselves to be wise, they became fools." As soon as man trusts in the conceit of his own wisdom, he abandons himself to spiritual and moral folly. True wisdom begins in the knowledge and the fear of the Lord and it continues with a humility in which man holds his place in relationship to God, but the conceited wisdom which sets itself up in judgment upon God is the kind which turns a man into a fool in both what he thinks and does. God counts the wisdom of this world foolishness and spurns it when it comes to the matter of salvation. There has always been a contrast between the wisdom of this world and the wisdom of God. "They became fools." In the Scripture, the fool is the man who says there is no God. Thus, in God's sight all those who account for the universe without God, who can explain life on a natural basis and who reason God away are fools.

The last step was, they "changed the glory of the incorruptible God into an image made like to corruptible man, and to birds, and four-footed beasts, and creeping things." This shows where heathenism ended up. Heathenism did not spring up over night. It was a long process of rebellion, of seeking one's own way without God. The degradation of worshiping lions, or frogs, or flies, or leopards, or trees, or the sun, or fetishes, in all of which stages we find men today as well as in the stages of idolatry, is due to the rejection of the light of God. The first step in the degeneration of the worship of God is to change His image into that of a man. It is this stage which we see round about us on every hand today. Men are making God finite, are limiting Him with human characteristics. Once this is accomplished through our present theories it will be but a step in the further degeneration of our worship. It is no wonder that the wrath of God is upon our generation.

IV. The Wrath of God in Operation.

As soon as Paul gives the cause and the process of the degeneration of man he then names the effects from the wrath of God. Three times he says that God gave them up. This is a terrible thing because no souls seek God, but turn away from God, and when God gives men up they are lost. Then God's wrath abides on them. Then they are just as much condemned to punishment during life as they will be in the life to come. It is interesting to note the three things to which God gave them up, which also will be steps in the process of His giving up people today.

First, it says, "God also gave them up to uncleanness, through the lusts of their own hearts, to dishonor their own bodies between themselves." When men will to worship the creature rather than the Creator, when they will to worship an eternal process of nature as the pantheists do, they will become like that process of nature. Man today says that God is a product of man's mind and that man is a product of the brute beast, and he is turning back to the brute beast practice in life. He dishonors his own body through lust. The dishonoring of the body has been a mark of corrupt society in every decadent period of history. The process of changing God's truth into a lie and worshiping the creature is continuing now. This is the devolution rather than the evolution of man. He is turning to an unclean animal. History is one of the greatest arguments against any thought of the evolution of man.

Secondly, God gave man up to vile affections. Not only lust, but the very vilest and unnatural kind of lust consumed man. We can only read this but not expound it. This is the story of improper sex relations which go beyond all such standards as fornication and adultery and reach the very bestial life of abnormal minds. "Their women did change the natural use into that which is against nature. Also the men, leaving the natural use of the woman, burned in their lust one toward another; men with men working that which is unseemly, and receiving in themselves that recompense of their error which was meet." All we wish to say is that this is going on in a very widespread way in America today and those in public life have ample illustrations of it called to their attention.

Lastly, God gave up man to a reprobate mind, to do those things

THE WRATH OF GOD

which are not convenient. Look at the list of sins and their manifestations, fruit of the flesh, listed here. First there are the four governing forms of evil. Injustice or the disregard of human rights; wickedness or the absence of all principle, namely, moral rottenness; covetousness, or selfish greed, whether to acquire wealth or to satisfy lust; and maliciousness, the lack of that which constitutes human excellence. Then are listed eight anti-social sins of a bitter nature, three sins of selfishness or pride and finally six sins which are against the natural principles upon which society is based. All of these have their source in the rejection of God. It is possible to point out illustrations of practically every sin, which reveals that there are multitudes of people whom God has given up to iniquity. The great tragedy of it is that many of these know the judgments of God, that those who commit such things are worthy of death, and they not only do them but have the pleasure in them that do them. Thus God's wrath is revealed.

All who despise the goodness of God which leads to repentance in order that the righteousness of God might be exercised in the forgiving of sin, treasure up unto themselves wrath against the day of wrath and revelation of the righteous judgment of God Who will render to every man according to his deeds. In the knowledge of this, how can any man expect to escape?

III
THE FALSE SECURITY OF THE SELF-RIGHTEOUS

TEXT: *"Therefore thou art inexcusable, O man, whosoever thou art that judgest: for wherein thou judgest another, thou condemnest thyself; for thou that judgest doest the same things."*—ROM. 2:1-16.

THE first half of this chapter introduces to us the moral man who holds a false security concerning his salvation. The body of teaching follows the declaration of God's wrath on all ungodliness and unrighteousness of men. The first application of this was made to the heathen who had descended to the depths of moral and spiritual degradation. Now its application is made to moralizers who are no better than the heathen.

The text describes a man who criticizes those who do the wickedness described in the first chapter of Romans beginning with fornication and ending with being unmerciful. This moral individual is willing to judge such outright sinners and to look with disdain upon them from his heights of moral achievement. He carefully distinguishes himself from all such overt sinners. It is his belief that the wrath and the judgment of God on such wicked men is just and righteous, but he does not believe that this judgment and wrath is also upon him. This moral man is blind to his own state and to his sins which in the eyes of God, though not as revolting as those of the heathen, are as guilty. Being outside the household of faith, being without Christ and salvation and not possessing the righteousness of God, however moral this man is, he too is under the judgment and the wrath of God. His false hope is a form of self-love and self-flattery, in placing himself upon a pedestal of unique relationship with God and this renders his condition more dangerous and more fatal than that of the wicked man who knows he is under wrath.

The condemnation of self is included in this moral man's condemnation of the overtly wicked because the governing principles of both lives are the same. The moral man is also without the righteousness of God and thus is inexcusable in his sin, no matter how refined

FALSE SECURITY OF THE SELF-RIGHTEOUS

that sin may be and no matter how censorious and disdainful he may be of other gross sinners. The very act of condemning another condemns himself. This principle applies to all impenitent persons who, however respectable in their own eyes and before the community, yet judge others. The purpose of this section of Paul's epistle is to cut off from escape all moralists, all moral philosophers and all self-righteous souls. Paul leaves no avenue of escape by showing that all men are under the condemnation of God and need the righteousness of God which is in Christ.

The moral man also is under the judgment and the wrath of God. That God is a judge and that such a thing as judgment will occur, the first chapter of the Roman epistle clearly declares. That the wrath and the judgment of God is altogether proper on such individuals as are there described, many will admit, while excusing themselves from this judgment and wrath on the grounds either of morality or of religion. It will be necessary in the next section of the book of Romans to deal with religion as a means of escape from the wrath of God. Here it is our intention to consider morality by showing from the Word of God that those who trust in their own works are under the wrath of God. This trust in one's own morality and works you may call self-security or self-righeousness. Self-righteousness is the pit into which many fall to their own destruction, and death, having already escaped the grosser sins of life. Those who from pride disdain the awful sins so hideously described in this previous chapter but fail to see their need of a Saviour and fail to trust in Christ are likewise under God's wrath. God's purpose is to include all under judgment that He might include all under mercy. Therefore, if God is to judge the world in righteousness it is essential for us to know the principles of that judgment. This will remove all false security and delusion among men. It must be made plain to moral men that judgment upon them is also imminent and that according to the word of God their place is in hell with the violent sinners.

I. THE DIVINE JUDGEMENT OF ALL MEN.

Paul said, "We are sure that the judgment of God is according to truth." The certainty of this judgment Paul based upon common knowledge. He did not say, "I am sure" but "we are sure." Natural reason and Divine revelation agree in the acceptance of the certainty of Divine judgment upon men. If there is a God and if man is a moral being, created in the image of God, God will hold him accountable for the deeds which he has done. Humanity has always believed in the judgment. You may go where you will among the tribes and nations of the earth and you may read their religions and their mythologies and will realize that there is a universal dread of an inevitable judgment-day. Phillips Brooks told of an Austrian noble who was dying at the age of ninety-three after having spent all of his life in pleasures and delights, never being troubled with any infirmity. Concerning him Frederick the emperor said, "From hence we may conclude the soul's immortality, for if there be a God that ruleth this world, as divines and philosophers do teach, surely there are other places to which souls after death do go and receive for their deeds either reward or punishment. For here, we see that neither rewards are given to the good nor punishment to the evil." There must be a future reckoning when the scales of justice are balanced for individual life.

The Scripture is full of declarations concerning that judgment. It is called a Day of Wrath, of Indignation, of Punishment, of Reckoning and of Retribution. Jesus described it as "That Day." This judgment comes after death and must not be confused with any justice which is meted out to us in this life. "It is appointed unto men once to die, but after this the judgment." The judgment concerns our eternal life. Jesus said, "It shall be more tolerable for the land of Sodom in the day of judgment, than for thee." Paul said, "He hath appointed a day, in the which he will judge the world in righteousness." This judgment will concern men and angels. It will be absolutely universal, including the small and the great and all generations. Even the angels which are confined with chains in darkness are reserved unto that judgment.

The Scripture also says that Christ is to be the judge in that day. "The Father judgeth no man, but hath committed all judgment unto the Son . . . and hath given him authority to execute judgment also, because he is the Son of man." Christ as the God-Man has full knowledge of all the limitations of man and will judge righteously in that day. How appropriate it is that he who stood condemned before the judgment bar of Pilate should have authority in that day to settle the eternal destinies of man. This judgment will not be exercised until after His second coming. "The Son of Man shall come in the glory of his Father with his angels; and then he shall reward every man according to his works."

The standard of that judgment of God is truth. It will be according to truth. This describes reality or fact, not appearance or imagina-

FALSE SECURITY OF THE SELF-RIGHTEOUS

tion. The truth means the facts about God, that He is not only loving but also just and severe. If God spared not His own Son but freely delivered Him up because of sin, are we to think that He shall spare the impenitent sinner who spurns His Son? If God is of eyes too pure to behold iniquity, how can the unforgiven sinner stand in His presence? The truth concerns the facts about man. It shows that the morality of the impenitent man was a sham, a screen to give him a reputation before others when in reality he loved sin. Instead of loving his neighbor he disdained him in pride. The fact that Christ as the righteousness of God has no appeal to the moral man reveals him as sinful in his own nature. The truth is that God's fundamental attribute is righteousness and not love. The righteousness of God alone can guarantee the consistency and the permanence of love. Were it not for that truth of righteousness in God, His love would be capricious. That judgment according to the truth will concern the facts about you. You know the truth about yourself and God knows it, and the judgment shall be according to the truth. Christ knows the secrets of all hearts and He shall judge them righteously. Mr. Moral Man, can you stand upon your record by saying that you have not hated or envied or lied or coveted or foolishly sinned? The reason we urge you to face the truth now is that you may meet God in Christ first and remove the guilt and penalty of your sins from your life. The whole reason for thinking about the judgment of God which is according to truth is to bring us into the arms of a Saviour who has endured the wrath of God for us.

If that judgment is certain, if the standard is the truth, what are the principles upon which it will be conducted? Paul declares three of them in this most explicit passage of the Scripture concerning the principles of the judgment of God. It will be according to works, it will be with no respect of persons, and it will concern obedience. Paul said, "God . . . will render to every man according to his deeds." This could not be otherwise. God knows all the facts in regard to man and His judgment must be in accordance with them. Those who come up to the last judgment will be judged according to the things which are written in the books, according to their works. If, however, the judgment is to be according to works, how is this to be reconciled with the doctrine of justification by faith? This is well explained by the theologian Hodge. Notwithstanding the doctrine of vicarious justification, the apostle teaches that the retributions of eternity are according to our works. The good only are saved and the wicked are condemned. The wicked will be punished on account of their works and according to their works. The righteous will be rewarded not on account of but according to their works. Good works are to the righteous the evidence of their belonging to that class to whom for Christ's sake eternal life has been graciously rewarded. Evil works are evidence of the contentious, strifeful and unregenerate heart of the wicked. The fact is that the apostle is not here teaching the method of justification but is laying down as general principles of justice according to which, irrespective of the Gospel, men shall be judged.

Another writer emphasizes that here the life as a whole or the life choice is in question. Thus Paul tells of two great classes, the patiently enduring and the rebellious, those whose life practice is good and those who work evil, those who obey the truth and those who reject it in order to remain in the unrighteousness. Paul says, "God . . . will render to every man according to his deeds: to them who by patient continuance in well doing seek for glory and honor and immortality, eternal life: but unto them that are contentious, and do not obey the truth, but obey unrighteousness, indignation and wrath." Patient continuance in well doing is not the means of procuring eternal life, but is a description of the life of those to whom God has rendered eternal life. Well doing is obedience to the light which God has given. With Abel it meant performing a sacrifice pleasing to God; with Noah building an ark to save his house; with Abraham leaving his country and kindred; with Peter and John leaving their fishing nets to follow Jesus. It means obedience to the will of God as revealed. Likewise, contentious describes those who are disobedient to the truth as revealed to them, as were Cain, Esau, Saul and Judas. The retribution and the reward promised to these two classes are according to their works; reward to the righteous, punishment to the wicked. The description of the punishment is terrible,—wrath, indignation, tribulation and anger. Whereas the gracious blessings bestowed upon those working good are radiant life, honor and incorruption. Thus works may be considered the basis of that judgment.

The second principle is that judgment will be with no respect of persons. Earthly justice is often dispensed with regard to position, wealth and standing. Recognition and honor is bestowed with respect of persons. It is very hard to do otherwise in this world, because man looketh upon the outward appearance, but it shall not be so with God, for God looketh upon the heart and God's judgment will be according to the secrets of men's hearts. Here a moral man

FALSE SECURITY OF THE SELF-RIGHTEOUS

may not be distinguished from a truly regenerate man, but it shall not be so in God's sight. What a comfort this should be to the poor, to the persecuted and to those discriminated against. Almighty God will judge according to our conduct and not our person. Various responsibility has been given to different individuals in accordance with their light and their opportunity. To whom much has been given, from him much will be required, and the proportions of retribution and reward will be made according to this responsibility and privilege. Sin, disobedience and failure, whether found among the enlightened or the unenlightened, brings condemnation and death. Thus the distinguishing characteristic will be the life choice either of sin or of obedience, according to the manifestation of the righteousness of God in the Lord Jesus Christ.

The third principle of judgment is that it will be according to obedience. Paul clearly states that not the hearers of the law are just before God but the doers of the law shall be justified. The class who have the truth but disobey it are under God's wrath. Merely possessing the truth gives one no advantage over him who has not the truth. Advantage comes by obedience, by a life in accordance with the truth. One of the subtle dangers is for those who possess the knowledge of Christianity to have a false confidence in that knowledge rather than in the Person of Christ and the righteousness of God. When we know about Christ and when we know the truth, we must act in accordance therewith. We must walk as a Christian should walk. Paul also mentions the class who have not the truth, but from the constitution of their nature obey the truth. Said he, "When the Gentiles, which have not the law, do by nature the things contained in the law, these, having not the law, are a law unto themselves: which show the work of the law written in their hearts, their conscience also bearing witness, and their thoughts the meanwhile accusing or else excusing one another." God has placed a work within man which is the basis of his conscience or his knowledge between right and wrong, so that his knowledge of his transgressions is not dependent upon his environment but upon his very nature. Thus when the moral heathen are judged, their hearts will acquiesce in the justice of God's judgment. Moral men will recognize that their attainments have left them far short of what their own consciences have demanded. This conscience is not a means of justification, but gives the principle of condemnation, so that all men may know that they have sinned and need a Saviour. Yes, when the secret councils of men are revealed at the judgment bar of God, He will be shown to be just.

II. THE REASON FOR FALSE SECURITY IN THE FACE OF THIS JUDGEMENT.

Paul asked the question, "Thinkest thou this, O man, that judgest them . . . and doest the same, that thou shalt escape the judgment of God?" The first reason for false security is the expectation of escaping the judgment of God. In spite of what nature, conscience and Scripture declare about God and the inevitability of judgment, some think that they have a ground on which to escape. With not a few this may be a trust in a morality. Often one hears the response from a respectable person, when talking about the need of Christ as a Saviour, "I'll do what I think is right and then I'll take my chance." That is a hope to escape judgment on the ground of morality. Others have a false hope because of the performance of some great work of atonement such as the building of a church or the leaving of a large sum of money to a benevolent cause. In Cairo, Egypt, there are at least one hundred mosques which have been built by individual Moslems who believe that thereby they purchase a ticket straight to heaven. Yet others are willing to make an exception of self, deeming that by some means they are favorites of God and will not be brought into judgment. It takes the work of the Holy Spirit to show one the culpability of his sin, his lost condition and his need of the Saviour. That this false security of expecting to escape is ineffectual is evident by the Scriptural teaching that there is only one bridge from earth to heaven, one door to the mansion of God, one ark which preserves from the flood, one way out of the tribulation, and that one Saviour is Christ, the righteousness of God.

Second, Paul asked, "O man . . . despisest thou the riches of his goodness and forbearance and long-suffering?" The riches of God's goodness are manifested in numerous ways. His goodness is evident in our conscience which prohibits us from indulging in the self destructive process of sin. The moral precepts enjoyed by multitudes who are not Christians are an evidence of the goodness of God. The common mercies of Providence in life reveal His goodness. But the crowning act of God's goodness is the continued offer of the Gospel for salvation which came by the incarnation, life, death and resurrection of Christ. That God should continue to offer this salvation and forbear to punish unrepentant men in the face of their

FALSE SECURITY OF THE SELF-RIGHTEOUS

evil is a manifestation of His goodness. To despise God's goodness means to treat this Divine wealth of grace, of forgiveness, of mercy and of salvation lightly. Continued action such as this necessitates Divine forbearance and long-suffering. Why God does not smite men for despising the wealth of His goodness is a wonder. Some interpret this as an easy, good natured indifference to sin, but that is to misunderstand the attributes of God, for His goodness is a withholding of wrath, rightly deserved by men. Whoever thinks that he does not need God's goodness and mercy, either because there is no God, or because all shall be saved, or because life ends at death, is despising His goodness offered in the Gospel.

Third, Paul asks if this moral man does not know that the goodness of God leads him to repentance. Here is a false security derived from a tragic ignorance of the right action of the goodness of God on the human soul. To accept all the Divine benefits without repentance, faith and obedience reveals a life choice of sin, the reward of which, however moral the life may be, can only be wrath and indignation. Such ignorance is the result of wrong thinking. We do not imply that man who despises God's goodness, or who thinks he can escape, or who accepts God's goodness without repentance, does not think, but his thinking is declared by the Bible to be erroneous, to be opposed to God's revelation. Never think that the goodness of God is a sentimental attribute which implies that He will not punish, but rather consider the goodness of God as the means of leading you to forsake sin and to receive the assurance of acceptance in His sight.

III. THE PUNISHMENT OF THE SELF-RIGHTEOUS IN THE DAY OF JUDGMENT.

To such self-righteous individuals who think they will escape God's judgment, Paul said, "After thy hardness and impenitent heart, treasurest up unto thyself wrath against the day of wrath." Whosoever defers his salvation or despises God's goodness gradually adds up for himself a treasure of wrath. The picture is that of building up a fortune little by little until one possesses great wealth. Each small part in itself is insignificant but the cumulative effect of the addition is great. Such is the cumulative culpability of impenitence. There is a piling up of the wealth of wrath. Here is the contrast. The riches of God's goodness or the riches of His wrath. Which will you have? The growth of accumulative wrath is in proportion to the hardening of the heart. Man can resist and harden his own heart in impenitence until he builds up with God an opposition, antipathy and necessary severity because of his obduracy. When mercy in a great treasure could be built up, how senseless it is to build up wrath! On the believer, the one who by patient continuance in well doing demonstrates that he is a believer, there is no wrath, but on the unbeliever, or them who are contentious, there is no mercy.

Finally this punishment shall be manifested in the great outcome of wrath. Paul says the impenitent treasures up wrath against the day of wrath and revelation of the righteous judgment of God. These words "indignation and wrath" are so stated in language as to be earned as a reward by man instead of being sent by God. God permits man to earn the riches of wrath because of his willfulness in rejecting Christ. The word describes the intensity of Divine opposition to such impenitent souls. To them may be added the word "tribulation," bespeaking an irrevocable calamity for the soul, telling of the fearful visitation of horrible suffering, because of which it would have been better had one not been born.

This punishment will occur at the day of judgment. It is called wrath in the day of wrath. There will come a time of revelation of that which is now veiled from the eyes of men. What will the day of judgment be? We remember the flood in which all perished but eight souls, and Sodom and Gomorrah in which all perished but three souls. The twentieth chapter of Revelation describes that judgment. The evil works of all sinners in their influence and their ramifications will be completely revealed. The dread outlook for such whose works were written in the books will be torment day and night forever and ever. These words, torment, gnashing of teeth, outer darkness, fire which is not quenched, are words the meaning of which we do not profess to know, but they are severe enough for us to want to escape the awful wrath to come by fleeing to Calvary and the loving arms of a Saviour.

In the light of such a judgment how long will you defer your life choice of righteousness? Every moment of impenitence adds more to your treasure of wrath. Escape for any soul is impossible. Absence of privilege which others possess will not excuse you. The greater your privilege the more searching will be your judgment. You must have more than a mere profession of reality or religion. You must have obedience to God in the Lord Jesus Christ. Even if you have never heard of the Divine law, the commandments and the righteousness demanded in the Bible, the constitution of your own nature condemns you and tells you that you need a Saviour. How then shall you escape if you neglect so great a salvation, even that which God in his goodness and mercy has provided through the Lord Jesus Christ?

IV
RELIGION VERSUS SALVATION

TEXT: *"For he is not a Jew, which is one outwardly; neither is that circumcision, which is outward in the flesh; but he is a Jew, which is one inwardly; and circumcision is that of the heart, in the spirit, and not in the letter; whose praise is not of men, but of God."*—
ROM. 2:17-29; 3:1-8.

THIS text manifests that there was no essential difference between Jesus and Paul. We have often heard that Paul's religion was different in kind from the religion of Jesus, but this is not true. We could almost imagine Jesus speaking these words of our text, for they are very similar to His teaching in the Sermon on the Mount. There He told us that God looketh upon the heart, that the matters of value in the external exercises of what is called religion depend upon one's inner relationship to God. Prayer is not to be made for the eyes of men, but in secret unto our Heavenly Father, who in turn will reward openly. Alms are not to be given before the eyes of men but before the eyes of the Father who seeth in secret and will reward us openly. Likewise, when we fast we are not to appear unto men to fast. We are to wash and to anoint our faces and let fasting be a matter of our heart attitude. Jesus emphasized that as soon as these exercises were externalized, they became religious formulas with their reward only from men.

That is exactly what Paul is saying in this text, for being a Jew outwardly does not mean that one is a Jew or a child of the covenant inwardly, for the true relationship with God must be of the heart, in the spirit not in the letter.

For this reason Christ set Himself against the religion of His day by denouncing its practices, condemning its attitude and separating Himself from it. He acknowledged the truth which was included in Judaism. He practiced spiritual exercises in His own life and He believed the Scripture which the Jews also claimed, but He rejected their externalized religion. Paul also did all of these things. He said, "If any other man thinketh that he hath whereof he might trust in the flesh, I more; circumcized the eighth day, of the stock of Israel, of the tribe of Benjamin, an Hebrew of the

Hebrews; as touching the law, a Pharisee; concerning zeal, persecuting the church; touching the righteousness which is of the law, blameless. But what things were gain to me, those I counted loss for Christ." Paul, having excelled above his brethren in the Jews' religion, set his face against all these things in order that he might gain Christ.

There is also a similitude of cause in the rejection of Paul and of Jesus by the Jews. They were rejected because the Jews did not want heart repentance, Christ as the Son of God and salvation through the Cross. Their rejection of Christ sent Him to the cross. Their rejection of Paul sent him as minister to the Gentiles. The heart message of Jesus and of Paul necessitated the excluding of sin from one's life, but the Jews' religion had been so externalized that religion and sin were compatible. It is often true that religion comforts one in his sin. Salvation, however, makes sin incompatible with the saved one. This may be something of the cause for the progressive degradation in religion, for it seems that the earlier period of each great religion of the world has been the purer, nobler and better period when it is compared with the latter state of religion. Early Buddhism was both spiritually and ethically noble, but Buddhism two millenniums later was degraded to the worship of human follies and lust. Thus it was with the Greek religion and with the Egyptian. The history of religions is that of progressive deterioration rather than development. Men love to rationalize their sins and to protect themselves in their sins by rituals, sacraments, forms and ceremonies. They allow these things to mediate between themselves and a holy God in whose presence their conscience convicts them of sin.

Jesus and Paul had a controversy with the religion of their day and those who experience a heart relationship to God in Christ today will have a controversy with Christendom. What called forth these statements of Jesus and of Paul, about the necessity of a right relationship with God existing in the human heart, is recurring in Christendom today and must be exposed. It is externalism in religion. A false hope from religion is being given to millions of men who in reality are under the condemnation and wrath of God. Just as we learned in our last study that there were many moral men who thought because of their morality that they would escape the judgment of God, so we now learn that there are many religious men who hope by means of their religion to escape the judgment of God. God's controversy is not with any branch of Christendom particularly but with all religion which substitutes formalism or privilege for a true, heart salvation among men.

The particular class which Paul here brings under condemnation is the religious Jew who rests in his privileges of having the law, knowing the will of God, possessing the circumcision and being entrusted with the oracles, but whose heart is not right with God. Rather than confine our thinking to merely this one religion, we wish to suggest a larger field under the following titles: first, Religion Versus Christianity; second, The Church Versus Christ; third, Salvation Versus Magic.

I. RELIGION VERSUS CHRISTIANITY.

Since we use the word religion, we perhaps ought to define it. Many different definitions have been given by philosophers and religious thinkers. The derivation of the word itself has been ascribed to two Latin words: the first, "religere," which means to gather up again, to consider or to ponder; the second, "religare," which means to bind back, to restrain and which puts a certain sense of obligation on man. Some have used the first sense and some the second, but the general summary of definitions is that religion is an attempt to solve the problems of human existence, a searching for truth or a philosophical effort to explain God, the universe, man, his origin and relation to the Supreme Being. It is really the groping of the human spirit after God. Thus religion deals with the spirit of man and is confined to the realm from which he has fallen.

Morally, as we have seen, there is a work of God written on the human heart which lets man know the difference between right and wrong and because of this moral conscience all men have a sense of condemnation. This leads them to seek a religion which will bind them back to God. Their moral nature is not veiled but their spiritual nature is. In the spiritual nature they reach out for God and can not find Him. Thus, they create religions which are means of finding God or of being restored to God. The various religions of the world, from the base fetishism and animism to the high spiritual religions of the east, are attempts to go beyond the clouded, veiled relationship of the soul and God, to build a bridge back to God, and to reconcile a Deity which conscience says is offended by man's actions.

Here we make a differentiation between religion and Christianity. Christianity is not a religion. It is a Divine revelation. It is a bridge from heaven to earth. We can not say that Christianity is

RELIGION VERSUS SALVATION

one of the religions of the world, naming Moslemism, Buddhism and Hinduism along with Christianity. We can not say that Christ is the founder of a religion, as Zoroaster, Buddha, Mahomet and Manu were founders of a religion. Qualitatively, Christianity is utterly distinct from the other religions of the world. They are like in kind. Christianity is different in kind. We can not even say that Christianity has been founded on Judaism. Rather it was founded upon Biblical revelation which Judaism also claims. Jesus and Paul both rejected Judaism, but they claimed the Old Testament was the revelation of God and it was not in any sense identical with the Judaism of the day of Jesus and Paul. Thus Christianity professes to be not a religion of the world or a groping of man for God, but a supernatural revelation of God and God's will to man.

This leads us to consider briefly the origin, universality and history of religion. The origin of religion is held by the evolutionary school to have commenced with fear in the heart of primitive man as he cowered, a poor, jibbering, half ape in some cave, nursing his wounds which he had received in the struggle for existence. This theory has been carefully expounded in a book by Lewis Browne, called, *This Believing World*. He tells that this primitive man who was a poor half ape had a conception that all of the things in nature bore him malice, that he looked upon sticks, stones and storms as animate and that only gradually he found that he could not fight back against such things as boulders which crushed him or lightning which struck him, so he peopled these objects with spirits to whom he addressed groans, shouts accompanied by the beating of tom-toms, and words. From this he proceeded to the use of luck charms and wild dances. From this he stepped up to fetishism, thence to the medicine-man, and finally, because of times of drought and of pestilence, he began to offer sacrifices to the sun and moon and stars. Later each tribe had its own god and after many centuries some few began to think of one God of the universe. This theory holds that all primitive religions today are akin to the first religion of mankind. That this is contrary to the facts of history we have already mentioned, for the latest developments in both anthropology and archeology have revealed that the earliest recorded religions of mankind in the cradle of the race were monotheistic and only after many centuries did polytheism enter.

Thus we are still constrained to accept the Biblical teaching that religion had its origin in man's moral sense of obligation and spiritual sense of guilt or sin. The Bible tells us that in the original state man was innocent and righteous, but when the fall occurred he received the knowledge of good and evil. This is innate in all mankind, leading to a sense of offense, of guilt and of the need of propitiating Deity. The resultant shame from this sin which came upon the first man in knowing that he had done evil caused him to attempt to hide from God. Religion ever since has continued upon this line of covering and protecting man from God. In the beginning the Lord gave a promise of redemption and he instituted a sacrifice as a type of that redemption and the religions of the world hold in common the idea of sacrifice, although degraded in many forms. These four facts of man's original relationship with God; first of righteousness and fellowship, second of the fall and the knowledge of good and evil, third, of the resultant shame and effort to hide from God, fourth, the promise of redemption and the institution of sacrifice, are the facts which are back of all of the religions of the world and account for their similarity.

That religion is now universal among all men everywhere is admitted. Though some tribes have been suspected of having no religion, after investigators have lived in their midst for a while, they have been proved to possess a religion more or less crude or refined. No less an authority than Prof. Max Muller said, "We may safely say that in spite of all the searching no human beings have been found anywhere who do not possess something which to them is religion; or to put it in a most agreeable form, a belief in something beyond what they can see with their eyes." However degraded the particular religion which we may find among certain people of the earth, the presence of religion among men shows the sense that all is not right between man and God. Surely if there were ever any evidence which proved the fall in the history of man this is it.

The archeological excavations at Kish and Erech in Babylonia uncovered tablets of writing from a period as early as 3000 B.C., revealing a primitive monotheism. There are many cylinders and monuments of great antiquity gathered from Egypt, Babylon and Assyria which vindicate the common tradition among early mankind of the events which in very clear language are given to us in the book of Genesis, such as the existence of one God, the fall of man, the coming of a flood and the dispersion of the human race. One particular cylinder of great antiquity in the British Museum represents a man and woman by a tree. On one branch of the tree are two large fruit toward which they are stretching their hands. Behind the woman appears the serpent. This cylinder is held to antedate the Genesis account by hundreds of years. Likewise the story of the deluge has been reconstructed almost entirely by fragments of a poem found in the library of Ashurbanipal in Assyria. Bible scholars might go on giving the confirmation of the early evidence of a unity in the knowledge of God, of the fall, of punishment and of the promise of redemption from early archeological discoveries. Does this mean then that the Old Testament Biblical account was woven out of whole cloth, by the writers thereof? Such could hardly be true, for by the time the earliest books of the Old Testament were written these early evidences were completely obliterated in a common polytheism of heathenism. Out of this God called Abraham. It was four hundred years after Abraham that the revelation of the Pentateuch was given to Moses.

Thus we believe that Christianity is unique in its nature, that it is a Divine revelation and supernatural throughout. It has a supernatural basis in the Old Testament revelations made by God to His prophets from Moses to Malachi. It has a supernatural Person at its center who is Jesus Christ, declared by His mighty works, by His Person, by His teachings and by His resurrection to be the Son of God. It has a supernatural message of redemption through the loving act of God, Who Himself carried the condemnation of sin in order that man might be justified. It has a supernatural power which is vested in the Person of the Holy Spirit, who is able to work in the life of the individual, bringing supernatural life and experience to pass. Unique in its origin, its center and its workings, Christianity is altogether different from the religions of the world.

II. THE CHURCH VERSUS CHRIST.

Since Christianity has been established as the means of reconciliation between man and God, a theory has been advanced that the church is the one means of salvation. This is evidence of man's turning the revelation of God into a religion which is as external as the other religions of the world. Again it is a degeneration, a deterioration. This reaches its height in those branches of Christendom which offer salvation through the magic of baptism, of sacrament, of the authority of the clergy, regardless of their character, and through the confines and boundaries of the church and that alone. This theory is present in a measure in all branches of Christendom, giving a false encouragement to men because of their privilege in belonging to a particular organization.

There is a distinct parallel between what Paul discovered concerning the Jews and this modern teaching. He declared, "Thou art called a Jew, and restest in the law, and makest thy boast of God, and knowest his will, and approvest the things that are more excellent, being instructed out of the law; and art confident that thou thyself art a guide of the blind, a light of them which are in darkness, an instructor of the foolish, a teacher of babes, which hast the form of knowledge and of the truth in the law." These Jews had everything. Abraham was their father; they were children of the covenant. Circumcision was the external seal of their being the children of God. The oracles, or the word of God, were in their care. Of them the Messiah came. Great is the advantage of those who have such blessings. Every Jew whose heart condition corresponded to the covenant privilege enjoyed that salvation, but the pity of it was, as Paul said, "Thou therefore which teachest another, teachest thou not thyself? Thou that preachest a man should not steal, dost thou steal?" These Jews trusted in their privilege and continued in sin, with hearts that were far from the Lord. This, of course, made their condemnation all the greater. However, this is merely another way of saying the same thing about professing Christians who live under the baptismal covenant, who were born into Christian families, who have been received into church membership, who have a knowledge of the truth and yet whose actions declare their hearts are far from God.

Privilege in this regard is not without advantage but it gives no security. What advantage had the Jews? Much every way, for they had a great opportunity for salvation. What advantage has the baptized church member? Much in every way for he is sanctified by the positional covenant which ought to make him bear fruit for the Lord, but there is no security in these advantages. Just as the circumcized Jews were judged by their keeping of the law, so church members will be judged by their knowledge and privilege. Paul went on to say about the Jews, "The name of God is blasphemed among the Gentiles through you." They were dishonest, greedy, and immoral, and thought that because they were children of Abraham they would be saved. Thus innumerable multitudes of professing Christians, indulging in things which are contrary to the will of God, think that they will be saved because they are in the church organization, because they have religion, because they partake of the sacraments, when at the same time they are causing the name of Christ to be blasphemed among the heathen and leading pagans into condemnation because of it. Churchianity, the opposite of Christianity, instead of manifesting the revelation of God in Christ may become, as it often has become, a degenerated, deteriorated religion of the world, full of idols, incense and priestcraft, undistinguishable from heathenism.

As against all this, the Bible presents Christ as the means of salvation. When Peter was preaching to Cornelius' household about Christ, who was to be the judge of the quick and the dead, he said, "To him give all the prophets witness, that through his name whosoever believeth in him shall receive remission of sins." Christ is central to the Old Testament revelation. All the prophets bore witness to him as the means of salvation. Christ is exalted in the New Testament preaching and life. It is by His incarnation, His atoning sacrifice, His resurrection and His authority that we have salvation. Now Christ is the head of the spiritual Church which is His body and He is exalted at the right hand of God giving life to His own. Salvation comes to the individual by Christ and not by the church. It was not the Old Testament church organization or nation which brought salvation to the individual but his faith in the divine revelation concerning Christ. It is not membership in the New Testament church organization which brings salvation to an individual, but when he is saved by Christ he becomes a member of the true spiritual Church. Thus salvation is not a matter of submission to the ordinary ordinances of religion, but of submission to the person of Christ. In the Bible, salvation is a personal matter between God and the sinner wrought out by the Lord Jesus Christ. All saved Christians bear such a testimony to the Person of Christ. Paul said, "Be it known unto you . . . that through this man is preached unto you the forgiveness of sins: and by him all that believe are justified from all things, from which ye could not be justified by the law of Moses."

Church privilege or position within organized Christendom may easily keep one from true salvation. Some trust in their privileges rather than in Christ, as did the Jews, but there is no excuse for it. This fact will not invalidate church membership, baptism and the ordinances of Christianity, for in spite of men's failure, God will fulfill His purpose with Christendom as He did with Israel. The Jews ask, "Shall their unbelief make the faith (faithfulness) of God without effect?" Paul answered, "God forbid: Yea, let God be found true, but every man a liar." If every Jew had failed the Lord, He would still fulfill His purpose which had been foretold in His prophets to Israel. If the vast mass of Christendom apostatizes, God will still fulfill His purposes and promises in relation to the true

Church. Then the Jews asked, "If our unrighteousness commend the righteousness of God, . . . is God unrighteous who taketh vengeance?" This meant that if the unbelief and evil of the Jews actually forwarded the plan of God, how could God still judge them as sinners? Paul replied that the Judge of all the world will do right and the fact that God's purposes were promoted in their wickedness will never excuse them. Likewise, though the apostacy rapidly gathering momentum in Christendom will actually bring about the prophesied future events, this will not exclude individuals from the judgment of the Lord. It is true that the rejection by the Jews brought about Calvary and was included in the plan of God, but it did not lessen one whit the culpability in the Jews' sin. Therefore, if any one takes the attitude, "Let us do evil, that good may come," he will be justly condemned in the judgment.

III. SALVATION VERSUS MAGIC.

As soon as true religion degenerates from the revelation of God magic receives a large place in it. The religions of the world exalt the idea of magic. The initiatory ceremonies in the ancient religions were magical ceremonies. In the Eleusian religion, there was first of all the ceremony called the blood bath, after which the initiate participated in a sacred meal. This brought him into relationship with the deity. Similar rites were held in the cult of Isis and of Mithras. In the Eleusian mysteries the climax of the celebration was reached in the mystic plays. The initiates stood outside the temple. In the darkness the doors were opened and in a blaze of light there was acted before them a great drama of the festival. There were no words spoken. It was an acted parable in silence, but there was an awful individuality about it. The initiates saw the sight in common, but each one saw it for himself. The effect of it was to conceive a change in relationship to the gods. By it the initiated were made partakers of the life to come. Of course, the central figure in all this was the priest who was the mediator between the gods and the individual passing through the ceremony. He dispensed the magic. Much of this was transferred bodily from the heathenism to early Christendom, when Christianity degenerated from a pure religion to a world religion. Then baptismal regeneration was taught. Then through magic words and ceremonies individuals supposedly were saved. Then priestly power began to be exercised over souls for the present life and for hereafter. Then vigils were kept for the sake of receiving visions. The proportion in which this idea of magic prevails in the church is the proportion of Christendom's deterioration into a religion instead of being the custodian of the means of salvation.

Contrast this magical religion with the direct heart relationship of salvation through Christ proclaimed in the Bible. Biblical Christianity tells us to repent and confess our sins unto God and Christ, and to trust an atonement made by the Son of God by which our sins have been condemned and taken away. Here we are promised a complete, supernatural regeneration by the power of God and by the indwelling Holy Spirit who is God in us. Thus Paul said, "circumcision is that of the heart, in the spirit, and not in the letter." Not by obedience to the letter of the law nor to the external requirements of religion, but by the indwelling of the Holy Spirit we have the true change of heart which God requires and which alone will stand in our favor in the judgment.

Confidence of salvation is possible for a believer. This salvation is not given by the authority of men, the clergy, the priesthood, the religion. There can be no satisfying confidence from these external, human matters. Confidence of salvation is given in the witness of the word of God, concerning what Christ has done for us, which we have accepted, and which is attested by the evidences produced in our lives in accordance with that word. This confidence of salvation is the result of a direct, personal relationship to God through His Son, the Lord Jesus Christ, and removes one from all condemnation.

Just as we have seen the heathen world under condemnation, the moral world under condemnation, we now see the religious world under condemnation. Whoever is outside of Christ is under the wrath of God which is revealed from heaven against all ungodliness and unrighteousness of men. Therefore, come out from your shelter of church membership, from your confidence in your baptism, from your false trust in man's authority; seek Christ the righteousness of God; know that your sin has been condemned in His Cross, and that through His blood you are saved. He is not a Christian who is one outwardly by his religiosity, but he is a Christian who is one inwardly in the heart and in spirit.

V

THE SINNER'S PICTURE PAINTED BY GOD

"All have sinned and come short of the glory of God,"—Rom. 3:9-23.

PICTURES are very fascinating. Even pictures of ourselves have a peculiar interest for most of us. When one is in the presence of the art masterpieces of the ages, he is overwhelmed with the sublimity of expression, the keenness of insight, and the clarity of vision such men had. Raphael, the painter of madonnas, has a most wonderful work in the Dresden Zwinger gallery called the "Sistine Madonna." It was painted for an altar piece. He had the popes kneeling beside it and the angels in light clouds behind it. Most of us have seen the reproductions of it without these two phases. His "Transfiguration" is the greatest of his works. You who have seen it, or prints of it, with the Christ suspended in mid-air just after Moses and Elias have departed, know what the touch of an artist hand means.

In St. Peter's is that great painting, the "Last Judgment," by Leonardo da Vinci, a fresco with one hundred figures on it representing the nations of the earth come for judgment. His "Last Supper" is the most famous of his works. Partly defaced from whitewash which covered it when the Graecia-Maria Church in Milan was used as a stable, it still reveals the master's hand. It pictures Christ saying, "One of you shall betray me," and the reactions of the disciples are shown by their hands. They are seated on one side of the table in groups of three each. It is an epochal work and has never been surpassed. Then there are secular paintings of great note. Some of us have spent hours in the various galleries of the world—in the Hermitage, the Trechikov, the Zwinger, Versailles, Potsdam, the Huntingdon, the Tuilleries, etc., trying to absorb some of the genius behind such pictures as the "Blue Boy" by T. Gainsborough; the "Scene on the Tours" by Constable; and "Red Riding Hood" by Sir Joshua Reynolds; "The Hunt" by van Eck; the "Night Watch" by Rembrandt; and scores of others. It is only now and then that one can break through his limitations and see the wonder of them.

THE SINNER'S PICTURE PAINTED BY GOD

Often we have watched nature paint her pictures in spring and fall with color, harmony, and beauty which mortal artists cannot reproduce. We have watched the sun rise out of the ocean, or hills, or canyons, sometimes guarded by the dogs of war, sometimes preceded by the rainbow, enchanting the world, but always casting its cheering light. We have seen it drop slowly and peacefully through the Golden Gate or behind trees or lakes, always spreading the peace and calm of an evening twilight. A tinge of frost, a covering of a blanket of snow, a dead tree silhouetted against a gray sky, a blossoming plant, a blooming flower—truly nature reveals God to the opened eye. Word pictures are hardly less vivid at times.

But of all pictures those in the Bible are most wonderful. They have been the inspiration for the artists of all ages. Take for example such scenes as the Flood, the Destruction of the Tower of Babel, the Bondage of the Israelites, the destruction of Jerusalem by Nebuchadnezzar, the prophet Jeremiah seated in the ruins of Jerusalem lamenting, the Crucifixion, the Ascension, and finally, such as the Four Horsemen of the Apocalypse. Some of these appear in almost every gallery, but they are more real in the Word.

The picture to which I draw your attention is the clearest depiction of the human soul in language. It is as if we took a mirror and gazed into it, discerning the thoughts and intents of our hearts; it is as if we stripped the covering from our souls and saw their hidden secrets; it is as if we turned our hearts inside out to private and public gaze. It is a picture of your soul and my soul held before us to gaze upon. It is the most true picture we shall ever get because it is sketched by the hand of God. It is as true as the writing upon the wall of Babylon during Belshazzar's feast. It cannot be sidestepped so we must face it. It is the most terrible picture ever drawn of the human soul. Thus it is an argument for the inspiration of the Bible, for no man would ever describe himself as such.

There is a difference between portraits and photographs. A portrait emphasizes the main characteristics while a photograph includes all details. In this picture God has painted the portrait, we shall supply the details. We can grasp the portrait clearly from God, we can apply it to ourselves as we see the details. Now we shall turn to the sinner's picture as it is painted by God, and to its implications. These are: Our picture; our propitiation; and our plea.

I. OUR PICTURE.

"There is none righteous, no, not one." This picture as drawn in Romans 3:10-18, shows what men have not done, what they have done, and what they are by nature.

They have not been righteous. "There is none righteous, no, not one." We may try to be righteous and some men may even think they are. But I have never found a man who would not admit that he was a sinner. God says, "The heart is deceitful above all things, and desperately wicked: who can know it?" (Jer. 17:9). And, "If we say that we have not sinned, we make Him a liar, and His Word is not in us," (I John 1:9). Also in Isa. 64:6, "All our righteousnesses are as filthy rags." Thus God makes His first bold stroke and says, "none are righteous."

Then God says man has not understood spiritual things; "there is none that understandeth." This agrees exactly with Paul's words, "The natural man receiveth not the things of the Spirit of God: for they are foolishness unto him: neither can he know them, because they are spiritually discerned," (I Cor. 2:14). One summer I was thrown into contact with an educated doctor from Chicago University, who was a rationalist. We discussed philosophy by the hour, but when I would try to swing him around to the philosophy of the Cross, he would call me "a fool," and that argument, "stuff." He would say, "Can you never leave that alone? You argue intelligently enough on other subjects. Why must you return to that?" The preaching of the Cross was to the Greeks foolishness and to the Jews a stumbling block. Why? Because they were natural men and could not discern spiritual things. No man without the Spirit of God understands spiritual things. As an animal such as a horse or a dog cannot understand the things of men, so men cannot understand the things of God.

Then another base line is put in and God says, "There is none that seeks after God." We have a peculiar notion today, which is being propagated from our pulpits, that man everywhere is seeking God. God here says that is a lie. No man seeks God. Man is religious by nature, but instead of seeking God, he is trying to hide from God. Adam is an illustration of this. In the cool of the day after he had sinned, he did not go about calling, "O God, where are you?" No! God sought him calling, "Adam, where art thou?" And Adam was in hiding, trying to cover his wickedness with fig leaves. God has been seeking men ever since. This is shown in Romans 1:18

THE SINNER'S PICTURE PAINTED BY GOD

and following. When man is left to himself he entirely deserts God and gives himself up to wickedness. In this passage the philosophy of religion is presented. Man had revelation and was without excuse; he left God and sought sin, changing the glory of an incorruptible God to the image of corruptible things. And God gave him up to uncleanness. God stopped striving with him and left him alone, to himself. Then we read that man burned in his lusts one toward another, and God gave him up to vile affections. Leaving him alone to such an extent he did not even want to retain God in his knowledge, so the Word says God gave him up to a reprobate mind. Three times God gave man up and he went on down in his sin. This is a history of the race which once knew God, and it is the history of every individual who will not respond to God's seeking. Naturally, no man seeks God.

The negative preparation being finished by verses 10 and 11, God places some positive characteristics in. He tells us what man has done. "They are all gone out of the way." Man has erred; he has taken the wrong path. He has turned to his own way rather than God's way. It may have seemed smoother, but it led him astray. He has done this in face of the clearness of the way. Isaiah says, "An highway shall be there, and a way, and it shall be called the way of holiness; the unclean shall not pass over it; but it shall be for those: the wayfaring men, though fools, shall not err therein," (35:8). Man knows the way, but he prefers another, such as the way of pleasure, of sin and of riches. "Blessed is the man who walketh not in the way of the ungodly."

"They are together become unprofitable." Man is always a liability to God rather than an asset. You never do God a favor by accepting His salvation; you are benefiting yourself. It is true that God is pleased to bestow such upon us, but there is no room for boasting; it is pure grace. God would still be righteous if He blotted out the entire race; but He has seen fit to show us favor instead. Life at its best is a worthless, useless, wreck to God, if it is without Christ. We might crudely say, "God is in the salvage business, saving what He can from the wrecks of humanity." Once these wrecks are in Christ, they are worth the world to God for they are fit for His fellowship.

There is "none that doeth good, no not one." If man does no good, then he does evil continually. Gen. 6:5 shows this clearly. After the fall man had been left to himself. The line of grace soon faded away by intermarrying and intermixing with the line of sin, until just before the flood the Word says, "And God saw that the wickedness of man was great in the earth and every imagination of the thoughts of his heart was only of evil continually." Notice the superlatives in that sentence: great, every, only, continually. Can man with such a nature do good? The Bible never says that man cannot do moral good, social good, ceremonial good, but only that he can do no spiritual good. It is only God's common grace which prevents him from becoming so bad as to necessitate another judgment. Man militates against God.

Next we learn what man is by nature, (13-18). The rubric, or 13th verse, gives us the clue of this passage. It tells us what man's nature is. His nature is as rotten as an open sepulchre. Standing before the tomb of Lazarus, Jesus had ordered the stone rolled away. Martha, knowing that decomposition had set in, remonstrated, saying, "for the body stinketh." So it is with our nature. The seven statements under this rubric correspond exactly to the seven types of sinners in the lake of fire, (Rev. 21:8). When the list is inverted it shows that man does not become a liar after he has lied but is a liar by nature. In Romans, God tells us what the end of this nature will be unless changed. The bones of a dead man, and the fumes of the lake of fire constitute a terrible picture, showing man dead spiritually and doomed to hell.

Notice the close comparison. "With their tongues they have used deceit," and the last class in Revelation is the liar. There may be different categories of lies in our catalogue, but there is only one in God's—anything spoken with intent to deceive, whether insidious flattery or uncharitable falsehood.

"The poison of asps is under their tongue." This poison is no other than idolatry. That is, the false doctrine to other gods. It is the most deadly poison existing, far worse than the blue fluid spurting from the rattlesnake's fangs after he has struck. It can kill the soul. Cleopatra, when finished with the terrible folly of her life and being condemned to prison, had secreted to her in a basket of figs an asp. She had previously experimented upon her slaves to see what was the most deadly poison which killed without pain. She knew that such an end was coming so when the hour struck she allowed the asp to bite her. Almost instantly she was dead. Such is the poison covered under the idolatrous lips of the false religious prophets of the day.

"Their mouth is full of cursing and bitterness." They are sorcerers, bitter against God, trying Spiritualism and magic arts, sold

THE SINNER'S PICTURE PAINTED BY GOD

out to the devil and hell. They are twentieth century Dr. Fausts. In common their mouth is full of profanity.

"Their feet are swift to shed blood." Revelation is plainer, it calls them murderers. Ever since Cain, man has been a murderer. The fact that God restrained it in Noah's day by civil government and capital punishment is all that keeps the natural man from murder. The heart of man without God is full of hate and murder. Today, murder is carried on in the mass. Blitzkrieg is a lightening mass murder, regardless of the nation which conducts it.

"Destruction and misery are in their ways." They are abominable. They make pretenses of religion and yet carry on injustice. They indulge in sin and yet think God will hear them pray when they are in need. One fraternal order asks the initiate, "On whom do you put your trust in times of peril?" "On God" is the answer. Unless such a man knows God through his daily life, his prayer in time of peril is an abomination to God. Misery follows in the train of man's history. What a judgment on his nature!

"The way of peace they have not known." Revelation calls them unbelievers. This is more definite. Who has the peace of God in his soul? Only he who believes on Jesus Christ. "Being justified by faith, we have peace with God through our Lord Jesus Christ." Then God gives us "the peace which passeth all understanding." No unbeliever can know the way of peace.

"There is no fear of God in their eyes." They are fearful because there is no fear of God in them. The man who fears God fears none other, but the man who fears not God fears everything. He has no security whatever.

Thus with such a nature we can never inherit the kingdom of God, for the Scripture says, "The fearful, and unbelieving, and the abominable, and murderers, and whoremongers, and sorcerers, and idolators, and all liars, shall have their part in the lake which burneth with fire and brimstone." This picture shows the results of sin, but we are sinners by nature and are included in this class unless redeemed by the blood of Christ.

II. OUR PROPITIATION.

But even with so dismal a picture we are not left without hope. God has provided a propitiation. That we need this is evident. The text says, "All have sinned and come short of the glory of God." We have all fallen and are now unrighteous. Our picture shows us that.

This throws us into a difficult case. God is a righteous Judge or He is not perfect. Being righteous, He must punish sin. This is a law of His nature. If He is the Creator, Ruler, and Governor of the universe, His law of righteousness must be sustained. Every theist admits this.

But by the above Scriptural proof, man is fallen and sinful and deserving of punishment regardless of what he can do. Justice demands the punishment of man.

However, God being perfect must be merciful, and if merciful must forgive sin. Here we have a dilemma; God must forgive and must punish. How can He do both to one man? There is only one escape and that can come through a substitute who makes propitiation. It is here that Unitarianism fails; it can never meet this difficulty. The substitute must be God to atone for all men, to make an infinite satisfaction; and he must be man to represent man. Therefore, He must be a God-man. Such a Person we find in Jesus Christ. And it was in Him that mercy and truth met, that justice and peace kissed. Here the natural mind rebels and calls this philosophy of the Cross and of a suffering God a trick of legerdemain; but though to the wise it is foolishness, to those who believe, it has been proved to be the power of God to salvation.

This propitiation cannot come by the law. By the law every mouth is stopped and men are made guilty before God. They have not lived up to the law and thus cannot be justified by it. The law makes conscious of sin; it is a schoolmaster which leads to Christ, (Gal. 3:24). By the deeds of the law no flesh shall be justified in His sight. For if it is by law, it is reckoned of debt and not of grace (Rom. 4:4). And this debt could never be paid (Eph. 2:8,9). By the law is the knowledge of sin. It leads directly from Sinai to Calvary. The rumblings of Sinai can only throw one upon Calvary in flight (Rom. 7:12). No propitiation is ever made by the law.

But propitiation is made through Christ. "Being justified freely by His grace through the redemption which is in Christ Jesus: whom God hath set forth to be a propitiation through faith in His blood." Righteousness can come only without the law and through faith. Abraham was justified through faith before the law existed. But the law came to witness to the righteousness of God, that is, His justice. This justice is satisfied in Christ's propitiation and is applied unto those believing in declaring them to be righteous. The answer to the above dilemma is manifested here in that justification of sinners is given through the redemption which is in Christ Jesus. He

THE SINNER'S PICTURE PAINTED BY GOD

bore the penalty, He took man's place in death. He made redemption possible. Through His sacrifice we are set free.

And propitiation is made in the forbearance of God. He did not judge the world of mankind because He looked forward to Christ. It is made for the remission of sins. The blood of bulls and goats had covered the sins of the past, but the blood of Christ now removes them all, both past and future. It is made through faith in His blood. This is the way of application. It is made for all men, but applied only to those who have a saving faith in His blood.

This is to declare God righteous (just) and the justifier of those who believe in Christ. It is the marvelous philosophy of the Cross.

III. OUR PLEA.

What then is our plea? Do we have a right to salvation because of our works? "Therefore we conclude that a man is justified by faith without the deeds of the law."

This removes our boasting. All boasting is excluded. Where are the sacraments then? They are excluded, being only symbols, with no virtue in a priest's blessing. Where are works then? They are excluded, being only expressions of love which Christ has put in the heart. We work out salvation according to the power that worketh within us. Where is self then? It is excluded, buried deep in the grave of Christ. "I live, yet not I, but Christ liveth in me."

This rests our salvation in Christ. "Jesus Christ my wisdom, my righteousness, my sanctification, my redemption." He becomes my wisdom, my guide through life; not a professor, not a college education, not a philosophy, but the teachings and work of Christ. He becomes my righteousness, my guilt of sins. He bore my sins, lifted the ban, set me free. He becomes my sanctification, my guardian from evil. He will not let my foot slip. He will defeat the enemy. He will keep me. He becomes my redemption, my glory. He will swing wide the gates of heaven and take me in. He is my all in all.

This reveals God and man in the correct relationship. God is just, merciful, perfect, the omnipotent Creator and Preserver of the universe. Man is a sinner lost and condemned, but is justified and declared righteous through a substitute whom he accepts and in whom he trusts. God and man are in harmony; God sovereign and ruling, man obedient and humble, but glorious in the image of God.

VI

THE RIGHTEOUSNESS OF GOD

"Whom God hath set forth to be a propitiation through faith in his blood, to declare his righteousness for the remission of sins that are past."—Rom. 3:24-27.

THIS text brought Martin Luther into the glorious liberty of the sons of God. This text thrust Karl Barth into the forefront of the ranks of living theologians. And this text has brought peace to the hearts of countless multitudes who have meditated upon its truth. It is taken from the most wonderful passage of Scripture in the Bible, that which declares a truth which could not be set forth until the time in which the Apostle Paul proclaimed it.

We should bow our hearts in reverence, prepare our minds in solemnity and catch our breath in expectancy before this wonderful and awful truth, for here we see God in all His holiness and unapproachable majesty as well as in the condescending mercy and love which proceed out from Him as a billowing ocean. Here the preacher stands before the center of Divine wisdom, the flower of revelation, the climax of history, with the riches of grace and the end of the plan of the ages. This truth will melt the heart of stone and will summon the hatred of the damned. It will turn the hardened sinner from his ways and will enrage the self-righteous. It will manifest infinite love to fallen man and will win the lost and wandering prodigal. How can the preacher speak this truth in a faltering, human tongue? He must cry, "Oh God, visit me with illumination of Thy Holy Spirit, anoint my lips, quicken my mind, chain my enemy the devil and release the words and the thoughts that will convey thy heart of love, thy majestic justice and thy unspeakable way of redemption. Let the people hear and understand even what thy servant is incapable of expressing."

It is clear from God's revelation that Divine wrath rests upon the heathen, who have not retained the knowledge of God in their mind but have turned to worship the creature rather than the Creator, whom God has given up to uncleanness and to a reprobate mind. It is clear that condemnation and wrath rests also upon moral men who by their philosophy rest in a security of self-righteousness when truly

THE RIGHTEOUSNESS OF GOD

they are guilty of the sins which they condemn in others. Their true state will be revealed at the inevitable judgment. It is also clear from the Divine revelation that there is a lack of escape from the Divine judgment and condemnation for the religious man. External religious privileges and relationships will never save the man who is not in Christ. Thus the Scripture declares that all men are depraved, that they are unable to save themselves, that they are sinful and unrighteous, and therefore are under the wrath of God which is revealed against all unrighteousness.

Man has been manifested as not having the right relationship to God or to his fellowmen. He is not righteous, that is, he has not discharged his obligation and his duties and his debt to others. The terrible denunciation from heaven on the children of men, because of what they have not done, what they have done, and what they are by nature, we have seen in the sinner's picture as painted by God. This terrible unrighteousness confines all men under Divine wrath. We must remember, however, that the word, "wrath" contains no notion of an incensed Deity in fury, but it reveals justice requiring its demands in moral universe. Throughout this entire passage there is no thought of placating a vengeful God, but only of doing right by God's holy law and so making it possible for him righteously to show mercy upon sinners. God's wrath is most clearly manifested in the Cross in that He spared not His own Son but made Him the object of righteous punishment and the example of what holiness requires on behalf of sin. His wrath was not against the Person of Christ, for he was only drinking the bitter cup which it was necessary to drink, nor was God's anger manifested against the sinner, for God loved the sinner, but the Cross reveals God's wrath against sin. It was the going forth of the infinitely holy nature of God against sin and this necessary wrath fell full on the Person of Christ. Justice in operation means for the soul bitterness, woe, torment, and hell because of unrighteousness.

The question dealt with in this passage of Scripture is how unrighteous, wicked, depraved mankind, which deserves judgment and death, can be declared righteous before the Divine tribunal. Let us remember that justification is purely external and deals with man's relationship with an infinitely holy, just and righteous God. That is why justifying faith is a faith relating to God. It is the belief in and the acceptance of what God declares Christ has done for the sinner. The means of obtaining this righteousness for man must be worthy of God and must shew forth not only His moral consistency, but also His goodness and mercy which are at the heart of the universe. Hence it is with a sense of great relief that we turn from Divine revelation which speaks forth condemnation, guilt and wrath to the Gospel which speaks forth mercy, life and salvation. It is like emerging from the gloom of a Swiss mountain tunnel into a sun bathed valley of Italy in all the glories of spring. Here we see the goodness and mercy of God at its height.

The words of this passage of Scripture begin with the phrase, "But now." These are both descriptive of a temporal transition and of a linguistic change. Now a new point of emphasis was to be made. As the extremity of man's condition was fully manifested in the development of the argument, the point came to declare the wondrous plan of salvation. Similarly, temporally, when man reached the lowest point of his extremity, God undertook for him in history. In the "fullness of time" Christ was born. "In the last days" God sent forth His Son.

Man had failed in every way under God's tests, previous to this final manifestation of salvation. First, man was tested in innocence in the garden of Eden under one commandment, "Of the tree of the knowledge of good and evil, thou shalt not eat," but man listened to Satan's suggestion and sinned. Under the first test man was a failure. Then, with the knowledge of good and evil, man was tested as to whether he would live according to his conscience or not. He still had the original knowledge of God but no direct revelation was given to him, and within a few generations, the Lord's estimate of man was, "the wickedness of man was great in the earth, and every imagination of the thoughts of his heart was only evil continually." Man had again fallen. Later, the law was given as a direct revelation from God concerning the measure of righteousness which God demands from men, but the chosen people to whom the law was given broke the law, slew the prophets, whom God sent to recall them to Him, and became hopelessly corrupt. Finally, in the consummation of the ages, God sent forth His Son in order to manifest in the flesh His righteousness, but Him they hated, rejected and crucified, revealing that in man there was no good thing. Hence, after all these centuries in which man proved that he had no righteousness, the only hope which remained was that God should undertake for him and we have the words, "But now." This God now did and by the incarnation, the life, the death and the resurrection of Christ, God's righteousness was so manifested that a new ground of righteousness could be offered unto men which never was possible before.

Now when man has been shown unrighteous, the righteousness of God could be manifested. This, then, is the place to set forward God's great work in bold relief. God's righteousness is to be obtained as a free gift, available for all. Christ died for all men. The propitiation was made that righteousness be available for all, although it is not applied unto all. Corresponding to this great "Now" in which redemption is wrought out, other "Nows" of the Scripture are announced. The first is that "Now" God no longer winks at the times of man's ignorance, but calls upon him to repent because he will be brought into judgment. Moreover, "Now" is the time of salvation. Today is the day. Now that the righteousness of God has been revealed whereby a guilty man may be declared righteous, there can be no excuse for man remaining unrighteous. If we neglect this means of righteousness, we can not escape the judgment of God.

This reveals a new way of God's dealing with men. No longer will men be dealt with on the principle of law, but now of grace. The righteousness of God utterly apart from the law is now manifested to the world in the cross of Christ. It becomes our duty and our privilege to show forth this Divine way of reconciliation of wicked men to absolute righteousness through the Cross.

I. THE RIGHTEOUSNESS OF GOD.

When we speak of the righteousness of God we must consider it from three aspects. First, as a characteristic of God, Second, as a characteristic of Christ. Third, as a characteristic of the justified sinner. In connection with God, righteousness signifies His action toward the man Christ Jesus in raising Him from the dead and exalting Him to the right hand of glory, and in giving to those who believe on Christ the same relationship to the Father as Christ actually bears. This is the attribute of righteousness or self consistency operating in the nature of God as it relates to man. Concerning Christ, righteousness means the declaration of the self consistency of God in dealing with sin, for Christ is the Lamb slain in satisfaction for the demands of God's holiness and justice. Publicly before the universe, God is declared as righteous in passing over the sins of justified sinners and of judging the unjustified in accordance with His holy law. The righteousness of the justified sinner means that he is now accepted by God as in Christ, justified from all of his past sins by the blood of Christ, accepted on the ground of the resurrection of Christ, and given a new life in this federal head. Thus the righteousness of God is a provision of God for sinful man, which we call salvation.

Our Scripture says "the righteousness of God without the law is manifested, being witnessed by the law and the prophets." The emphasis here is on the words "without the law." It is very hard for man to understand that he can be righteous without fulfilling the requirements of the law, whether that is manifested in commandments or in character or in good deeds. God specifically says that righteousness is without the law. If man is to be justified at all it must be apart from any principle of obedience to Divine law, whether it is one written in his heart or one given to him on tablets of stone. The law of God has nothing to offer sinful man but condemnation. It shows up the sin that is in our hearts. It reveals our lost condition and it never justifies. Hence, whatever God's righteousness is which He gives to man, it is not the making up of defects in man's standing before the Lord.

We all know how perverse and wicked Israel was, yet when Balaam spoke for the Lord he said, "He hath not beheld iniquity in Jacob, neither hath he seen perverseness in Israel: . . . Let me die the death of the righteous, and let my last end be like his!" There is an acceptance which is not based upon the fulfillment of the requirements of the law. If the righteousness which God gave to men only made up man's defects it would only give him a righteous standing in the flesh, as a child of Adam, and this is invalidated by the sin principle. In the flesh there is no good thing. Hence God's righteousness must be upon a new principle of grace and faith through Christ. This was declared in the key verse of the book of Romans, "Therein is the righteousness of God revealed from faith to faith," that is, "on the principle of faith to those believing." This righteousness must be in accordance with God's justice. If wicked man is to be saved at all, his salvation must be in harmony and in consistency with Divine justice and Divine righteousness. A way must be found to satisfy the claims of justice, declaring guilty man to be righteous. God's righteousness applied to Himself must be His consistency with His own law and His own holiness in freely justifying a sinner who believes in Christ.

Though this gift of righteousness is utterly apart from the law and must never be associated with the law, yet it is witnessed by the law and the prophets. It was purposed by God from before the foundation of the world. In the eternal counsels of God Christ was

THE RIGHTEOUSNESS OF GOD 63

the Lamb slain. In the first promise made unto man the Messiah was to be bruised. This righteousness of God was manifested in the law. There was the testimony of the coats of skin whereby our first parents were clothed. There were the sacrificial victims accepted because of the faith of those who offered them. There was the wonderful symbolism of the tabernacle into which the guilty person could come only by a blood atonement. The entire law witnessed to a kind of righteousness obtained apart from the law. This was also true in the prophets. The prophets declared that His name whereby He shall be called is "Jehovah our righteousness," Jer. 23:6. "By his knowledge shall my righteous servant justify many," i.e., "make many righteous," Isa. 53:11. "To bring in everlasting righteousness shall Messiah be cut off," Dan. 9:24,26. It was in perfect accordance with Divine justice and holiness that He should have smitten every sinner as Sodom and Gomorrha was destroyed. God was not obliged to save any man but it was His purpose to reveal Himself, for He is love. Therefore God's full nature comes into evidence at the Cross, where His love and His holiness meet in providing a way of salvation for guilty, sinful, wicked men.

But this Divine righteousness provided for man is a "by faith righteousness." Paul says, "Even the righteousness of God which is by faith of Jesus Christ unto all and upon all them that believe." Here is a return unto the declaration made in the opening verses of this book of the Gospel of God concerning His Son, Jesus Christ our Lord. The faith is the taking of God at His Word. It is not the looking to Christ to do something to save. It is the believing of God's testimony that He has done something for us. It is the conviction that God's Word concerning what God has done on the Cross is true. God freely offers salvation, His righteousness, the acceptance in the beloved to all who will believe that He has done this. Hence, all of the verses in the Bible which proclaim salvation by faith. Jesus said, "He that believeth on me, believeth not on me, but on him that sent me." The Gospel concerning His Son is that Jesus Christ was the Son of God, that He overcame sin by His blood, that He is our very own so that what He has done was really done for us.

All need this, Paul declares, for "all have sinned and come short of the glory of God." Hence, all are concluded under the necessity of grace for there is no other means of justification. One would like to speak of the meaning of "the glory of God," that is, the state of innocence from which man originally fell and which is a sharing of fellowship and presence and being with God. This, of course, is the heavenly hope of the Christian. The glory of which we fall short now is to be given through the righteousness of God on the new principle of grace. Thus, in the first place, we conclude that God has provided righteously for the salvation of man.

II. THE RIGHTEOUSNESS OF GOD IN CHRIST.

The means of mediating God's righteousness to an unrighteous man is the Lord Jesus Christ. Paul said, "Being justified freely by His grace through the redemption that is in Christ Jesus: whom God hath set forth to be a propitiation through faith in His blood." Our righteousness is given freely and without price on our part by the loving grace of God, but it is not without price on the part of God Himself. If it were without price then God would be unrighteous. The moral universe would tumble about our ears. But a satisfaction has been made and God set forth on Calvary the exhibition of His justice in punishing sin. Our justification is through the redemption which is in Christ Jesus.

Redemption means to deliver by paying the price. On Calvary the God-man paid the price of sin. He endured the wrath of God. To whom was that ransom paid? The picture is that of redeeming one from bondage by the paying of a ransom. Several words are used in the Bible to depict this redemption. One means to purchase in the market, with the thought of paying the price of a slave. The other is to release or to set free through the paying of a ransom, so that the individual will never be in bondage again. Now to whom was the ransom paid?

Some have said that the ransom was paid to Satan and thus they have exalted Satan to a position of equality with God. The ransom was not paid to Satan, for his power is an usurpation, and he, too, is under the same bondage to the Divine morality and righteousness which requires a satisfaction. The ransom could only have been paid to the demands of law, to the righteous throne of an infinite God, to Him who is the personification of the moral universe, in order that the power of sin might forever be broken over those who have been slaves of sin. The price of that redemption was the blood of the Redeemer who died in the place of those in bondage.

On Calvary a more profound event occurred than the human mind imagines. To call the death of Christ an example of sacrifice, or a martyrdom of a man, or a persuasion by suffering is a terrible sin. On Calvary Christ carried the wrath which is manifested against unrighteousness. He became sin for us although he knew no sin. He

THE RIGHTEOUSNESS OF GOD

was the object of offended justice in action. He carried the brunt of broken law. When man sinned in the garden of Eden, God drove him from the garden and set cherubim with a flashing sword to guard the way. That sword was Divine justice and it has been flashing over the way of life, keeping man therefrom, until it was awakened against the Shepherd and then forever sheathed in the heart of God, smiting Him on Calvary. Now the way back to innocence, the way back to glory, the way back to the Paradise of God is open for those who will believe because the sword no longer flashes in judgment. Only God himself could do this mighty work of redemption for man. The God-Man Christ Jesus, was set forth as an eternal exhibition of the justice and the love of God.

The Scripture says that this righteousness of God in Christ was brought about by means of a propitiation by blood. The word, "propitiation" was common in the Old Testament. In Hebrew "capporeth," and in Greek "hilasterion," designates the mercy seat in the ancient tabernacle and temple of the Jews. This place of mercy or of propitiation was very important. It consisted of a golden altar in the holy of holies placed between and under the wings of the cherubim. These cherubim were the agents of justice and judgment as we have said. Within the golden altar was the Ark of the Covenant containing the Law and the Covenant on the basis of which man must be judged.

No man could enter that holy of holies where the glory of God dwelt between the cherubim, unless he entered with the blood of the sacrifice to be sprinkled upon the holy altar. Long preparation was made once a year for the entrance of the high priest into this sanctuary of God to make an atonement for the people. Christ fulfilled the figure both of the sacrifice which was offered and the mercy seat on which the blood was offered. Hence the ground of mercy before God, in the temple not made with hands, is the blood of Christ which was shed for the remission of our sins. The only blood which ever had any value to God throughout the history of His dealings with man was the blood of Christ, for it was this blood alone which made an atonement. The blood of bulls and goats was used typically to teach men that they must have faith in a God who would send His own Son to bear wrath upon their sins. Because of this, God was righteous in pretermitting, or passing by, or winking at, or overlooking, or not imputing the sins which were past. That does not mean the past sins of the present sinner. That means the sins of the saved saints before the Cross. Adam, Enoch, Noah, Abraham and

David were all sinners, identified in the flesh with Adam and under the wrath of God, but God passed by their sins because He foresaw a sufficient and a complete satisfaction made through "the Lamb of God who taketh away the sin of the world." Thus, though the high priest entered once a year into the holy of holies to make sacrifice, Christ in the consummation of the ages, once for all, suffered without the gate, and through the eternal Spirit, offered up the blood of the new covenant on the Cross. Thus both as the place of appeasement and as the ground of appeasement Christ is our propitiation through faith in His blood. This Christ exalted in His humanity to His right hand, where he will be clothed with the glory which he had with the Father before the world was, and it is in that position as in Christ and heirs of the Lord, on the resurrection and exalted ground, that the justified sinner takes his place before God.

This exhibition of Calvary was made "to declare" His righteousness: that he might be just, and the justifier of him which believeth in Jesus. This, then, was the purpose of the Cross. By the philosophy of the Cross we retain a righteous God who is able to declare a sinful man to be righteous in his sight. Thus Christianity proclaims what can be proclaimed by no other religion, the way of salvation. The throne of God's righteousness is unmoved and our moral universe is unshaken. The full demands of the law have been met and yet man can be saved, though he is a sinner, fallen and unable. What wonder there is in this salvation which declares that a guilty sinner is righteous. Look at Christ in the garden of Gethsemane when he shed drops of blood foreseeing what must occur on the Cross. Witness Him as he tasted the dregs of the cup of bitterness. Hear Him as He cried, "Why hast thou forsaken me?" There you see something of the wrath which He endured but that shed blood met every claim of justice on the deepest sinner and need never be repeated and never will be repeated for those who are saved.

III. THE RIGHTEOUSNESS OF FAITH FOR THE BELIEVER.

We recognize that there is no righteousness in us and that only in Christ can we be saved or declared righteous. In the flesh or in the Adamic nature, as we are born into the world, we are dead in trespasses and in sin, aliens from God, slaves of evil and in need of redemption! But now in Christ we are dead to sin, dead to the flesh, dead to Adam's nature, for which there can only be condemnation. The means of this change is faith in Christ. By faith we have been crucified with Him, have died, and have been raised again, so that now we stand on resurrection ground. Christ is the end of the law for righteousness to every one who believeth. "He made him to be sin for us, who knew no sin, that we might be made the righteousness of God in him." Only on this ground, and on no other will we have salvation. Thus there is no room for pride or boasting, for we are but sinners, saved by faith through grace. In all this, of course, we are not talking about practical sanctification, but righteousness before God. When once saved by faith in what Christ has done, we become new creatures with a new acceptance and place in Christ.

That this justified sinner has something performed in him as well as for him is also an important truth and one to which we will come at at later time. That truth is the inward renewal by the Spirit of God who makes salvation a powerful experience, a positive aspect of salvation, but nothing experiential can occur until after the great forensic phase of justification is completed. It is in the realm of practical holiness, in manifesting this new acceptance as the righteousness of God, that works take on new value.

Let us reemphasize that all of this is received by faith through grace. It is the free gift of God. It is through Christ. It is sufficient for all because Christ was sufficient. It is received by all those who believe God and who trust the Lord Jesus Christ as their Saviour.

We summarize the righteousness of God. In the abstract, the righteousness of God is an attribute or a quality of God. In the concrete, the righteousness of God is Christ exhibiting God's justice in forgiving sin. In application, righteousness of God is the righteousness given to us in Christ through our faith in what was done for us on Calvary.

> "My hope is built on nothing less,
> Than Jesus' blood and righteousness.
> I dare not trust the sweetest frame,
> But wholly lean on Jesus' name.
> On Christ the solid rock I stand;
> All other ground is sinking sand."

VII

THE RIGHTEOUS SHALL LIVE BY FAITH

TEXT: *"We conclude that a man is justified by faith without the deeds of the law."*—ROM. 3:28-4:25.

OUR text says that "a man is justified" or declared righteous "by faith without the deeds of the law." The book of Romans clearly declares that the law condemns all because all have sinned. Whatsoever the law saith, it saith to them who are under the law, that every mouth may be stopped and all the world may become guilty before God. If there can be no righteousness for those who are under the law by obeying the law, which was a holy instrument of God, then surely all other works which are on a lower scale than the law are excluded as a means of righteousness also. This book leaves no doubt that men are lost, either because they have broken the law under which God has placed them by His providence, or because they have disobeyed their own consciences which are a work of God written in the heart.

It is true that where there is no law there can be no transgression, but that does not mean that there is no sin and no guilt, for all the world is brought under guilt and under sin by God's plan. Hence, if ever there is to be a means of justification, it must come outside of the province of the law and without works which always leave men as sinners. Thus Paul asked, "Do we then make void the law through faith? God forbid: Yea, we establish the law." When Christ died upon the Cross where He endured the penalty of law and the wrath of God, He established rather than voided the law. Thus also, when we turn to faith acknowledging our guilt and the impossibility of any salvation or righteousness by means of works, we also establish the law in its truth and righteousness. All of us are included under sin. We ought not, therefore, to mourn over our bad works and our failures but we should turn in faith to Him Who justifies the ungodly. Inasmuch as we are included in the ungodly and recognize ourselves as such we have hope to receive a righteousness from God on an entirely different principle.

We have also seen that God, being righteous, declared sinful man or the ungodly righteous through His righteousness in Christ, Whom

He hath set forth as the propitiation for sin. That teaching declares the great means of redemption whereby God can remain righteous and still justify or declare righteous sinful men. Divine mercy may be extended unto sinners through the mercy-seat, which is none other than Calvary where the blood of Jesus was sprinkled to make a satisfaction for sin. Justification and righteousness are inseparably connected in the Bible, both of them coming from the same root word, one meaning righteous and the other to justify. The believing sinner is justified because Christ, having borne his sins on the Cross, has been made unto him righteousness. Christ is the one means by which God can justify a sinner. Because of the propitiation made by Christ upon the Cross, justification may be a judicial act of God before a moral universe whereby He declares righteous an ungodly person who believes in Christ.

The principle by which the believing sinner is declared righteous is that of faith. Justification and righteousness are, on the principle of faith alone, available for the sinner. This designates the gift of righteousness as something which God, the Judge, has done for us, rather than something which we have done. Faith is passive, not active. Faith is not a meritorious work, but it is a heart attitude induced by God. Righteousness or justification is what God does for us when we trust ourselves to Him. This righteousness before a holy and a just God, through faith, is for the Jews and heathen both. Whenever a Jew was saved, it was not because he obeyed the law, but because he had faith in the coming Christ. Thus, also, heathen who may never have heard of the law of God may be saved through faith in the promise of a Saviour. The acceptance of this message of a righteousness of God which is by faith vindicates the law which condemns us before God and tells us that we are sinners. What a wonderful message this is that there is a means by which we may be declared righteous before the God of the universe without works of the law; a means by which as a free gift we may receive a standing of perfection in His sight.

The great illustration of faith is Abraham. Abraham was made righteous by faith. Abraham knew the blessedness of imputed righteousness and Abraham lived righteously in faith. As the great example for us, we must turn to his life as it is given to us in the fourth chapter of the book of Romans, illustrating the truth of justification by faith.

I. The Declaring of One Man Righteous—Abraham.

The position granted to Abraham was "the father of the faithful." Paul here calls Abraham "our father." He, of course, is speaking as a Jew according to the flesh, but Abraham is also the father of Christians as well as the saved saints of the Old Testament. If Abraham is set upon such a pedestal, then surely the examination of the righteousness which he received before God should be helpful to us.

Whatever righteousness Abraham had was before the law, for the law was not given until four hundred years after the time of Abraham. If Abraham was declared righteous by God, it was by some other principle than obedience to the law, so that the example of Abraham will again vindicate the argument of Paul that the righteousness of God is manifested without the law. Moreover, Abraham was justified while he was yet uncircumcised and circumcision was only given to him as a seal of the righteousness which he already possessed. It was not by means of any formality, ceremony or rite that Abraham was declared righteous in the sight of God. Abraham was a raw heathen when God called him. Everything which is written in the first chapter of the book of Romans about the degraded state of the heathen might have been written concerning the conditions in Abraham's own day. How far he participated in these things there is no way of knowing, but he was a heathen and it was out of heathenism that God called Abraham and then justified him or declared him to be righteous in his sight.

God did not call Abraham because he was a monotheist in the midst of idolatry, or because he was morally pure in the midst of impurity, or because he was honest in the midst of thieves and liars. Abraham was not righteous when God called him. Neither did God declare Abraham righteous because of the righteousness which he would ultimately attain to in obedience to the Divine command. The righteousness which Abraham had was an imputed righteousness, something which was reckoned to him or accounted to his credit on a certain principle, which principle was that of faith. We read, "Abraham believed God, and it was counted unto him for righteousness."

Whatever righteousness Abraham had, it came because he believed the promise of God. Hope played a prominent part in the salvation of Abraham. God spoke to him about something which would occur in the future and Abraham accepted the naked word

THE RIGHTEOUS SHALL LIVE BY FAITH

of God and believed that word. It was this faith in God and God's Word which was accounted to Abraham for righteousness. That promise which he believed was of a seed through whom all the nations of the earth should be blessed, so that Abraham should be called, "the father of many nations." This included, of course, the Messianic promise of a Redeemer.

The difference between Abraham's faith and ours is very simple. Abraham waited for the accomplishment of what God promised, sure that He could not lie and was able also to perform. He was expecting One who was promised, but had not yet come. It was this faith of Abraham which was reckoned to him for righteousness. Our faith is exactly the same with one distinction. The object of faith has come and has wrought the Infinite work of redemption. This, of course, is fraught with mighty consequences. The foundation of all that God ever expects to do is now already done in that He hath perfectly wrought out a redemption. This is the gospel of the grace of God and it is not a promise, but an accomplishment. In Christ's atonement, God hath already put away sins, so that they are gone forever for the believer. This does not become a question of hope, but is one of faith in the efficacy of a redemption which has already been accomplished through the shedding of His blood and the giving of forgiveness.

Yet because Abraham believed God's promise, that his seed should be as the sand of the sea and the stars of the sky, and that in them all the nations of the earth should be blessed, he was accounted as righteous. Every child of Abraham from that day to this, whether Jew or Gentile, must be saved on the same principle of faith. There is no other means. Abraham believed God concerning what was impossible outside of God's own activity and he was declared righteous. When we believe God's word concerning what was impossible outside of His own activity and what He has accomplished on Calvary, then we, too, may be declared righteous in His sight.

The principle of Abraham's justification is that of faith. "Abraham believed God and it was counted (reckoned to him) as righteousness." Here it is specifically stated that there is no ground for boasting because of works or of character. Abraham had no righteousness in the flesh, but his faith was reckoned to him as righteousness. That word, "reckoned," is a court word. It describes God acting as a judge and accounting those who believe in Him as righteous, or those who do not believe in Him as unrighteous and iniquitous. The great Judge of the universe on the principle of faith is able to account a sinful individual as righteous in His sight because of what Christ did upon the Cross. There is no merit of righteousness in faith itself, but faith is reckoned as righteousness. Abraham simply believed that God would do what He had promised to do. This was a heart attitude of Abraham, not a particular act. Because of this heart attitude God reckoned Abraham as righteous.

Works are ascribed to a different principle from faith, namely, that of debt. Paul said, "Now to him that worketh is the reward not reckoned of grace, but of debt. But to him that worketh not, but believeth on him that justifieth the ungodly, his faith is counted for righteousness." Strange as it seems, one can not earn righteousnes by good works. That is very hard to get into the human head. We always think of doing something, of earning something, of receiving salvation because of what we attain to, but let us remember that works are on the principle of wages, due as a debt. God never owes a man salvation or righteousness. All God owes to man is judgment and wrath because of his iniquities and of his sins, and hence righteousness and salvation can only come as a free gift of God, without any works on man's part. If we work on the principle of wages and of debt, let us remember that daily we are piling up a larger debt of sin and unrighteousness than we can ever begin to pay with the wages that we might earn by certain deeds of kindness and of righteousness. God demands absolute perfection of man and we fall so far short of this that our debts increase rapidly.

Yet there are multitudes who by self-denial, morality, kindness and good deeds seek to be righteous before God. These multitudes are acting on the principle of works and of debt. They are asking God to judge them on the basis of the things that they do. Poor, benighted souls! What awful judgment awaits them regardless of the height of their morality to which they may attain in this world! Such a great gulf separates them from God and from God's standard that they can never bridge that gulf by their own attainments. This idea of working for one's salvation is utterly different from being justified by believing on a God who says He will declare the ungodly to be righteous.

What a wonderful gospel this is! What a wonderful thing for God to do! What an unspeakable gift for a sinner! Only an Infinite God could have worked out such a plan whereby sinful and ungodly man might be called righteous in His sight.

This provision of righteousness and justification is only for the

THE RIGHTEOUS SHALL LIVE BY FAITH

ungodly. He justifieth the ungodly. Notice that God does not justify the godly, whether they are Presbyterians, Methodists or what. Until we can see ourselves as sinners, as ungodly, as no better than the worst human being who is of the dregs of outward sin, because we are unrighteous in His sight, we can not be justified by His shed blood, but wherever an ungodly man, no matter what his former condition has been, comes to trust the promise of God and His provision through Jesus Christ as a propitiation for sin, he is declared righteous on the principle of faith. The moment one ceases from his own work and rests on what God has done at the mercy-seat, he becomes righteous in God's sight. Thus it is that a righteous God declares an unrighteous man as righteous in His sight through Christ.

Even though one is not justified by works, nor is reckoned as righteous because of the deeds which he does, there is a practical attestation of saving faith. Abraham performed great acts of faith. His first magnificent response was in leaving his native land and kindred and friends at the call of God to go out into a country which he did not know. This was an act or a work of faith which demonstrated that Abraham believed God. Later he also believed God's promise, in spite of his advanced years, that Sarah would bear him a son of promise. Humanly speaking, this was utterly impossible for both were too old to have children. Nevertheless, God promised Abraham that he should have a son and Abraham believed that promise, so that it was counted unto him for righteousness. Finally, the greatest act of Abraham's faith was his willingness to surrender the son of promise, at the command and bidding of God, as a living sacrifice on Mount Moriah. Here was an old man with but one son, of promise, and all of God's purposes converging in that son, and yet the command came that he should be put to death. In utter faith, believing that God could raise the dead, Abraham went about the act of sacrificing his son. These were works which Abraham did and they demonstrated both to God and to the world that Abraham believed God. This is the reconciliation between the teaching of James and of Paul concerning faith and works.

In Abraham's life of faith there were many testings. Some of them might be called lapses of faith. He did not have the greatness of faith at the beginning. He grew in faith as the years went by. When God first called him out of Ur of Chaldees, he went as far as Haran and waited there until his father died. These were wasted years as far as God's program was concerned. Then after going into

Canaan, instead of tarrying, he went down into Egypt. In Egypt he lied concerning his wife Sarah and he was ultimately expelled from the country in humiliation as not being worthy of the presence of the Pharaoh. It was in Egypt that Abraham took Hagar to wife, which was an act according to the flesh, hoping that God would accept the child of Hagar as his instead of the child which was promised to be born through Sarah. These were all lapses of faith and because of them God chastened Abraham, but though he had such sins and failures it did not remove from him the gift of righteousness which was by faith.

II. The Blessedness of Imputed Righteousness.

To be declared righteous in the sight of God is extremely blessed indeed. David said, "Blessed are they whose iniquities are forgiven, and whose sins are covered. Blessed is the man to whom the Lord will not impute sin." If the righteousness can be imputed, or reckoned, unto a man, sin and iniquity can also be reckoned unto a man, and for those who deal with God on the principle of works, such a reckoning will be revealed at the day of the judgment. Thus it was that David cried out, "Oh, the blessedness of the man to whom God doth not impute sin!" for David had sinned. He had committed adultery. He had committed murder. He had violated the commandment of God and his heart was heavy and sore within him as he was under the conviction of God for what he had done. Yet after this experience, David was restored to God's fellowship and God's blessing through his confession and his belief in the mercies of the Lord.

When sin is not imputed, it is covered. That was the word used in the Old Testament to describe the forgiveness of sin and it meant that the blood of bulls and goats covered sin until Christ's sacrifice took it away. The propitiation made upon Calvary took sin away. Christ put away sin by the sacrifice of Himself. The Lord will bury our sins in the deepest sea. He will remove them as far as the east is from the west. He will remember them no more. God could cover the sins of Old Testament saints because He knew that Christ's death was to come and in forbearance He overlooked these sins in the light of the future sacrifice. God will never bring those sins up again. He will not reckon them to the sinner. What this must have meant to Peter, to Paul, to David and even to Abraham!

The most important thing in the fourth chapter of the book of Romans is what is left out. If you will notice that in this fourth

THE RIGHTEOUS SHALL LIVE BY FAITH

chapter God never even mentions the sins of Abraham, his sins of unbelief, of going into Egypt, of lying, of taking an Egyptian woman to wife in order that he might help God by some work of the flesh. Wonder of all wonders, God lost His memory at Calvary, His memory of our sins! He forgot them. They are taken away. They shall never be brought up again. If Abraham's and David's sins are not imputed to them, mine shall not be imputed to me when I believe in Jesus Christ. Oh, the blessedness of it all, to know that my failures, my sins, my unrighteousness, the wrongs which I have done are remembered no more!

Then there is the blessedness of being righteous in God's sight. Abraham received a seal of righteousness which God had given him while he was yet in uncircumcision. This meant that in the sight of God Abraham was uncondemned. He was certain of acceptance. He was pure as snow, washed clean and made whole. What this means to a burdened soul, suffering under the conviction of his sins is beyond all description. The blessedness of knowing that before God we are uncondemned, standing as Christ stands, is a wonderful thing.

Luther, who scourged himself, flagellated himself, did penance, prayed and obeyed the ordinances of the church, one day recognized what it meant to have the imputed righteousness of God in his heart, to be accepted as God can accept one by faith, and from that day he was a changed man. To know that we are in Christ, that Christ Who is the righteousness of God is now ours, that we are accepted at His right hand and are perfect in His sight, is beyond all comprehension. To have such a blessedness rests not in the circumcision, in the law, in baptism, in the Lord's Supper, in confirmation or in any other ordinance of the church, but it rests on simple faith in God Who justifies the ungodly. This blessedness comes utterly without the law and without ordinances and without works through the simple exercise of faith in God.

To be declared righteous means to have the blessedness of being heirs of the promise through the righteousness which is of faith, for the promise that he should be the heir of the world was made to Abraham and to his seed. Think of it, the children of Abraham shall inherit the world, the meek, the lowly, the righteous, the merciful, the peacemakers. These are the ones that shall inherit the world; not the children of Adam, not the murderers, the greedy, the ambitious, the violent, but the children of Abraham. All the promises which were made to Abraham and which converged in Christ are ours and will be fulfilled in the believers, the children of Abraham. Moreover, the promise is sure to all the seed, to all who believe because it is of grace and not of debt. Remember that we do not have to win the world. We inherit the world. Abraham, Isaac and Jacob shall come and sit down in the kingdom of God and there shall be a recognition of the fact that Abraham inherited the world and we shall inherit with him. Yes, the promise to Abraham was partly fulfilled in Calvary, when God wrought out redemption for His people, but it will be totally fulfilled in that better city which hath foundations and which Abraham sought while he was here upon earth. While Abraham was on earth, he lived as a pilgrim, in a tent, looking for that city and if we are to follow Abraham as his children we, too, must live as pilgrims in the present age, looking for the glorious time to come.

III. THE LIFE OF RIGHTEOUSNESS IN FAITH.

This verse describes Abraham's life in faith: "He staggered not at the promises of God through unbelief; but was strong in faith, giving glory to God; and being fully persuaded that, what He had promised, He was able also to perform." The literal translation of the words "was strong in faith" is "finding strength in faith." As we read about Abraham's exploits we notice that there is a great gap between us ordinary mortals and Abraham in the practice of faith, yet he is held up as our example. Why is it that there is such a great gap? Why is it that Abraham could take his only-begotten son Isaac and be willing to sacrifice him, when we know that we would not? The answer comes, in this statement, "he found strength in faith." Remember that the righteous shall live by faith. From faith to faith we shall go on and as we conquer in our testings and our trials and mount up in faith, we shall find strength to do the seeming impossible which God expects us to do. Abraham believed in a God who quickens the dead and calls things which are not being into being. Here is the creative fiat of an omnipotent God. Here is One Who has all power in heaven and earth. If we believe in such a God we shall find strength to do the impossible. It is faith such as this which enables one to expectantly await God's activity in one's own behalf and to act in accordance with that, great hope.

Abraham did not stagger at God's promises. God promised to this old man and to this old woman a child and they laughed at God. They laughed out of unbelief, because of the incongruous thought of their having a child, yet in spite of the impossibility of it, Abraham

THE RIGHTEOUS SHALL LIVE BY FAITH

believed God. He did not regard the conditions, which would have overcome any one's faith causing him to doubt and to resort to human devices. He did not think of Sarah's age and of the deadness of her womb, but he looked only unto God, the God who was able to do these things which He had promised. Abraham staggered not at the promise of God. Faith means that we are to reason from God and His word and not from self or from circumstances.

In all this, Abraham gave glory to God, because he was fully persuaded that what God had promised He could also perform. This difficult though blessed pathway of faith includes trials and tests and uncertainties, but always fulfillment on the authority and the power of God. To God we must give the glory for whatever is accomplished in the life of the Christian as he lives by faith, for it is His power and His faithfulness that has performed it. To give God the glory is to count on God and to bring His promise to pass. We may even go so far as to thank Him for the answer and to thank Him for His undertaking on our behalf before it has actually come to pass. It was this which was reckoned for righteousness to Abraham, for he believed God and it was imputed to him for righteousness, but the Scripture says that it was also written for us, to whom righteousness "shall be imputed, if we believe on him that raised up Jesus our Lord from the dead." Thus we are returned to that central fact of all, the Cross of Calvary, where God set forth His only-begotten Son as a propitiation and raised Him for our justification. Our sins were imputed to Him upon Calvary, where He carried their penalty in His death, and His righteousness, the righteousness of God, is imputed to us by God's raising him from the dead. A free acquittal from all guilt is declared for us. Righteousness in the sight of God is the state of all who will believe in Christ and in God Who gave Christ to us.

Why then should we go on trusting the miserable works of our wicked hearts? Why, then, are we trying to earn our salvation? Why, then, are we trying to steal into heaven by some forbidden door? Rather let us confess, let us believe on what God has done, and let us trust God that He may impute His righteousness to us and that the blessedness of sins forgiven may be ours.

VIII
THE GLORIOUS BENEFITS OF BEING RIGHT WITH GOD

TEXT: *"Being justified by faith, we have peace with God through our Lord Jesus Christ."*—ROM. 5:1-11.

THIS text proclaims what it means to be right with God. The most important question any man can ask and answer is, "Am I right with God?" Do you know that you are right with God? Are you justified by faith? Has the righteousness of God become your righteousness through the righteousness of Christ? Have you been cleansed by the blood of the Cross?

The question, "Am I right with God?" involves one's present condition and future state. Is my present condition such that God looks on me with displeasure because of my sin? Is the wrath which is revealed from heaven against sin impending over me so that death would place me in hell? Much importance is placed upon death in the thinking of the average individual, but death itself is much less important than the destiny of my soul. Death is emptied of all of its meaning and power and fear if I know that after death I shall be in heaven in the presence of Christ and if the wrath of justice has been emptied of all of its sting. The sting of death is sin, but the victory over sin is given to us in the Lord Jesus Christ. If there is a way to become right with God in spite of my sin and evil this consideration outweighs all others at the present moment. I must give my attention to it. According to the Bible the certainty of being right with God and of treating this matter in my own life as settled is available. That certainty arises from the belief in what God has said His Son did for us on the Cross. It means that any one who is to have this certainty must accept the gospel of God in Christ.

To be right with God means to be justified or to be declared righteous in His sight through faith. Such righteousness is declared by our text to be the result of justification. We read, "Being justified by faith, we have peace with God." Justification, then, must be the basis of our future relationship with God. The past tense is used. This declaring of the sinner to be righteous by God must come before there can ever be any peace between the sinner and God. Justification is a declarative act of God before the tribunal of the universe, setting the sinner forth as righteous. It is defined, "Justification is an act of God's free grace, wherein He pardoneth all our sins, and accepteth us as righteous in His sight, only for the righteousness of Christ imputed to us, and received by faith alone." The word "justification" never means to make morally upright. The character producing power of the gospel does not emanate from justification itself. Justification only changes a man's standing in the presence of God and the moral universe, but it is the necessary foundation of all future relationship with God. This justification is through faith, not on account of faith. Justification is God's work and faith is only the mediating cause. We are justified on account of the sacrifice of the Lord Jesus Christ on Calvary. This is the effective cause. It is through faith that the blessings of justification are appropriated, but a man might have plenty of faith if he had no Saviour and never be justified. Modern teaching that we are saved by the attitude of faith is absurd. Faith must rest in an object and that object is the Lord Jesus Christ.

The need for justification is abundantly clear from the condition of man as it is revealed in the first three chapters of Romans. There we see him sinking in unspeakable degradation because he turned his back upon God in heathenism. There we see him in the moral life still unable to rise higher than the wicked heathen. There we see him with religious knowledge and external environment, but with a heart that is far from God. There God said that all men have sinned and come short of His glory, that every mouth is stopped and that there is none righteous, no not one. With this background it is obvious that humanity has a need for the setting forth of Christ as the righteousness of God in making a propitiation for sin. God did something which is able to make us righteous. If we believe what He did His unmerited favor will be extended toward us.

The benefits of being right with God now will occupy our attention. These constitute the climax of what God has done for us in redeeming us from our sins. The instrumental and effective cause of our justification has been clearly presented. Now the apostle is saying, "therefore." This connects the results with the cause. At the conclusion of the list of these benefits Paul said, "We exult in God through our Lord Jesus Christ." If these benefits are yours, your spirit will rise in prayer and praise and exultation because of the goodness and wonders of God's grace. What then are these benefits? Justification enables us to have peace with God, to have access by faith into grace, to rejoice in the hope of the glory of God, to receive the gift of the Holy Ghost shed abroad in our hearts, to experience the love of God within us, to possess salvation from the wrath to come and to be utterly reconciled to God by the death of His Son.

I. We Have Peace Toward God.

It is impossible to over emphasize the extreme blessedness of peace toward God. In fact, it can only be known by those who are aware of the enmity toward God which preceded it. Later we shall learn that the carnal mind is enmity to God. This carnal mind was in complete control of the sinner before his justification, before a new principle was infused into him. Search as he may, the unregenerate man can never know the peace toward God. Only turmoil of soul grips him when he seeks to obtain peace.

Only the individual who has known the extreme enmity toward God will appreciate the blessedness of obtaining peace after this struggle. However high the moral life of the individual before this justification he will now recognize that the end of enmity has come. Peace is experienced.

The object of this search is a new relationship toward God. This new relationship arises because of the expiation for sin and its guilt made by a Saviour. It constitutes a state of no longer being enemies but now objects of favor with God. It involves a complete change of our standing. If this great experience could only be broadcast and accepted by the men of our age what a benefaction it would be to our nervous, distraught people, for surely the meaningless motions of excited men are due to the lack of peace in their soul.

The possession of this peace is a precious blessing greater than which there is none. The justified soul has no more upbraidings of an unappeased conscience and no dread of divine wrath. Instead of condemnation there is now justification. Instead of the guilt of our deeds there is now forgiveness and a contentment arising therefrom. This peace towards God is different from the peace of God which passeth all understanding. It is quite possible for one to be at peace toward God without having the peace of God. We shall see this more clearly when we enter into the trials and temptations of the regenerated man, as illustrated in Paul's own experience. Temptations and distractions, failures in prayer and supplications, disobedience and wilfulness may cause us to fail to enjoy God's peace. Yet all this will not invalidate the fact that we are at peace with God himself. The enmity now is within our own nature, between the old man and the new man, instead of toward God. This peace toward God should normally produce the peace of God in us. Our pious affections should be the result of our reconciliation to God and not the cause of it. Therefore we may rightfully expect them to follow our justification. If they do not we must learn what the reason is and we shall find it in the latent sin nature residing in us. But this peace toward God is founded on an atonement, by which the enlightened conscience is put at rest in seeing that a just God is able to forgive the sins of a wicked man. It is all of grace and it is all through our Lord Jesus Christ.

The result is peace which comes after a conflict or a war. Natural man, who is at enmity to God or in rebellion against Him, stands as a criminal does to a judge. He fears him because of his acts of disobedience and because of the just powers wielded by the judge. A usurper is ruling in his heart in the place of God and he must be subdued before there can be ultimate peace.

The way of obtaining this peace toward God is the exercise of faith, which is described as allowing Christ to enter the soul. Christ has certainly won a victory over Satan upon the cross. Potential justification has been accomplished, but it only becomes applicable to the individual through the act of committal or the act of trust which is called faith, on the part of that individual. We alone can let Christ into our life. In the moment in which that decision is made and that action taken, the potential victory of Christ upon the cross is accomplished in another individual life. Satan is vanquished for the believer. Then the debt and the guilt of the individual's life are completely discharged by what Christ has done as substitute upon the cross. Objectively Christ has already accomplished this, the debt has been settled, Satan has been defeated, peace has been made possible, but it becomes the possession only of the man who opens his heart to Christ, or who believes upon him. For such a blessed individual justification has come and he is at peace toward God. The war of sin is over and we shall soon see that perfect peace will come only by perfect submission to the new master and the understanding of our position in Him. With Him as our advocate and with Him waging our battles there can only be peace and security.

II. WE HAVE ACCESS TO GRACE.

The second great benefit mentioned is, "we have access by faith to this grace wherein we stand." This is the picture of a place of favor. Grace is the undeserved favor of God. Whereas we were at enmity and under God's wrath we now are under His blessing and His favor. This free grace flows from God toward us. It is conceived of as a realm having frontiers which may be crossed. We have access into the realm of grace, having been introduced to it by the Lord Jesus Christ. Grace came by Christ and we make our entrance into grace only through Christ.

Again faith is emphasized as the key or the instrumental cause. It is obvious that there are no blessings of salvation save through faith. This is merely repeating in other language what we have already expressed. The way of entrance is through Christ. Being justified, we have the privilege of entrance through Christ into this realm of grace and favor. Jesus said, "I am the door: by me if any man enter in, he shall be saved." Any one attempting access by any other way than by Christ is described as a thief and a robber. He is like the one in the parable of Jesus who came to the wedding feast without possessing a wedding garment. He has crept in stealthily and does not belong there. All access to God and God's grace must be by way of the Lord Jesus Christ as mediator.

The justified man abides in the favor of God. Paul said, "Wherein we stand." Christ is not only the door to the realm of grace, but on account of Him we stand in grace. We have a new position. He is our all in all and since grace came by Him and we are now in Him we remain in the realm of grace. As believers we are firmly and immoveably established. No longer are we under the works of the law, but we are under grace. Our position is no longer precarious. It is now on firm ground and in the divine strength. Recall that when Elijah appeared before Ahab he said, "As the Lord God of Israel liveth, before whom I stand, there shall not be dew nor rain these years, but according to my word." It was because Elijah was living and standing in the presence of God that he could be sure of the answer to his prayers. Likewise when the believer is living in the realm of grace he may be sure that he has God's favor and God's blessing. Enoch walked with God. This is held out before us as the highest privilege of man, but it is our joy to walk with God though the benefits of justification, for being justified by faith we have access to grace.

III. WE REJOICE IN THE HOPE OF GLORY.

Joy or rejoicing is the natural result of justification. We observe that the word used for rejoice is not the ordinary word for joy, but it is the word for boast. We boast in the hope of glory. Obviously this is not a boasting in oneself, which is objectionable in any one, especially in a Christian. It is boasting in God. The action is more than rejoicing. It is self-felicitation and exultation in view of the exaltation which Christ has obtained for us in our new standing. Formerly the glory of God was unapproachable holiness and the object of fear, for we had fallen short of His glory, but now it is our hope and to it we shall ultimately be conformed. The highest ambition and the end of the believer is to share in the divine glory. Now we may be partakers of His nature. Now we may be the children of God, but ultimately we shall be made like Him in glory. That glory in an objective sense is the glory which God possesses, which Christ had with the Father before the world was. In a subjective sense it is the glory which God gives to the believer. Jesus said, "The glory which thou gavest me I have given them." May God help us to let our hearts be the abiding place of His present glory until we shall be transformed from glory unto glory into the same image even as by the Spirit of the Lord. Because of what Christ has done for us we have hope and look into the future with the assurance of participating in His glory. This is the great privilege and end of the Christian.

The necessary counterpart of heavenly glory is tribulation on earth. Just as with the Israelites the glory of their deliverance from bondage was followed by the wilderness experience, so the discipline of tribulation is necessary for the Christian. It does not originate from God, but from Satan. It may be accepted as the earthly counterpart of heavenly joy which arises from our contact with sin. Yet even this according to Paul should be the cause of rejoicing. All afflictions which God permits to come to us are benevolent manifestations of His love. They are intended to have a sanctifying power for the believer, chastening and purifying him that he might be fit for the very presence of God.

Moreover, "tribulation worketh patience." That is an oft repeated suggestion in the Scripture. Evil is permitted in the life of the believer for the development of his character. These trials and tribulations work out patience. Patience is a perfect work of grace. We know that the Lord Jesus Christ was perfect in patience, giving us the highest example thereof, but patience was also found in the lives of the heroes of the faith. With patience Moses chose "to suffer affliction with the people of God, than to enjoy the pleasures of sin for a season; esteeming the reproach of Christ greater riches than the treasures in Egypt." Whatever our present sufferings may be, let us remember that they work out for us "a far more exceeding and eternal weight of glory." Paul said, "the sufferings of this present time are not worthy to be compared with the glory which shall be revealed in us."

He goes on to say, "patience worketh experience" or approvedness. When one is truly patient he gains the approbation of his own conscience, of his Christian brethren and of God. The man who proves the good, perfect and acceptable will of God in experience, obviously is approved of God; and if we Christians are to judge our brethren according to the Christian standards, we must approve those who are living in accordance with God's revealed will.

Tribulation worketh patience and patience worketh experience or approvedness, and approvedness worketh hope. The Christian religion is a religion of hope. We are saved by hope. We abound in hope. We live by hope and hope abides within us. This is true because we have an adequate ground of hope in our justification, in our abiding in the realm of God's favor. Thus being approved before God, we hope for special blessings and benefits from Him through grace. Thus though we started with tribulation, we end with the greatest benefit which can be received, namely, our hope to be transformed into the glorious image of the Lord Jesus Christ, at His coming.

Then Paul announced that there is no shame in such hope, "because the love of God is shed abroad in our hearts by the Holy Ghost." With the hope which is anchored in the Person of Christ and the promise that we shall be like Him through this wonderful gospel of God, there is certainly no need for the Christian to be ashamed. The only source of shame to him could be his weakness, his sins, his failures and these belong unto us as human beings and not unto Him. They do not impugn Christ or the gospel. They merely emphasize the need of such a gospel and such a Saviour. Along with hope, love is shed abroad in our hearts by the Holy Ghost. First comes righteousness. Then comes love. Before we can have Christ's work in us we must accept Christ's work for us. Hence, love comes after justification. Christ performed His work

BENEFITS OF BEING RIGHT WITH GOD

for us on the cross, but He performs His work in us by the Holy Spirit.

This is the first mention of the Spirit in the book of Romans. The Spirit of God in our hearts stimulates within us a love for God. In a truly justified man there is no need to work up our affection for God. Love is automatically present through the Spirit. When the Spirit of God is given unto us we have received the Divine nature, and no man ever hated his own nature at any time. Therefore it is only normal that he should love God. This love is not present in a sample form. Instead it is shed abroad through our hearts by the Holy Ghost. We are permeated with it.

Following this Paul developed a symposium on love, manifesting and illustrating the reason for our love of God. The height of it is, "God commended His love toward us, in that, while we were yet sinners, Christ died for us." When we were helpless, without strength and yet weak, Christ died for us, the ungodly. This weakness of men consists in their helplessness to save themselves. They were powerless. It has been and is the case of the human race. Man is utterly helpless spiritually. Still in the appointed time Christ died for us. It was with a view to this that God overlooked the sins of the past. The substitution of Christ for sinful men is the greatest manifestation of God's love that there has been or ever can be. "Herein is love, not that we loved God, but that He loved us, and sent his son to be the propitiation for our sins." In the natural flesh one man would hardly die for another and he will only consent to do so when the man to be rescued is a good man. Thus Sidney Carton died for Charles Darney in the *Tale of Two Cities*, according to Dickens. The Scripture says, "Greater love hath no man than this, that a man lay down his life for his friends." Such action reveals supreme love and only a few people ever love that way. How much less would a good man give his life for some reprobate sinner! Humanly speaking we would say, "Let him take the consequences. He deserves it." Yet in this very fact we have the greatest proof of the love of God. Though we were not righteous, not good, not deserving of any love, while we were in this state of rebellion, God demonstrated His love toward us, in that He, in the person of the Son, died for us on the cross. Thus we know that God loves us and, because this love of God is shed abroad in our hearts by the Holy Ghost, we in turn become the examples of divine love before our fellow men and illustrate to them what the love of God is.

IV. We Shall Be Saved Through Him.

This salvation is both present and future. The full effect is much more than being now justified by His blood. "We shall be saved from wrath through him." The most important item in the salvation of the soul is the future aspect, that of salvation from wrath, from future judgment. There is an eschatological element in salvation which if overlooked would empty it of its main content. The importance of the death of Christ on the cross as a means of our salvation is that He endured the wrath of God, the pains of hell and the demands of justice, thereby revealing a suffering God making satisfaction. Hence the blood of Christ upon the cross is Deity justifying believing men. We must never omit the blood, for by faith in His blood we are saved.

If this postulate be true, as Paul declares it is, the contrast of the following teaching is greater. "Much more then . . . we shall be saved by His life." This is easy to understand; if we are saved from the penalty of our sins by Christ's death, then we are much more saved by His life. The life of Christ may be considered from three ways. First, we are saved by the earthly life of Christ. Our salvation rests not only upon Christ's death. That is primary. Just as Christ fulfilled all righteousness and gave a perfect satisfaction to law according to morality, so that righteousness is ours today. We have two representatives. The first was Adam and inasmuch as his sin was imputed to us, so now by faith the righteousness of Christ, the second Adam, is also imputed to us. Second, we are saved by Christ's glorified life. Christ in the tomb was unable to save. Had He stayed in the tomb our faith would be in vain and we would yet be in our sin, but when he emerged, the victor over the grave and death, rising to a new life of glory, he brought immortality and life to light, so that we, by faith sharing that death and resurrection, now live in His resurrected life. We are now in Christ, identified with Him by faith and because He lives and is subject to death no longer we also shall live with Him. Thus our salvation rests in His present resurrected life. Third, we are saved by the life of Christ in us. He now abides in our hearts. His desires, His love, His attributes are incarnate in us, working themselves out through us. Because the Spirit of God and of Christ is given unto us at the moment of our justification, he begins the regenerating and transforming process to make us like unto Jesus Christ.

Thus if we are saved by His death much more shall we be saved by His life.

The climactic benefit, is that of reconciliation, "for if, when we were enemies, we were reconciled to God by the death of His Son, much more, being reconciled, we shall be saved by His life." Reconciliation, personal, present and ultimate; what a glorious fact! The propitiation of Christ is the ground for it. The presence of the Holy Spirit is the evidence of it. The hope that we have in Christ is the object of it. God is now propitious toward us and we are standing in the position of favor, in spite of our sin, because we have been reconciled by the death of His Son.

Considering these great benefits of having peace with God, of having access by faith into this grace wherein we stand, of rejoicing in the hope of the glory, of recognizing tribulation as a means toward glory, of experiencing the love of God shed abroad in our hearts and of knowing that we are saved from wrath through Him, is it any wonder that we exult in God through our Lord Jesus Christ? All that we could ask for, God has done. All that we could seek, He has given. We have become the recipients of salvation. It now remains to us to leave the matter of our justification and consider what God does in us, to take up this word "Spirit" and follow His works in the Christian through all of its phases. We shall next consider sanctification.

IX

THE REIGN OF GRACE THROUGH CHRIST

TEXT: *"As sin hath reigned unto death, even so might grace reign through righteousness unto eternal life by Christ Jesus, our Lord."* —ROM. 5:12-21.

ADAM and Christ are our federal representatives. The wonders of man's relationship to God are here shown under the doctrine of two men. The teaching draws an analogy between them. It involves two races or families, two heads, two acts, two results, two sovereigns and two kingdoms. The families are the family of Adam and the family of Christ. The representatives are Adam and Christ. The two acts are disobedience and obedience. The two results are death and life. The two kings are sin and grace. The two realms or kingdoms are condemnation and righteousness.

The transfer from one to the other of these kingdoms or families is made by justification and the new birth. On the basis of a finished justification, we are now about to discuss the truth of the deliverance from sin, the sin which plagues a born-again believer, casting him down into misery and despair. Sin is mentioned for the first time in the book of Romans in verse twelve of this fifth chapter. It is the sin out of which all other sins come. Salvation would be incomplete without dealing with the source of sin in order that we may gain complete deliverance therefrom. He who is a new creature soon discovers that carnality exists in his own old nature and is very interested as to how to deal with it. Many great saints have wrestled with this problem, with groanings and cries unto God for deliverance, but the deliverance may be just as simple as our initial regeneration and forgiveness of sin.

These two men, Adam and Christ, are representatives of the whole race in their acts and in the results thereof. The consequences of the act of each head of the race flow out toward all the race. "As the sin of Adam brought sin and death to all mankind, so the redeeming work of Christ brings righteousness and life to all who are united to Him by faith." These few verses of our Scripture constitute one of the profoundest paragraphs in the Bible. They

THE REIGN OF GRACE THROUGH CHRIST

are the arena in which Arminians and Calvinists, Universalists and particularists have struggled. It is impossible to sound the depths of the teaching of this paragraph, but certainly it is possible to make the outstanding truth of it plain and clear to all. We believe that it will continue to be the battle ground for theological controversy, but it will also continue to be the high ground from which the delivered Christian shall praise God for His infinite grace, over abounding sin, which was brought to pass through the Atonement of our Lord.

This passage constitutes the climax of the argument on justification by faith and the transition to the teaching on sanctification and the life of holiness in which justification issues. Here is shown that the same principles are involved in justifying and delivering man as in condemning him, namely, the representative character of two heads of the race through whom God has dealt with us as individuals. Here the groundwork in truth is laid for the wonder of the believer's union with Christ which means that before God Christians are accepted as one with Christ. His nature, His standing, His perfection, His inheritance are all ours. In this union, we are able to say that nothing can "separate us from the love of God, which is in Christ Jesus our Lord." The means by which this union with Christ is consummated and made effective will be discussed in our sermons on chapters six to eight, but here, we must lay the foundation for that discussion. Our ability to receive the deliverance through the second Adam is based on our willingness to be identified with the first Adam in the responsibility for his sin.

In the development of this analogy between the two heads, the two kings, the two kingdoms and the means of change from one kingdom to another we have some comparisons to make between them. In some ways they are strictly alike. In other ways they are completely different and on that basis we must make some contrasts.

I. THE REIGN OF SIN.

The reign of king sin was initiated by Adam and came as the result of one of two deeds. Let me speak of one of two deeds, namely, disobedience; of one of two results, namely, death, and of one of two kings, namely, sin. We read, "By one man sin entered the world," and, "By one man's disobedience many were made sinners." Let us note at this point the change from sins to sin. Here it speaks of sin entering the world, not sins. Hitherto, our responsibility, our guilt, our actual sins have been the apostle's subject.

What follows this verse relates to sin, namely, that evil principle in us for whose presence we are in no wise personally responsible and which we inherit from Adam who is the head of the race. For the justified man, no claim of God can ever again rise against him because of his sins. His responsibilities for his sins have been fully met in Calvary. Nevertheless, sin still has power over him. He still possesses his carnal nature. Hence, it is necessary for us to return to Adam, the source of all sin. The Bible teaches that sin entered by Adam's disobedience to a specific commandment which was, "Of the tree of the knowledge of good and evil thou shalt not eat." How and why Adam disobeyed this commandment we are not concerned with in our present discussion. That would come under the topic of temptation. Suffice it to say that Adam disobeyed this commandment. As a result, came the fall. From the fall issued a depraved nature, sinful, condemned and wicked in all men. This sin passed on to all of Adam's posterity, you and me included. The Bible says, "Adam begat a son in his own likeness." This means the son was sinful, fallen, corrupt and, knowing the difference between good and evil, being wholly inclined to do the evil. Adam had no children before the fall. His entire posterity was conceived in sin.

What then is the case of man since Adam? Our Scripture says, "Until the law sin was in the world; but sin is not imputed where there is no law." Antediluvian mankind was held under conscience which was his inner knowledge of the difference between the right and the wrong. This power of discernment was given to him in the fall, but we are told that without the law there can be no transgression. Sin, however, can exist without transgression of a particular commandment. Sin consists of self-will, of lust and of pride. This sin constituted human history before the flood a sea of violence until God wiped it out in a great judgment. Man sinned by following the wrong and not the right before the flood.

The post-diluvian men until the time of Moses were held under human government. As a restraining influence over sin, God ordained, "he that sheddeth man's blood, by man shall his blood be shed," but death still continued to reign over all men because of sin, for all men were sinners. Man was also a failure under this condition and turned away from the knowledge of the true God received in the family of Noah, to idolatry, pride and to evil. The great judgment came in the incident of the Tower of Babel.

Through Moses, God gave His law to a specially called-out people who were chosen for this purpose. The law was not given as a

THE REIGN OF GRACE THROUGH CHRIST 91

means of salvation, but in order to reveal the offense or to show up sin. Its purpose was to reveal the mighty wickedness of men's hearts. Grace was already existent before the law and was manifested in God's calling out a people from this depraved, human race, in manifesting His power for their salvation at the Red Sea and throughout the wilderness in answer to the prayer of Moses, but law was added to show sin, to manifest the transgression and to make evident a need of salvation by grace through an atonement. All this was clearly revealed in the Mosaic Laws concerning the tabernacle. Before the law, man's sin was revealed in lawlessness. Under the law, it was revealed in a violation of the Commandment which restricted his sin. After the law was given, the Israelites sinned after the similitude of Adam, whereas between the time of Adam and Moses sin was not in the transgression of a specific law.

Finally, mankind was tested under the very presence of Christ. The goodness of God made its final movement toward man in the Person of Christ, full of mercy, compassion, love, sinlessness and grace, in order that men might have confidence in and trust God, but fallen, wicked man again did not turn to God in love and in repentance, but rejected, hated and crucified the Lord Jesus Christ, thus revealing his awful wickedness.

This sinful condition of man has been confirmed in the case of you and of me. According to conscience and also to God's revealed law, each one of us must confess personal disobedience and lawlessness. Sin, of course, has a wider and deeper concept than merely the transgression of the law. It really is a heart attitude of lawlessness, as was revealed by the teaching of Jesus. The vindication of God's including all under Adam's sin as a federal representative in guilt is that all have sinned and thus confirmed it since that time. In whatever age we look at man, we find lust, pride and self-will bearing their fruit in man's life, revealing him to be a child of Adam, possessed of the Adamic nature.

Second, we look at one of two results which is death. Our text says, "Death passed upon all men . . . death reigned from Adam till Moses." Death's reign over mankind has been universal. Even the holiest and the best of the ancients died. Death has been and is a terrible reality for the sons of men. Once a preacher was reading the fifth chapter of Genesis where it speaks of the antediluvian characters all of whom died and a man heard those words, "And he died" repeated again and again. He wondered why the preacher should read such a chapter, but as he continued and he heard the words repeated again and again, "And he died," he began to think, "I, too, must die. Then I had better get right with God." And he did. The thought of death is ever before all of us. Even where there was and there is no law, death holds sway because of the universality of sin.

The Bible says that the death penalty passed upon all men because of the conduct of the head of the race, not because of our own individual sin or responsibility. It is not due to an actual transgression of a command upon our part that we die. This clearly shows that all of us were involved in Adam's sin. How were we thus involved? There are two primary answers. One says, all men were in Adam physically and by physical inheritance this was passed down. This is called, Realism. There is some support for it in the Bible, for in the Book of Hebrews we read that Levi paid tithes in Abraham. Now Levi was not born until four hundred years after the time that he was supposed to have paid tithes in Abraham. This appears to teach that Levi was in Abraham as the oak is in the acorn. Some men, therefore, teach that all of us realistically were in Adam. However, most theologians have held and this passage seems to teach that all men were only represented in Adam and thus fell with him, receiving by imputation a guilt and by inheritance a corrupt nature. At least of one thing we are sure. Man is not a sinner because of environment, but because his nature is depraved and fallen through sin.

The power of death holds over you today. "It is appointed to men once to die." We simply can not get around this fact regardless of the cults who deny it. It is easy to say, "There is no death" but all men die and you shall die, too. From the smallest child to the most valuable man death holds sway. On a tombstone in St. Andrew's Church-yard in Scotland marking the resting place of the bodies of four young children are the words:

> "Bold infidelity, turn pale and die.
> Beneath this stone four sleeping infants lie:
> Say, are they lost or saved?
> If death's by sin, they sinned for they are here.
> If heaven's by works, in heaven they can't appear,
> Reason, ah, how depraved!
> Turn to the Bible's sacred page, the knot's untied:
> They died, for Adam sinned; they live, for Jesus died."

THE REIGN OF GRACE THROUGH CHRIST

Only those who will be translated at the second coming of Christ, like Enoch was translated before the flood, will escape death and that only if they are living when Jesus comes. Death has sway over all other men. When will you die? Will it be today? Will it be tomorrow? Are you then ready? Are you justified? Has death lost its sting and the grave its fear for you, or are you a child of Adam under the sovereignty of death today?

Now let me speak of one of two kings, namely, that of sin in the realm of condemnation. There is a parenthesis in our text from verses thirteen to seventeen. Hence, if we go from the twelfth verse to the eighteenth verse it brings us immediately to the subject of judgment. We read that by the offense of one judgment came upon all men to condemnation. This judgment passed on all men who are represented by Adam whether by realism or by imputation. In Adam we all stand condemned, no matter how high an ethic we hold or how great and beautiful a character we have achieved. All of us outside of Christ are in Adam and the Adamic nature is condemned and lost before God even before he comes into judgment.

This judgment which is spoken of is not according to our works but according to our nature. Man's works, which are deeds of evil, are settled in one of two ways. If he is a believer, his sinful works were settled at Calvary and if he is an unbeliever they will be settled at the great white throne judgment spoken of in the twentieth chapter of Revelation. Hence, judgment which was passed upon all men in the fall certainly does not deal with our works, but deals with our nature. By the judgment of the offense of one, all the race is condemned and is judged as lost, sinful and needing salvation. Hence, before one ever sins, in God's Presence he is a sinner. Thus, David could say, "In sin did my mother conceive me."

This judgment was passed upon all men in the fall of mankind. However, its effect will come at the judgment which follows death. "It is appointed to men once to die and then the judgment." Hence, we see that from our first representative came sin, death and judgment before ever we sinned in our own right or on our own responsibility. Thus we must have a new representative in order to receive grace, righteousness and life. Thank God, that new representative came in the Lord Jesus Chist. He was the One of Whom the first Adam was a figure. Now we have seen one act which was disobedience, one result which was death and one of two kings which is sin, who has control over us.

II. The Reign of Grace.

In this passage, we have three times the words, If such and such happened, how much more will this happen? These "much mores" of comparison are most vital to our text. If God condemns men through a representative, how much more will He justify him and give him life and consider him to be righteous through a second representative.

Thus, let us look at the other of two deeds which is obedience, at the other of two results which is life, at the other of two kings which is grace.

We are speaking about the reign of grace. Grace means favor, unmerited favor as it is manifested in God's nature, for God is love. If God will condemn, how much more God must be ready to show mercy. The first representative, namely, Adam, was permitted in God's wondrous plan in order that he might include all in the possibility of mercy and grace by a second representative. Hence, just as we are held responsible for the deed of Adam which is disobedience, we are given the privilege of the blessing of the deed of the second Adam which is one of obedience. This deed of obedience is the one act of Christ, namely, the one in which He died on the Cross to bear the guilt of Adam's sons and to found a new family in grace. Yes, the Cross was an act of obedience on the part of Christ. When He came into this world He said, "Lo, I come to do Thy will, O God," and Paul said, "He humbled himself, and became obedient unto death, even the death of the Cross." That Cross of Calvary, with the blood of Christ shed thereon, established the possibility of grace or favor from God while still retaining His righteous character. God's law and justice were satisfied while He was able to manifest favor toward men. Thus, the gift of grace abounds unto many by one man, even Christ Jesus.

The application of this act of obedience, however, is given through our trusting Christ. God has commanded men to repent and to believe on Christ Who is the Divine offering for sin as well as for sins. By the accomplished obedience of Christ there comes an offer to all of justification from our sin as well as our sins. God offers a free gift to all who are involved in the consequences of Adam's sin which is eternal life manifested in the Son of God which also is a state of grace at the present experience of those so delivered. To this new life, sin can never be attached.

The other of two results, then, is life. Life is the very opposite

THE REIGN OF GRACE THROUGH CHRIST

of death. It is called in our Scripture justifying life. It is the life of Christ in us and justifying us. This is different from physical life and from physical death, for a man may be living in spiritual death without Christ when he is physically alive, and a man may have eternal life now though he is facing physical death. If Adam's act results in a state of condemnation to death, Christ's act results for us who believe in "the righteous title to live." Hence, Paul says that they which receive abundance of grace shall reign in life by Christ. This does not describe life as reigning, but believers as reigning in life. Christ makes the believer a king and a priest unto Him. Just as death no longer has any dominion over Him, death has no longer any dominion over us. Our eternal life has begun and it will never end. Thus by Christ Who is the second Adam grace is on the throne. Mercy is being manifested. Patience and love of God is shown to all men. Thus the free gift comes through grace unto life.

The other of two kings is grace which reigns in righteousness. The Scripture says, that, as by the disobedience of one many were constituted sinners, so by the obedience of one shall many be constituted righteous. This means that we are made righteous in constitution, just as we were sinful in constitution from Adam. Every one unified with Christ through the new birth is in principle made righteous in constitution. Herein the comparisons are of value. The first one consists of the comparison between the gift of life by Christ's saving work and the penalty of death by Adam's disobedience. The second comparison is between the condemnation which came through Adam's offense and the justification unto life which came by Christ. The third comparison is between being sinful and being righteous from these two federal heads. Thus their deeds were similar in the effect which they had upon us from the source, but they were different in other ways and the contrasts are marked. First, there is a contrast in quality. The first deed was one of sin. The second deed was one of bounty and of grace. Thus Paul says, "Not as the offense, so also is the free gift." Then there is also the contrast of quantity. From one act of disobedience, condemnation came unto many, but from many acts of sin justification came unto life. Third, there is the contrast of consequence. Whereas death reigned by one over all, now many reigned by one in life, even Jesus Christ. Here then we have seen the second of two deeds, the second of two results and the second of two kings. Grace is king in the believer. God's favor outstrips all evil and all sin.

III. THE MEANS OF THE DIFFERENCE.

The only difference between being in Adam and being in Christ is that one has taken his position by faith with Christ on Calvary which means that he has died to Adam, has died to the flesh, has died to the old man and has died to sin by faith. The believer has died with Christ on the Cross. Paul said, "I am crucified with Christ: nevertheless I live, yet not I, but Christ liveth in me: and the life which I now live in the flesh I live by the faith of the Son of God." Paul was crucified with Christ on Calvary. Thus also by faith we have died to Adam and to sin, but we shall say more of this later when we come into the great teaching of the sixth chapter. Our Bible does not say that righteousness reigns. If it did, then no one would reign in life. But it says that grace reigns in righteousness. Yet, it is God's favor through the Cross which reigns. God's goodness came to meet man in his wickedness at the Cross and by the dying of His only begotten Son God righteously was able to manifest His favor and mercy toward sinful man, declaring him to be righteous. One act of Christ on the Cross was the means of righteousness by which grace moves toward all and reigns in those who believe.

After the believer has taken his position with Christ, he assumes a new standing before God. He is now in the second Adam, in Christ Who rose from the dead. Thus, our present position is in His resurrection life. When we speak of being, "In Christ" we mean that we are invested with His nature. We are made to be the sons of God, eternal, living and triumphant. These are the benefits of union with Christ. Just as we were united with Him in His death, so we become united with Him in His resurrection and in His triumph. It is the apprehension of this great truth that settles the question of the believer's security. Once he is risen with Christ, no man can touch him. Thus, the Bible says, "If any man be in Christ, he is a new creature: old things have passed away; behold, all things are become new," and "As in Adam all die, even so in Christ shall all be made alive." This is not Universalism, but is restricted to those who are in Christ. As resurrected and exalted, Christ is now the fountain of life to all who believe. Wonder of wonders, this is in full accord with the righteousness of God.

Then the new position of the believer is under the reign of grace, in the kingdom of righteousness, under the nature of Christ. Until the coming of Christ, sin ruled in this world as a pitiless monarch,

THE REIGN OF GRACE THROUGH CHRIST

but since the redeeming work of our Lord, grace has been enthroned and has been given sway over the followers of Christ, so that they are delivered from death and made heirs of eternal life. We, then, are either in Adam, belonging to his race, receiving death and condemnation and judgment, or we are in Christ, the head of the new race and are subsisting in a state of righteousness. Paul thus tells us the true purpose of the law, saying, "the law entered, that the offense might abound. But where sin abounded, grace did much more abound." Wherever sin reigned to death, grace now is able to reign to life in Christ Jesus. Law deals with an individual and his sins, not with our sinful nature. It only shows up the sinfulness of our nature. By fettering our nature it makes sin abound, but once we have died with Christ we are freed both from sin and from the law.

Hence, Paul is able to say, "As we have borne the image of the earthy, we shall also bear the image of the heavenly . . . for "that was not first which is spiritual, but that which is natural; afterward that which is spiritual." Every man who comes into the world comes with Adam's image and with Adam's sinfulness. Of this we have no more to say than we have to say of our physical birth. It is the nature of things. We simply must accept it and the consequences. Moreover, each one of us must bear Christ's image in God's way if we would escape death and judgment. We must be justified from sins and from our sin. We must be born again. We must be transferred from one kingdom to another by faith and begin the life of holiness in sanctification. Earth's and heaven's highest blessing is thus a free gift of God. His plan is life available to all, even to those who lived before Christ, but who believed God's revelation to them concerning the coming Christ. Oh, wondrous plan of God! Oh, marvelous grace and love! These words in the fifth chapter of Romans tell us the source, the way and the end of salvation. Yes, grace reigns in life through Jesus Christ.

X

THE QUALITY OF LIFE A CHRISTIAN SHOULD POSSESS

TEXT: *"How can we that are dead to sin live any longer therein?"*
—ROM. 6:1-23.

THE life about which we are to speak today begins when justification is over. A Christian may now be assumed to be right with God. This means that he has taken his position with the second Adam, being justified by Christ's deed of obedience, that he has reiceived grace and enjoys life unto God. Just as the believer has accepted his identification with his first representative, namely, Adam, so now he has accepted his identification with the second representative, even Christ. These are his two federal representatives. Justification by faith was the act whereby the righteous deed of Christ upon the Cross was imputed unto the sinful believer so that he in turn is declared righteous in the eyes of God through the propitiation which is Christ. His relationship with the first Adam has been utterly broken and he has taken his place in Christ to reign in life. This means that now he is dead to sin, that he died in the death of Christ and he is now alive unto God. This last truth is the truth about which we are to concentrate.

This high position and blessing of the Christian was brought to pass only by justification by faith, for as an individual he was condemned in nature and in deed to both physical and eternal death, for he was a child of Adam both in nature and in act, but having accepted a substitute for himself, the demands of that death and sin were fulfilled in the death of Christ, who was the propitiation for his sins. This teaching about the death of Christ is called the Gospel and it is revealed to us by Almighty God. The believing of God's Word in reference to what Christ has done is the accepting of the Gospel and the means of our translation from death unto life. This becomes personal through faith. Therefore, the believer is declared righteous through his faith, from all sins, but, more than this is included. The believer is also justified, or declared righteous from sin, which is the truth which must now be examined.

It is this death unto the old man and present union with Christ,

QUALITY OF LIFE A CHRISTIAN SHOULD POSSESS 99

the new man, which begins the sanctified experience for the believer. Thus, we might call this union with Christ sanctification, or the quality of life a Christian should possess. The believer is dead to the Adamic nature. He is a new creature in Christ Jesus. Old things have passed away and all things have become new. Sin is no longer reigning as king over his life, but grace reigns through Christ Jesus. This does not mean that his person is not exactly as it was before, physically, mentally, and emotionally. This is a change which deals purely with our spiritual nature. We learned that through the offense of one, namely, Adam, many are dead. Yes, all men outside of Christ are under the dominion of death. They are dead spiritually and dying physically, but as soon as they come "in Christ" they are alive, resurrected, living unto God. Thus our text says literally, "How shall such ones as we who died to sin, live any longer therein?" Every believer is now in a new class of people, those holding a new relationship to God through Christ. This, of course, means all Christians. The implication of the question is, that it is impossible for those who are dead to Adam and alive to Christ to continue in sin.

This relationship, called "in Christ Jesus," is a mystical, spiritual union with Christ which is the ideal position and privilege of the Christian, but there is much which interferes to keep the believer from the practical identification with his Saviour and Lord. This ideal is held out before us but there are many who never attain to the ideal. Hence, the inevitable question arises, "If the believer died to the Adamic nature in the death of Christ, how then can he now sin?" It would almost appear that sin would be impossible and no matter what we would do it would be no sin. This question immediately arises when one talks of ending his relationship to the first Adam or to the old man in us. It is due to the fact that almost every Christian finds a strife in his nature between carnality, or the desire to do evil, and spiritually, or the desire to do good. Hence we must study the doctrine of how we get out of the power of sin, which is given to us in the sixth chapter of Romans. This might be called the deliverance chapter. This begins a concrete section of teaching on sanctification which embraces the sixth, seventh and eighth chapters and which might be called, sanctification begun, sanctification hindered, and sanctification complete.

The fact that where sin abounds, grace does much more abound does not give us a warrant to live on in sin. It is very obvious that Paul means to teach that there will be a complete and utter break between the Christian and sin, because of the grace of God under which he now lives. In this portion of Paul's epistle we expect to find, The Fact of Deliverance, the Faith to Believe It, and The Force to Live It. We invite your attention to these three topics:

I. THE FACT—WE BELIEVERS DIED WITH CHRIST.

Considering the fact of this death with Christ, I call your attention to the doctrine, to the experience and to the application.

In talking of the doctrine of sanctification, we must distinguish between the fact and the experience of deliverance from sin. As soon as we come to think of complete deliverance from sin, as well as from the guilt of our sins, the very presence of sin in the regenerate life, in the form of evil desires and tendencies and acts which are contrary to God's revealed will, makes it difficult to grasp the truth that we have died to the old nature. The presence of sin makes this very improbable to us. Then also there is the horror with which saints have viewed evil in themselves and the earnestness with which they have struggled with it after they have been saved. A young man came to me from Harvard University, telling of his thoughts upon this matter of complete deliverance from sin. In the midst of the conversation he confessed that sin still had dominion over him and that evil desires were still present in his life, in spite of his belief that Paul was very clear in his teaching that the believer should be delivered from the old man or from his evil nature or his old manner of life. This young man does not stand alone in this experience, for there have been many of the greatest saints of the ages who, after they had been born again, wrestled with this great problem of wickedness, evil, and vileness within their own nature. Some were amazed at it and struggled with it through their whole lives, in pleadings and groanings, fastings and self-abnegation. Such in particular was the experience of David Brainerd. Nevertheless, God tells us that when we are justified by faith in Christ's work on Calvary, we have died to sin, whether we believe it or not. If we are Christians, if we are regenerated by the Spirit of God and yet still find sin in our members, controlling our lives, this does not alter the fact that we have died unto sin, according to God's Word. If we can grasp the teaching of God's Word, it will not only lift our experience to one of victory, but it will preserve us from much error and from much grief of mind, the kind of grief which has driven many men almost insane in their search after holiness, in order to be pure in the eyes of the

QUALITY OF LIFE A CHRISTIAN SHOULD POSSESS

Lord. Such searchings by prayer and fasting, confession and groanings, are not at all necessary that one might be holy before God, nor are they necessary to be holy in practice, for God has given us another way of holiness.

The fact is, if you believe on Christ, you died with Christ on Calvary. Paul said, "I am crucified with Christ: nevertheless I live; yet not I, but Christ liveth in me." Paul evidently said that he was crucified on Calvary, that he was there. Were you there? Were you crucified on Calvary? The Bible says that if you believe in Christ you were crucified on Calvary. If you died to sin, what died? It is obvious that your body did not die. There was no physical crucifixion of your body on Calvary two thousand years ago, nor is there any bodily deliverance from sickness, mistake, limitation and suffering now through our redemption, and there will not be until Christ comes again. Thus Paul said, "We ourselves groan within ourselves, waiting for the adoption, to wit, the redemption of our body." It is true that in the meantime, by faith and in answer to prayer, the Lord may deliver us from certain sicknesses, certain mistakes and certain limitations, but we still bear the image of Adam in the body and will until Christ comes again. So the body was not crucified on Calvary and did not die. What then did die? Paul said, "Knowing this, that our old man is crucified with Him, that the body of sin might de destroyed." Thus, it is the old nature, as I was in and from Adam, with the natural mind, tastes, feelings and desires apart from God, which was crucified on Calvary. My old nature, my old connection with Adam, was crucified that the body of sin might be destroyed. It is this old man which we are commanded to put off, for it is corrupt according to the deceitful lusts, and we must be renewed in the spirit of our mind that we may put on the new man, which is created in God in righteousness and true holiness. The old man is to be crucified and all that belongs to the old life. We can not crucify him today. We do not die today, but we believe that the old man was crucified in Christ.

What then remains of the sin principle in the believer today, for we never read that sin died, but that we died unto sin? In the body which is yet unredeemed and which waiteth for the redemption of the sons of God there is the manifestation of the sin principle which is called "the flesh," and though the old man, which is what we were from Adam, was crucified, this flesh or sin principle still abides in the unredeemed body of man and wars against the new man, namely, what we are now in Christ Jesus. Hence, there is a constant conflict set up between the flesh and the Spirit, or the Holy Spirit, which continues throughout life. Never think that sin as a principle was crucified on Calvary or has been destroyed, for it is very much alive. It is only in the power and the work of the Holy Spirit that this sin principle or "the flesh" can be overcome and subdued and defeated constantly by the Christian. When we come to the eighth chapter, we shall see how the presence of the Spirit in the life of the individual accomplishes this fact.

What then are we now, after we have been considered dead in the Cross of Christ? The believer is now a new man in Christ Jesus, having put on a new manner of life, of desire, or tastes, of habits and of conversation. He is now alive unto God. There has been a complete change from his former relationship to his new relationship. He is passed from the kingdom of Satan unto God, from darkness unto light, from death unto life, by having been identified with Christ in His death upon the Cross, through faith. The believer now becomes identified by faith with the life of Christ as risen from the dead. Having been unified with Him in His death, he is now unified with Him in His resurrection. Thus the body of sin, that is, his body, unredeemed and undelivered from sin, is annulled by the Spirit, Who indwells him and quickens him to do God's will.

However, it appears that most believers fail to realize that they are also justified from sin as well as from their sins. Most all believe, confess and thank God for forgiveness from the guilt of their sins because of the propitiation which is in Christ Jesus. They believe that He died for them on the Cross, carrying the penalty of their sins; but this is not enough, nor is it all that Christ did. To hold to this alone is a glorious fact, but it is not a sufficient fact, for this limitation will prevent one from the glorious liberty of the truth of God. To illustrate this class of people one may remember those who pray publicly, always confessing sinfulness of nature and shortcomings and failures. Inevitably we say in our own hearts, do they or we never arrive at deliverance from sin? Does the Gospel just simply bring us forgiveness and leave us short of attaining to a holy life? Most assuredly it does not and this is because of our failure. Paul knew, and taught here, that he was cleared from the thing sin itself. Being dead to sin, his former relationship to sin was ended. So is ours if we have died to sin. Sin has been judicially condemned and we are heavenly and righteous in our standing

QUALITY OF LIFE A CHRISTIAN SHOULD POSSESS 103

before God. The line of demarcation for sin is as definite as the line of demarcation for sins. Just as you may know that your sins are forgiven, so you may know that you have been cleansed from sin. Christ died for us that we might be forgiven, but we died with Him that we might be sanctified. Notice the difference of emphasis. It is because Christians have not died with Christ that they are not sanctified today. This does not teach a daily death. It teaches a completed act, a by-faith-sanctification brought about by our dying with Christ on the Cross. Contrast this by-faith-sanctification with a progressive sanctification, which so many seek by their own efforts and their own works, by dying out daily first to one thing and then to another thing. It is not thus that God gives us our sanctification. Christ is my sanctification and my righteousness. I enter upon this experience of sanctification when I realize and appropriate this great truth. There is no need to seek and to search and to plead for deliverance. God has given deliverance. I need only to believe Him.

What a glorious assurance this brings to the soul. We have a knowledge, on the authority of the Word, which is the same as that authority which underlies our salvation, that we are declared righteous from what we were as well as from what we have done. Henceforth, there is no more dejection, self-condemnation, for our own selves and nature. We may now stand in the presence of sinless angels, like Gabriel, or of a sinless Christ, or of God Himself, without fear for we are holy and just and perfect in His sight. Our sins are not only forgiven, but our sin has been cleansed and we are righteous in His sight. We have no longer any connection with Adam. We are now connected with Christ. This fact is true of every Christian on earth, just as it will be in heaven, whether he realizes it or not.

The experience of sanctification, or union with Christ, is brought about by the baptism of the Holy Spirit. One can be "in Christ" only by the baptism of the Holy Spirit, which is the new birth. The phrase "in Christ" means that one is out of the old nature and into the new, that he has a new standing and a new relationship with God. This was done at his justification by faith and the application of Christ's work on Calvary through the Holy Spirit Who regenerates the individual. Justification and regeneration are two sides of one great fact. Thus, we are led to believe, after much contemplation, that the baptism here spoken of by Paul is not water baptism but Spirit baptism. If this were water baptism it would teach baptismal regeneration. Paul said, "Know ye not, that so many of us as were baptized into Jesus Christ were baptized into His death? Therefore we are buried with Him by Baptism into death; that like as Christ was raised up from the dead by the glory of the Father, even so we also should walk in newness of life." Now a man becomes a new creature and has the benefits of Christ's death and resurrection only by the baptism of the Holy Spirit into the body of Christ when he is born again. To teach that this is water baptism would mean that by baptism a man is regenerated. The evidence against such consists of the vast multitudes of people who have been baptized but who today manifestly and confessedly are unsaved. Water baptism is not efficacious to place a man in Christ. It is only a sign and a seal of the fact that he has been saved and is now in Christ. Even should this apply to water baptism, which we can not see in any way, nothing is said about immersion. It simply says that we by our baptism, whether of Spirit or water, and you may judge which, are identified with Christ in a death to the old life and a beginning of a new. We believe there is a great mistake in using this as a proof text for immersion. The word "planted" literally means united with, or to grow with, showing that what is here taught is the union with Christ produced by the Holy Spirit and by Him alone. On this fact we must insist.

When we say that this describes the new birth by the Spirit let us remember that the Holy Spirit is given by God to the believer at justification, which begins his life of sainthood. He who has the Spirit is sanctified. He is a saint. He is united to Christ. Justification is always the means to sanctification and holiness is the end proposed by God in redemptive work of Christ. Hence the answer to Paul's question, "Shall we continue in sin?" It is impossible for a saved man to continue in sin. When a believer is "in Christ" God reckons all to be true of him that Christ passed through. Has Christ died? Then the believer has died in Him. Has Christ risen? Then the believer has risen with Him. Paul said, "If ye then be risen with Christ, seek those things which are above." Is Christ ascended? Then the believer also is made to sit in heavenly places in Christ Jesus. This is the great truth.

Let me apply this doctrine by asking, "Are you a Christian?" You reply, "Yes." You believe that you are justified by faith and born again. Then you are also a dead man. You are dead to sin, dead to Adam, dead to evil, dead to the old man of your former sinful practices which you have put off. Were you a Christian before

QUALITY OF LIFE A CHRISTIAN SHOULD POSSESS

you were married? Then your wife married a dead man, and here is a good suggestion for the separate life, for any young woman who is alive to the things of evil certainly would not want to marry a man who is dead to them. This becomes your protection. On the other hand, let me ask you again, "Are you a Christian?" You reply, "Yes." Then you are alive, alive to Christ, to God, to the works of Christ, to the wishes of God and to His purposes. This living unto God is the test which settles every action. Only true Christians will be willing to recognize that they were so corrupt, useless and wicked that they were good to God only as dead men. Yet in order to be sanctified you must recognize this truth of your death to the Adamic nature, to sin and to evil, for it alone has the power to deliver you from sin.

II. FAITH—RECKON IT TO BE SO.

We have declared this as a doctrine. Now we ask you to believe it. That is exactly what Paul did. He said, "Reckon ye also yourselves to be dead indeed unto sin, but alive unto God through Jesus Christ our Lord." This simply means, believe it. Consider it to be so. It speaks of the act of believing. Thus deliverance from sin comes about, not by feeling but by faith. Like our salvation it is a fact known by faith, apprehended and received by faith and that alone. As soon as the presence of sin in our body, inciting us to evil, is found, we find it most difficult to believe that the old man has been crucified and the body of sin annulled. Thus it is only on this principle of faith that you may be delivered from sin. It is a most hard thing to reckon and to keep reckoning that we shared Christ's death to sin and that we are alive to God. This is the only way of establishing our souls in deliverance. It is a sheer faith in God's Word, believing that God said we died with Christ on the Cross. To fail to believe this will land one in the experience of Romans seven, where Paul describes his ineffectual struggle to make his flesh obey God. To this we shall come in due time. It describes the Dr. Jekyll and Mr. Hyde of the Christian experience.

These teachings are astounding and amazing revelations but they must be believed. All of this is in the realm of revealed facts, not of experience. We have not been talking about your experience but about what you were to believe, first the doctrine, then the belief in that doctrine. Deliverance from sin is still no more an experience than it was before. God simply said that believers are dead to sin and alive to Him and He asked them to believe it. If sin were absent from us, we would not have to reckon ourselves as dead to it, but sin is present in our body and thus it calls for faith to believe that we have died to sin.

I am sure that I was not present on Calvary any more than I was present in the garden of Eden when Adam sinned, but I reckon that God counted me so. My presence was there by imputation, by representation, and this position must be held by faith. I hold it with Adam in order that I may hold it with Christ. If I repudiate it from Adam, then I can not possibly accept it for Christ. The lack of deliverance in our lives is because we do not believe God who says that this is so. By faith I am no longer joined to Adam, but to Christ.

The test of faith is to believe contrary to human experiences and consciousness, on the basis of the naked Word of God. This is what Abraham did when he believed that God could give him a son even though he was beyond the years of fatherhood and Sarah was beyond the years of motherhood. Abraham believed God contrary to all of these things and God counted it to him for righteousness. Thus you see believing does not depend upon feelings and feelings only lead to doubt, to struggle, and defeat. The man who looks at his own feelings as to whether he is dead in Christ or not, and is now alive unto God, will soon be a defeated Christian. It is due to this unbelief, to trusting one's feelings rather than the Word of God that most Christians still wander in the wilderness of defeat rather than entering into Canaan. They simply did not feel or think that God could deliver them. Just as the Israelites looked at the giants of Anak and turned back to the wilderness, so they look at their anger or their envy or their lust or their ambition or some other besetting sin, and they think or feel that God cannot or has not delivered them from these giants and they go back into the wilderness, defeated by them. God said they are defeated foes. Claim your victory. You are dead unto them and alive unto God in Christ. There is no sin that shall have dominion over you.

Faith must be kept and sustained as an attitude day by day. Since sin is not dead but merely defeated, and since we have died to sin, sin is able to reassert itself and make itself felt through the flesh. The old man, or the body of sin, is merely annulled and he must be kept annulled by faith and the power of the Holy Ghost. Since we are not in God's final place of rest and deliverance from the presence of sin, which comes only at the second advent, we retain what rest is possible for us in this world only in faith. Sin will

QUALITY OF LIFE A CHRISTIAN SHOULD POSSESS 107

try to renew the conflict and the struggle and the temptation in our lives, for sin has access to us through the flesh, but faith is the victory which overcometh the world, and faith through the Spirit unites us with Christ, Who is the great victor. As we live under the dominance of the Spirit, we have rest. Since this is an attitude of life, it must be commenced. There must be a time when we enter upon the believing life, when we believe that God cleansed us from all sin, as well as forgave our sins, in the death of Christ on the Cross. The act of so beginning to believe and to live a life unto God is a true crisis in the believer's life. It may be as great a crisis as the time when he believed on Christ as his substitute for the penalty of sins. This time it is a crisis when the power of sin is broken.

III. FORCE—ACT ON THIS TRUTH.

There remain several sentences of Paul concerning this, in which he gives us an exhortation, a command, and a promise. The exhortation says, "Let not sin reign in your mortal body, that ye should obey it in the lusts thereof." This exhortation would never be necessary unless sin were still alive and present. If sin were not alive, it could not reign as king. Some of the Belgians are saying today, "Let not King Leopold reign over you." They could not say that if King Leopold were dead, but he is living. It is merely a question of whether he shall reign or he shall not reign. King sin is located in our unredeemed body as the seat of the sin principle, which is the flesh. Sin through this avenue is ready to assume control of the believer at any moment. Temptation, trial and difficulty may very easily become sin, but we are not to let sin reign. Thus, you see, the believer has power over sin. He can let it reign or he can reject its reign. God has made it evident that it rests with us whether sin reigns or not.

Whether the believer has victory or not depends upon his own will. Being dead to sin, it has no claim or no power over the believer if he walks by faith. We have stated the doctrine. Doctrine is a matter of the head. We have urged you to believe. Believing is a matter of the heart. But now you must also act, and action is a matter of the will, whether that is action of word or deed. You may choose defeat or deliverance. Both are within your power, but there is no excuse for your defeat, no excuse for lust or anger or pride or sinfulness in the human heart. We need not let sin reign in our mortal bodies.

The command is stated in the following words, "Neither yield ye your members as instruments of unrighteousness unto sin: but yield yourselves unto God, as those that are alive from the dead, and your members as instruments of righteousness unto God." The word "yield" means to present yourselves or to stand before. Hence, the command is that you are not to present yourself before sin as a king in order to surrender your members as his servants or his instruments in accomplishing wickedness. This states that it is utterly wrong for believers to be servants of sin. We were bondslaves of sin before we were regenerated. Now we ought to be bondslaves of Jesus Christ. A change of masters has occurred. Paul later showed that if we are still serving sin, it is manifest that we are the servants of sin and that we have never been justified by faith or born again. That is a true deduction to make. Such yielding unto sin as our master can only mean that we have never been saved, or else that we are in a state of terrible conflict and of defeat with no victory nor rest in our lives. God pity the Christian who is walking in that state of affairs, for in order for a believer to sin he must yield himself voluntarily to sin, for sin's dominion has been utterly broken and taken away from him. If the believer does this, he invites God's chastening and punishment which inevitably will be his. Never envy a believer who voluntarily chooses to be the servant of sin.

On the other hand, Paul says that we are to present ourselves, to yield ourselves or to stand before another King, namely God, to yield our members as instruments of righteousness unto Him as those that are alive from the dead. Here we come in a certain class, which class consists of those who are alive from the dead. It is like a man who is poor suddenly receiving a notice from an attorney that he is the son of a very wealthy individual. He comes as a poor man presenting himself to the wealthy man as a son, because of the letter which he received. He now enters the class of sonship. Just so we consider ourselves to be alive from the dead. This takes considerable faith, for we may not always feel that we are alive from the dead. By this we are surrendering our bodies, minds, emotions, and powers to the service and will of God. Having been raised from the dead by the glory of the Father and having begun the new life, we set forth to do His will as bondslaves of God. Contrast life under the two masters. One is bound for death. The other is bound for life. One is a taskmaster. The other is a loving Lord. One was to do sin and the other to do righteousness. Again let me emphasize that to be in this attitude of presenting means a single act of surrender, which is

QUALITY OF LIFE A CHRISTIAN SHOULD POSSESS

based on our being alive from the dead. It is not a gradual improvement of our nature.

The promise given by Paul consists of the following: "Sin shall not have domination over you: for ye are not under the law, but under grace." Sin's lordship is ended. You are delivered. Many are the individuals who have claimed deliverance from their besetting sin when they learned this truth. First, they surrendered. They presented themselves as those who are alive from the dead, those who died to the Adamic nature and now live in Christ unto God. Then they claimed the victory of their great Saviour. Sin never had any dominion over Christ, but death, which was sin's penalty, did. Now since the believer is in Christ, sin has no dominion over him. Christ has carried death's penalty for him. He is now alive eternally. Thus deliverance is not found by fighting with the old master, but by merely recognizing that we have severed our connection with sin, with the old man, and with the body of sin, and are living unto God.

Does sin still rule you if you are a believer? Is it present in the form of wrath, of hatred, of lust, of spitefulness, of envy, or in some other form? Sin has no right over you. You owe it no allegiance. Your old man has been crucified. The body of sin is annulled. You have been delivered in principle. If sin reigns in practice it is your fault. It is your choice. It is your failure. Do not blame God for it.

The fruit of your life will designate you as under sin or under grace. The fruit of sin is unrighteousness. The wages of sin is death. The fruit of Christ is holiness, and the gift of God is eternal life, for we are under grace. The law is abrogated. Grace, life, freedom, holiness, belong to you if you are a believer.

Then take your place with the Lord Jesus Christ in the heavenlies and with victory and life. Here is your answer to the question, "Shall we sin because grace abounds? God forbid it." Can we sin if we are believers? Yes, but we also can have the victory. It is contingent upon faith, upon surrender, upon service to God as those alive from the dead and being in Christ.

XI

THE RULE BY WHICH CHRISTIANS LIVE

TEXT: *"Sin shall not have dominion over you: for ye are not under law, but under grace."*—ROM. 6:14, and 7:1-25.

THIS text correctly summarizes the seventh chapter of Romans, written "to them that know the law." Here is the key to the experience of being freed from the dominion of sin. Paul is not exercised about pardon of sins, but about deliverance from indwelling sin as a power over the individual. He cries, "Who shall deliver me from the body of this death?"

The narrative is the autobiographical description of Paul's experience after his conversion when he found a terrible conflict within him due to his sudden awakening to the spiritual nature of the law. This could not refer to his experience before his conversion for then he was a proud Pharisee regarding the law as a legal requirement and not a spiritual power. Then he considered himself to be blameless, but here he was condemned. He had been in the Jewish tradition which had externalized the law. How different from Jesus' interpretation thereof.

This chapter cannot apply to Paul's later life when the general stream of experience was triumph, peace, power, victory and blessing. Paul did not remain in this awful conflict, although he undoubtedly passed through it on the way to victory. No one could write as Paul does here, without having experienced this struggle.

The description must refer to an experience after the Damascus Road conversion, either before Ananias brought full enlightenment or during the Arabian sojourn, when Paul learned the truth of Romans six concerning his sanctification, namely that he was delivered from sin by dying with Christ. Once Paul fully grasped this truth, he never went back into the terrible state of conflict described in chapter seven. This is the story of Paul's experience as a converted Jew, still believing himself to be under the law. Since there is still so much legalism in Christendom, it aptly describes the state of multitudes of Christians today, and is of highest value for our consideration.

This teaching is included in Romans as a warning to believers to

THE RULE BY WHICH CHRISTIANS LIVE 111

avoid Paul's example, by the plain statement that we are not under law but under grace. The struggle with sin is usually initiated by the believer's being "convicted for holiness" after being saved. He realizes that he is not walking in holiness, and seeks deliverance from sin by compelling the flesh to conform to God's law, an impossible state. The struggle is not a necessary one. If the believer understands and pursues God's promises, he may immediately enter a state of deliverance at his regeneration. John Bunyan correctly pictured this in the journey of Christian who, when directed by Evangelist to the Wicketgate, missed the sound steps of the sure promises of God and fell into the Slough of Despond. Bunyon observes that nothing has been able to fill up this Slough so that spiritual travelers would not become besmirched, for it is "the descent whither the scum and filth that attends conviction for sin doth continually run, and therefore it was called the Slough of Despond."

Defeat by sin is not the normal Christian experience, that is, God's standard of experience. Nevertheless it is followed by most people in their distress and longing for a holy life. If we simply could believe the truth, that we died federally with Christ, that we are united to Him in resurrection life, we would immediately enter into the blessed state of deliverance, belonging to a regenerate one who is no longer under the law. From this universal condition we learn that we cannot be what we would be by personal effort, because of the incurable evil of our nature—"sin that dwelleth in me," except it be by identification with the dying and rising Lord Jesus Christ.

This struggle is commonly accepted as representative of the conflict between the higher and the lower natures in man. In so far as this refers only to the distinction between man's God-consciousness or his spirit and his animal consciousness or his body, it is fundamentally sound. The classic illustration of this in literature is Stevenson's story of Dr. Jekyll and Mr. Hyde. Any natural man has the choice of living at his best or at his worst. He may so descend into an animal place of living that he ultimately possesses what is called a disassociated personality. The classic case in psychological studies is that presented by Dr. Morton Prince of Boston. He had a patient known by two names and presenting two utterly different personalities, Christine and Sally Beauchamp. As Christine, Miss Beauchamp was intellectually and morally a most admirable young woman with a saintly character. As Sally, Miss Beauchamp was the complete antithesis of Christine; for every virtue of Christine, Sally showed a fault. Alternately, for hours or days or months these two different personalities occupied the same body. Over a period of seven years Dr. Prince studied this split personality in which time he became convinced that the Sally personality was the subconscious thrusting itself into the dominance in experience. Every one has such a subconscious self which is the reservoir of many suppressions and also untapped energies.

However, neither unregenerate nor regenerate man possesses two natures. Man is a unit and is fundamentally responsible for his actions at all times. Before regeneration a man is totally joined to fallen humanity and has a fallen nature only. After regeneration a man has a new nature and is able to do good or evil whether he obeys sin or righteousness. The conflict described in this chapter is the battle of good and evil in a regenerated man, a believer, a child of God, in which hopeless defeat is turned into victory by the power of Christ. Here is the picture of two laws struggling for supremacy in the arena of the Christian life. Such a state of conflict is a great hindrance to sanctification, and must be ended before the believer has full deliverance. God's promise is that sin shall not have dominion over us. The realization of this promise in experience is by living under the right rule, not law but grace, not of sin but righteousness through the Spirit of Christ. The acceptance of this truth will lead one to bless God for it forever. In classification thereof Paul tells us what "not under the law" is not (Cf. Rom. 6:15-23), what it is (7:1-25), and what "under grace" is (8:1-38).

I. THE PRINCIPLE OF DELIVERANCE FROM THE POWER OF SIN.

The law must be supplanted by grace in the believer's experience to bring about deliverance from sin. "Ye are not under law, but under grace." Law is an outward rule of conduct, and grace is an invigorating principle, not mere favor, but the activity of God in the Holy Spirit.

The law pertains only to the man in Adam, whether under a work of the law as written in his heart or under the Mosaic law. Grace only applies to man in Christ. Hence the law referred to by Paul can mean none other than the ten commandments. The illustration of covetousness adduced by him shows this. Though this law, strictly speaking, was only given to the Jews, all who are familiar with God's revelation, as the Romans were, must reckon with it. Moreover, though we speak of the Christian not being "under law,"

THE RULE BY WHICH CHRISTIANS LIVE

the law remains the permanent standard of what is right and wrong, a norm of judgment.

The law's purpose is to detect sin in man and to reveal him for what he is, a sinner. It was intended to show up sin; "it was added because of the transgressions" as a schoolmaster to bring us into Christ, that we might be justified by faith. The restraint of the law on the sinful nature provokes it to transgression. A motorist may never think of speeding till he sees a sign designating a slow course, and then it seems to be an obsession with him to exceed the limit. Something in most men causes them to rebel against the restrictions of the law. This does not make the law sin; rather, it is holy, just and good. But it shows that man is sinful in nature.

The law loses its power over the believer at Calvary. On the Cross the demands of the law were satisfied and those who died with Christ by faith, died to the law. Christ was born, lived and died under the law to redeem those under the law. The law has no authority over the believer. Does this mean that we shall sin because we are not under the law? Not at all, for grace has taken the place of the law as the rule by which we shall live.

The purpose of the law being to reveal sin, its power and dominion ends at Calvary. The believer is not to seek holiness by obedience to the law. Failure to realize this plunges one into this conflict of Romans seven, instead of bringing deliverance from sin, power, security and rest, as is depicted under the new rule in Romans eight. If one is in the throes of this dread conflict with reigning sin, it is because he has not appropriated this truth, namely, that he is dead to sin and the law, and is in union with the risen and living Christ. For the believer there is newness of life in Him. Defeat by seeking holiness through works of the law is due to ignorance of God's truth, and the yielding of allegiance to sin, when the Spirit can and will fulfill God's righteousness in us.

The place of the law as a rule of life is taken by grace. The transfer is effected by faith in the propitiation made by Christ and in reckoning oneself as dead with Christ to sin. Under grace the believer considers himself to have died to sin, to the law, to the Adamic nature, and to its power. This fact is made real by faith. No warrant is thereby given to sin, but an incentive to holiness. The new life is one of service or slavery, not to sin, but to righteousness. The believer merely exchanges masters and instead of being a slave to sin he is now a slave to righteousness and brings forth fruit unto holiness. Only as slave to righteousness and thus free to follow the true law of our being, can we cease to be slaves of sin. The rewards of this service make it wonderful.

> "My glorious Victor, Prince Divine,
> Clasp these surrendered hands in thine.
> At length thy will is all my own
> Glad vassal of a Saviour's throne.
>
> "My master, lead me to thy door:
> Pierce this now willing ear once more:
> Thy bonds are freedom; let me stay
> With thee to toil, endure, obey."

II. THE ILLUSTRATION OF DELIVERANCE FROM THE POWER OF SIN.

The simple analogy between the believer's condition and that of a woman married to an husband is drawn by Paul. The husband dies and the woman, who is bound by the law to that husband as long as he lives, is free. As a wife she died with her husband. Now she may be married to another. Likewise, we died with Christ to sin and are freed from the law which bound us to the old man. Now we may be united with the resurrected Christ as a new creature. The law only holds till death and if we recognize that we died to the law by the body of Christ we may now be free to live under grace. As the wife ceased to exist in the eyes of the law when her husband died, so our Adamic nature ceases to exist before God in Christ's death on the cross.

This death we reckon to have occurred for us in our crucifixion with Christ by faith. The old relationship to the law as to sin is thus destroyed and legally we are free to be joined to another, even Christ in his resurrection. Thus alive, the believer is bound to a new husband namely Christ, is in a new relationship and is under a new rule, grace. Freed from the law of the old husband—the Mosaic law—the believer is under the law of a new husband—grace.

This new law is called the law of the Spirit of God in Christ Jesus. The new union is to bring forth fruit in good works or holiness. It is the figure of a fruitful marriage. This fruit is the glad service of willing hearts, the end of which is eternal life. For the believer, walking by the Spirit has taken the place of walking by external commandments. The indwelling Holy Spirit is the gift of God to the believer, sealing him in this new union. The Spirit is the renewing power of the individual which produces fruitful life; as the invigorating power of grace the Spirit is shown in Romans eight.

THE RULE BY WHICH CHRISTIANS LIVE 115

The old letter, that is the law, killeth, never gives life. Only the Holy Spirit renews and quickens. It is a glorious day for the believer when he is no more in the flesh, but sees himself in Christ, dead, buried and risen.

All to which the believer was first allied is dead. "We are become dead to the law by the body of Christ." His relationship to sin, law and the world ended at the cross, when he died with Christ. The body of Christ takes a most important place in the plan of redemption. That body carried the guilt of our sins and died for sin. A final end came to the race of Adam. A new race was created with a new federal head in the resurrected Christ, this is a heavenly race. Our death with Christ by faith joins us to him in new life and standing. Therefore, the passions of sins, which wrought evil when we were in the flesh, are now defeated. Being in Christ, with the Spirit of God in us, and no longer in the flesh, we bring forth fruit unto life.

III. THE APPLICATION OF DELIVERANCE FROM THE POWER OF SIN.

The remainder of the chapter applies this truth to the condition of one who has been defeated in this struggle. The picture is of a converted man trying to live under both principles. He delights in the law of God, but he discerns another law in his members. He is defeated by that law in him, so that he does what he would not do. One cannot serve two masters any more than a woman can be married to two husbands. This is the story of carnality in the believer. Here sin takes its toll. Paul confessed, "I am carnal." He also accused the Corinthians of carnality, or fleshly mindedness. Whenever carnality appears, the believer, who is convicted of a lack of holiness, seeks sanctification by works. These works are the exercises of a quickened soul under the law, who knows not the way of deliverance. When this occurred in Paul's life, sin was revived by the revelation of concupiscence, or desire contrary to God's will for him. Sin is inert until recognized by the law. This tenth commandment shows the essence of sin to be desire other than the Divine desire.

Sin, lurking in the flesh, immediately revives in one who seeks to control himself in the power of the flesh. However much we attempt to be holy in our own strength we fail. We will do that which we would not. All good resolutions are futile when meeting this enemy. The flesh in the believer is no better than in the unbeliever. Only by union with Christ is the Christian delivered from sin in the flesh. The believer must come to the realization that under the law he is "sold under sin." Exactly this is what the new convert does not know. Forgiven and justified he knows himself to be. But to discover an evil nature of which he was not before conscious is a bitter shock. The nature of man is carnal. The law or commandments, showing God's requirements, produce despair in such a convert. Paul said, "And I died." All hopes in himself died with this discovery of the spiritual nature of the law. Honest resolutions were hopeless. To Paul the future was terrible, as it is for many Christians longing for holiness. Help, if any, must come from without. Who shall deliver? The truth concerning the indwelling Spirit answers this.

Note the conflict resulting from the realization of this lack of holiness under a spiritual law. First in a dirge Paul cries out that he is forced to do what he hates. The flesh forces him to do what he, a saved man, knows is wrong. What he did not wish to do he practiced. This reveals that something was within him, distinguishable from his real self as a child of God. Indwelling sin brought him into bondage. His second lamentation cries that he was unable to do what he most thoroughly desired to do. Constantly he went contrary to the newly implanted heavenly desires. In his heart he consented to the law and its goodness, but he failed to perform it. Evil prevented him from doing the good he would do as a child of God. What a terrible condition for a Christian! Only by the power of the Spirit is there a remedy.

The warring of two laws in one personality gives the suggestion of a split-personality, a Dr. Jekyll and a Mr. Hyde. The alternating state of obedience to one or the other of these laws presents the difference between a carnal and a spiritual man. The natural man is the unregenerate man who knows not the things of God, neither can discern them. The carnal man is the regenerate man obeying the law of the flesh. This is the man who wishes deliverance, but who fails. Sin dwelling in him makes him captive. The spiritual man is one in full deliverance from sin and the law.

If a Christian finds himself in this carnal condition, he should never stay there. But unwillingness to confess carnality is the greatest hindrance to the spiritual blessing of deliverance. In this condition a Christian can never know the peace which passeth all understanding. The condition of the conflict is as follows: with the mind the renewed man serves the law of God and delights in it, with the flesh the law of sin. But this should not be. It did not continue with Paul.

The cry of a converted man living in the flesh and facing this

THE RULE BY WHICH CHRISTIANS LIVE

condition for the whole of life is piteous. "Who shall deliver me from the body of this death?" The complete deliverance is offered in Christ. The contrast of Paul's use of the personal pronouns, "I," "me," "my," in chapter seven with the use of "the Spirit" in chapter eight gives a clue. In this condition he is living in the flesh. No one can force the flesh to obey the law of God. Only failure ensues. The experience is echoed in the lives of many Christians. Therefore do not fight the flesh; turn from it to Christ the Saviour. He is the deliverer. Paul answered, "I thank God through Jesus Christ our Lord." Not the law, but Christ in glory is the rule of the Christian life. Hence we immediately read, "There is therefore now no condemnation to them which are in Christ Jesus." And "the law of the Spirit of life in Christ Jesus hath made me free from the law of sin and death." The righteousness of the law is now fulfilled in those who walk not after the flesh but the Spirit.

The triumph and victory may belong to every Christian upon the realization of the truth of Romans six and eight. The gospel says, first, we died with Christ and now we are alive unto God with the risen Christ; second, those formerly under the law are dead to and discharged from the legal economy; third, the Holy Spirit indwelling the believer has taken over the conflict with the flesh and is the power of the believer's triumph; and fourth, there is no condemnation to them in Christ Jesus.

All this is by faith, by believing we died with Christ, and that there is no righteousness or strength in us. Christ is our righteousness. Allow God to show us how or wherein we are holding to any sin or indulgence in the flesh; then let us agree to the sentence of death on this particular thing, which was passed on Calvary. Finally if we reckon ourselves to be dead to sin, our hands may be cleansed and our hearts purified in the Holy Ghost, which is given unto us. No longer in Adam, not under the law, not in sin, not dying; but in Christ, under grace, walking in the Spirit, and looking to life. This is the normal Christian life.

XII

THE INDUBITABLE PROOF OF THE BELIEVER'S SALVATION, DELIVERANCE AND VICTORY

TEXT: *"Now if any man have not the spirit of Christ he is none of his."*—ROM. 8:1-26.

THE eighth chapter of Romans is the answer to Paul's cry, "Who shall deliver me?" This great deliverance is in contrast with the conflict of chapter seven. Here is victory and triumph in Christ. Here the believer stands in the glorious liberty of the sons of God, by birth and adoption, with a foretaste of the mighty glory which is to come. Nothing goes beyond what is revealed as the believer's possession in Romans 8. It is tragic when the believer stops before experiencing the great truth of this chapter.

It begins with the words, "There is therefore now no condemnation to them which are in Christ Jesus." This does not refer back to Christ's great work on the Cross for us in taking away our sins, glorious as that victory is. That standing won by Him is unshaken by anything. When the believer is in Christ he will never be brought again into condemnation of judgment. He has already met God at Calvary in his substitute, namely, Jesus. Hereafter for him there will only be the judgment of rewards when he must stand at the judgment-seat of Christ. This chapter does not discuss those who are not in Christ. Therefore it is clear that the heart condemnation spoken of here exists in the life of a believer who is walking after the flesh, from which he cries for deliverance.

The means of deliverance from sin, the law and condemnation, is the indwelling Spirit acting as the new law of life. The Holy Spirit is the new, uniform principle motivating the Christian life. Thus the Spirit's work is the important factor in this chapter. The part of the Holy Spirit, namely, the third Person of the Trinity or the Comforter, in applying what Christ did to us is described. This emphasis upon the Spirit as opposed to the self of the believer is made clear by the number of times in which the word "Spirit" is used in chapter eight over against the words for self such as "I," "me" and "mine" in chapter seven. It is made clear that when one believes, the Spirit as the power of life, is given to him. The Spirit is the

SALVATION, DELIVERANCE AND VICTORY 119

agent of the Godhead, making real the deliverance declared in the sixth chapter of Romans. Only by the indwelling Spirit of God may this become an experience for the believer. For the believer there is a law of the Spirit, that is, a uniformity of action, by which blessing, power and victory is given to the Spirit guided one. It is as much a uniformity of action as that under the law of sin by which condemnation comes. The believer who enjoys the new rule of grace and the uniform control of the Spirit will never be brought into the condition of conflict described by Paul in the seventh chapter of Romans in which he was defeated by the Mr. Hyde of his nature.

The end purposed by God in this great deliverance is holiness. Paul says, "that the righteousness of the law might be fulfilled in us, who walk not after the flesh, but after the Spirit." We have already shown the law to be ineffectual in producing holiness because it did not change a man's nature. It only attempted to curb it, thus manifesting or bringing into clear light the sinfulness which was there in the flesh. Law can never make a man holy. It can forbid, rebuke and curse, but it cannot remove sin by condemning sin. The law is a holy standard or a measurement of righteousness. Any one who would know God's standard of holiness should study the law which is amplified in the Sermon on the Mount. It is clear that lying, stealing, adultery and brutality are wrong for one under grace, as much as for one under the law, but the means to righteousness under grace is the Spirit of God who fulfills the law and not the law itself as a rule of life. The law or the Ten Commandments is holy, just and good. It is God's measure of righteousness, but it is unable to produce righteousness in man, although it is a measure of that very righteousness.

God, however, did by means of Christ what the law could never do. "What the law could not do, in that it was weak through the flesh, God sending his own son in the likeness of sinful flesh, and for sin, condemned sin in the flesh." This declares that Christ assumed flesh, not sinful flesh, but the likeness of it. His body was like our body, which in turn is under the dominion of sin. The Christ was identified with us in the incarnation that sin which has its throne in the flesh might be condemned. This sin has been condemned judicially. It has been dealt with by God on Calvary. The great fact of the deliverance of our bodies from the dominion of sin will become our experience at redemption, for which we wait. This factual and judicial redemption, having been completed for us, is the basis for the resurrection and translation of the body. It is also the basis for the availability of Christ living in our present bodies on earth, for potentially they are redeemed. Our sinful nature was atoned for and judged on the cross. Christ took the penalty of our sin in His atoning work upon the cross and He was judged or condemned for sin. Our sinfulness is thus condemned even though the sentence has not yet been executed. Nevertheless, there can never be any condemnation to those who are in Christ.

By this wonderful means righteousness of life, which God so thoroughly commanded in the Old Testament, is brought about as an experience in the Christian. It results in practical holiness produced by the Holy Spirit of God. One should never think that because the Christian is no longer under law as a rule of life that he shall violate the precepts of the law. Rather the Spirit of God fulfills the law in him. He has a new power to live according to the law. A steam-engine may find it difficult going in climbing the ridge of a mountain. That steam-engine has to contain within itself all of the power to propel itself. An electric engine, however, is able to draw on an external source of power to propel it when a steam-engine would fail. The simple reason is that one is dependent upon itself and the other one upon an unlimited amount of power. Thus it is that the Holy Spirit enables us to fulfill what we could not do in ourselves. God expects us to be holy, righteous toward our neighbor and upright. This is the first commandment of all. Righteousness is the goal of the Christian in all of his intercourse with his fellow men. There can be no basis for against-the-lawism or the excesses of liberty for those who understand the true teaching of the law of the Spirit in the Christian life.

The Holy Spirit empowers the Christian through obedience. Righteousness is fulfilled in those "who walk not after the flesh, but after the spirit." The Holy Spirit is the power of our sanctification, our transformation in accordance with righteousness. If we do not possess righteousness of life it is due to the fact that we have neglected the Holy Spirit. Paradoxically some people do not understand the work of the Spirit. They experience that work of the Spirit, however, and it is far better to be wrong in head and right in heart than to be right in head and wrong in heart. Others understand the work of the Spirit but they do not experience it, because they do not walk after the Spirit. Now we must determine what the Holy Spirit does in the believer which is declared to be as important as what Christ has done for the believer. In this chapter we see that the

SALVATION, DELIVERANCE AND VICTORY

Spirit gives victory over the flesh. The Spirit witnesses to our privileges of sonship. And the Spirit assists us in our infirmity.

I. THE SPIRIT'S WORK IN DELIVERING US FROM THE FLESH.

Paul said, "Ye are not in the flesh, but in the Spirit, if so be that the Spirit of God dwell in you." Here two classes of individuals are declared: one, those in the flesh; the other, those in the Spirit. The flesh, describes the natural man. Here is given a clear presentation of the kind of existence which has been left by the Christian, the fleshly state.

In the flesh we "mind the things of the flesh." The natural or unregenerate disposition of one causes him to be preoccupied with the lusts, the desires and the thoughts of the flesh. Being dead in trespasses and in sin, it is impossible to set one's affections upon things which are above. When these things of the flesh are listed for us they are very repugnant. Romans 1:29-31 described these fruits of the flesh, deeds repugnant to any right thinking man. Yet the unregenerate takes pleasure in them. A briefer list is given in Galatians 5:17ff., "The flesh lusteth against the spirit . . . the works of the flesh are manifest which are these, adultery, fornication, uncleanness, lasciviousness, idolatry, witchcraft, hatred, variance, emulation, wrath, strife, seditions, envyings, drunkenness, revelings and such like." They include the physical, mental and spiritual wickedness of man. In this tradition we may consider such individuals as Cain, Esau, Saul and Judas to be. Paul said, "They that do such shall not inherit the kingdom of God." It is absolutely impossible for the fleshly man to delight in the things of the Holy Spirit. They are foolishness unto him, neither can he know them because they are spiritually discerned.

In the flesh one is directed toward death, "for to be carnally (fleshly) minded is death." The end of this kind of condition, this living in the flesh under the dominion of sin or of the Adamic nature is death. Thus God said in the beginning, "In the day thou eatest thereof thou shalt surely die." Think of the terror of being in thralldom to death as the goal of one's existence, yet that is every man's condition before he becomes a Christian or is saved. He is already dead in trespasses and in sins. When we speak of fleshly-mindedness or the mind of the flesh it is not a state into which believers fall, but it is the life which characterizes an unregenerate state.

Likewise, fleshly-mindedness is described as "enmity against God." In this phrase we catch something of the antipathy, the rebellion and the hatred of fallen man to God. He is an enemy to God. No wonder that such wickedness as is the fruit of the flesh, such manifestation of enmity, should bring fallen man under the Divine wrath. Nevertheless, Paul declares that while we were in this state, while we were ungodly, Christ died for us, that by the Divine mercy we might be redeemed. We are not irrevocably condemned to enmity against God.

Likewise, he says, they that are in the flesh cannot please God. The religions of fleshly man which are nothing but mental gropings toward God, their religious offerings such as that of Cain, or their religious service such as that of Balaam, are not pleasing nor acceptable to God. Even the prayers of men in the fleshly state are unheard by God unless they be for the supreme matter of salvation. Even the philanthropies of the unregenerate such as the building of churches, the doing of moral deeds, or the sustaining of worthy works are not pleasing to God. The condition of the flesh is a condition to be shunned.

However, believers are not in the flesh, but in the Spirit. This is simply another way of saying in Christ or Christ in you. Here we note the difference in description. The individual becomes a different kind of being. He is in the Spirit, not in the flesh. That gift of the Spirit is the essential mark of a Christian and a believer is in Christ because of the gift of the Spirit indwelling him. Thus Paul describes one who is in the Spirit.

First, he minds the things of the Spirit. The Holy Spirit is by nature interested in the things of Christ and speaks of the things of Christ. If the believer minds these things he would be interested in salvation, in the fellowship of the saints, in the depths of the truth, in prayer, in evangelism, missions and in the second coming of his Lord to this distraught earth. Whenever one finds an interest, concern and care for these things of the Spirit he may be sure that he has found one who is in the Spirit. Many of us may fall short in our interest in these things, but such shortcomings are due to our deference to the flesh and may be called sin.

One who is in Christ and is spiritual minded is blessed with life and peace. Literally, the verse should be translated, "The mind of the Spirit is life and peace." He who is born of the Holy Spirit and thus has Almighty God in him has the source of life and peace. This life is eternal life and this peace is the peace which passeth all understanding. Only in obedience to the Holy Spirit may this be enjoyed.

Paul declares that such an one who is spiritually minded pleases

SALVATION, DELIVERANCE AND VICTORY

God. Note that the Bible declares God is pleased to find one bearing the fruits of the Spirit, yearning over lost souls, seeking to fulfill His program in the world. Do you want to please God? What a day it will be for that soul when, after suffering and serving here, God shall say, "My child, step up yonder. Well done, good and faithful servant." If, therefore, we would please God we must begin with faith in His gospel about Christ, for without faith it is impossible to please God, and thus being made spiritually minded we shall please Him.

Paul says, "The Spirit is life because of righteousness." Eternal life given through the Holy Spirit and sin do not go together. The gospel of the Lord Jesus Christ makes no room for unrighteousness. The difference between an unbeliever and a believer in his attitude toward sinful things is, though the believer can do all things and has perfect liberty, yet sinful things are repugnant to him. The Holy Spirit is the dispenser of all new life, given in the risen Christ because all righteousness has been met and fulfilled by Christ and now will be confirmed in the individual life.

Victory for the believer or complete deliverance consists in making the transition from the flesh to the Spirit complete. Believers may still be carnally minded. Thus Paul wrote to the Corinthians, "Ye are yet carnal." They were babes in Christ, needing to be fed milk instead of strong meat, for they were still having deference to the flesh. This state is not as it should be. One can not even be a believer unless he has the Spirit of Christ, but it is necessary for him to realize and appropriate the Spirit's power. I am constrained to believe that it is sometimes necessary for a man who believes to wait before God for the witness of the Spirit because of his faulty knowledge or because of his faulty consecration. This condition is illustrated by the God fearer, Cornelius, and the twelve disciples of John the Baptist at Ephesus. They believed, but their knowledge was faulty. The indubitable proof of one's salvation is the gift of the Holy Spirit, the seal of God on the redeemed.

If one is to have victory over the flesh, he must take the believer's attitude toward the body that the Bible here describes. "The body is dead because of sin." This language is used in contrast to spiritual life. A man may exist without having spiritual life which is the only thing that counts with God. He may exist physically in a body while he is spiritually dead. The body being unredeemed is therefore unquickened and is spiritually dead even now. We owe to the body no debt of service to pamper it. Our only debt is to God. But this very body is to be quickened by the Holy Spirit at the coming of Christ, so that it will be transformed into the likeness of His own body. The same Spirit which raised up Jesus from the dead shall quicken your mortal bodies in that day of the resurrection.

It is a magnificent truth to remember that the body is to be transformed, but we hold it also to be a truth that the Spirit can quicken one's body now as well as in the future. All faculties of the body including our moral judgment may be quickened by the Spirit. Men who walk by faith and are filled with the Spirit can often do the work of two men. There is no other way to explain the superhuman efforts of George Whitefield in preaching one hundred seventy-five times in seventy days in New England while he was ill in 1740, except by the quickening of the Holy Spirit. Sometimes this may even reach the proportion of miracles of healing, but our mortal bodies are subject unto death. They are not yet redeemed.

Therefore, the deeds of the body or the movements of sin must be mortified. Surely this does not teach an asceticism of medievalism in which it was the purpose to mortify the body even unto death, but it is to keep the body under the dominion of the Spirit. Any man may be thankful for a healthy body in which to do the righteous works of God, but the thought is that a holy life can only be lived in a God-controlled body. All sinful indulgences or bodily desires leading to sin must be mortified, denied, or sin will gain dominion over us in experience. Man is a spirit inhabiting a body. Happy is he whose body is the instrument of the Spirit. He who honors, obeys and grieves not the Holy Spirit may have power in this difficult task of ruling his body.

II. THE WORK OF THE SPIRIT IN WITNESSING OUR SONSHIP OR ADOPTION.

The Spirit not only delivers us from the flesh, but He witnesses to our adoption into the family of God. "As many as are led by the Spirit of God, they are the sons of God." Apparently there is a difference between the word "teknon" meaning "born one" and "huios" meaning "son" of God. In the Roman law, children of a man were acknowledged, but only when a man publicly adopted those children were they acknowledged as heirs. Thus the Caesars designated their successors to the throne. There was always a great rivalry as to who should become the adopted heir of the Caesar. Every man justified by faith and born again is a child of God and by the gift of the Holy Spirit he is adopted into the rights, privileges and inheritance of the sons of God. Without the gift or the witness of the Spirit, what God has vouchsafed to us in our justification is not yet ours in experience. This, also, is illustrated by the condition of the Samaritan believers who had been baptized in the name of Christ but on whom as yet the Holy Spirit had not fallen. So he is a son who is led and controlled by the Spirit. This means guidance but it means more than guidance, namely, general domination by the Spirit in all things. This control by the Spirit is quite in contrast with the Old Testament bondage to law and fear. In those days no saint called God "Father," but in Christ we believers may speak unto God as Christ did. Thus we have the witness of the Spirit or the assurance wrought by God in our hearts that God loved us, that Christ died for us, that our sins are forgiven and that we have been adopted into the family of God. "Because ye are sons, God hath sent forth the Spirit of His Son into your heart, crying, Abba, Father." This position as son is established by the presence of the Holy Spirit in our hearts. It is a position entered by His enlightenment, encouragement and energy.

The privilege of sonship with God enables us to claim a prayer relationship of a child to his father. Thus we may say, "our Father." We may ask things from Him as His children. We also are placed in the relationship of being God's heirs. When we remember what God is, this is almost beyond our comprehension. Here we understand how "the meek shall inherit the earth." No angel shall ever enter this privilege, but only the redeemed. This overbalances all which the true believer renounces in the world when he becomes a child of God.

This privilege includes our union with Christ as joint-heirs. God hath exalted Christ to a position above all hierarchies and beings in the spiritual world. With Him He will exalt the believers. Thus Paul says, "Know ye not that we shall judge angels?" When God is all in all, we shall be with Him ruling over this vast universe as our possession. Such union with Jesus Christ begins now by the Holy Spirit Who is given unto us, but it will be consummated in glory. "If children, then heirs; heirs of God, and joint heirs with Christ; if so be that we suffer with Him, that we may also be glorified together."

In becoming sons we have a very definite responsibility. That responsibility may include suffering which we will have to endure involuntarily as members of His body. As Christ is, so are we in this world, and if they hated Him they will hate us. There must, therefore, be in the believer a willingness to endure, to deny self, to take up his cross and to follow Jesus Christ now. Whosoever takes this path as a son of God is fitting himself for a high position of reigning with Christ in the future world.

Sonship with God brings hope. If the creature was subject to vanity, to frustration, the creature is also groaning for deliverance; if death is everywhere, redemption is promised. The believer along with all mankind and the creation is waiting for that glorious revelation when we shall be changed into the image of the Son of God. One may groan now in physical pain and suffering, but he has the true hope of the redemption of the body.

Thus the Spirit gives us patience. He teaches us to endure. We are to wait for the glory which shall be revealed, for the full manifestation of the sons of God. These descriptions beggar thought as the final rhapsody of redemption is sung. When we come to the full fruits of the Spirit, to the resurrection in Christ, to the loss of the last remnants of sin, we could wish for the tongue of angels to tell of the gospel by which we were redeemed.

III. The Work of the Spirit in Helping Our Infirmities.

Between, however, the time when we received the earnest of the Spirit and the time when we shall have the redemption of our bodies at the manifestation of the glory of Christ, we have an interim period in which the Spirit does a mighty work. The Scripture says, "The Spirit also helpeth our infirmities." The believer is full of infirmity and full of weakness here in life. Because he is redeemed he is not delivered from ignorance, weakness, faults and failure. These are still found in his life. Yet he has a marvelous encouragement in it all. God has given him a very present helper, the Paraclete, the Holy Spirit. Men like Francis Parkman, the historian who could only study five minutes at a time, were able to accomplish wonders by their perseverance. The believer can accomplish wonders by the presence of the Holy Spirit. Whether you are weak, lonely, impotent or discouraged, lean on the Spirit of God and you shall be strong. You shall even be able to overcome your besetting sin. With such a Person and power you can have victory.

The Spirit is the believer's help in prayer, for "we know not what we should pray for as we ought: but the Spirit itself maketh intercession for us." In the face of the need of the world today, one wonders how he should pray. He has a sense of ignorance, of helplessness, of frustration, yet if he is a true Christian he will find

SALVATION, DELIVERANCE AND VICTORY 127

that the intercessor is within. It is not necessary to pray in beautiful language of public eloquence. One need only pray or groan in the Spirit and the Spirit within us knows that which is most needed by us and makes intercession for us. Simultaneous with His praying, there is an intercessor in heaven at the right hand of God, our high priest Who ever lives to make intercession for us, and He understands the mind of the Spirit and makes intercession according to the will of God. Thus, as we are praying, the searcher of hearts is working. God is looking for our needs and is more ready to meet them than we are to ask in Christ's name. This threefold Divine cooperation in prayer and in help is to the purpose that God's will may be done, that all might work together for good for those who love God.

Thus we see that the Father, Son and the Spirit, the triune God, have undertaken historically in behalf of sinful, fallen man. The deliverance is complete. The goal is wonderful and the evidence is indubitable. No one could ever be satisfied outside this glorious redemption. The work of the Spirit is the indubitable proof of your salvation, of your deliverance from sin, of your victory over temptation. Without the Holy Spirit of God or the Spirit of Christ we are none of His.

XIII

THE HIGHEST, BEST AND MOST WONDERFUL REACHES OF CHRISTIAN DOCTRINE

TEXT: *"If God be for us, who can be against us?"*—ROM. 8:28-39.

WE HAVE now climbed the chief peak of doctrinal mountains. We may now survey the beauties of God's truth from this majestic height. We may now express the rhapsody of the redeemed soul. This is our emotion as we enter this last half of the eighth chapter of Romans.

Paul here gives an outburst of confidence astounding in its reaches and based on the full benefits of the gospel, revealed and declared in the previous chapters of his epistle, the gospel known as the power of God unto salvation. So far, that gospel has declared that all men are condemned in unrighteousness by a holy God, that some men are justified through faith in Christ, the righteousness of God, and that all such justified men must be sanctified through the indwelling Spirit who fulfills all righteousness in the believer. A further revelation of truth concerning the work of the holy Trinity is here completed. It contemplates the source of our salvation, namely, the divine purpose, the process of salvation, namely, the divine predestination, and the result of salvation, namely, our preservation in grace, all of which is manifested in the gospel of God. Commentators variously call this passage, "colossal," "profound," "inexpressible," and "transcending language." Not one word of this is hyperbole. The view from the mountain peak stretches beyond the sight of any but the keenest eye.

On some subjects I feel capable of teaching. On other subjects I forever feel that I wish to be taught. Whenever I come to the matter of the Divine decrees or the Divine purpose and Divine predestination I feel that I wish to sit in the learner's seat. Without assuming any note of authority or of finality, may I give a few suggestions concerning this magnificent passage of Scripture. I warn you that twenty-five years from now I expect God to give me a much greater, much deeper and much more satisfying understanding of this truth. I do not believe that this truth will ever change, but

I do believe that my apprehension of it will grow as I come to know my Saviour more and more.

It is well to note that we are brought to the matter of Divine election last in the order of doctrines. Hence it is only to be presented when the full gamut of truth has been preached and men have responded to the love of God. Once a man is saved, he will rejoice that God has included him in His love. To reverse the order and to preach the decrees and the predestination of God before a man has learned the love of God through Christ, is incorrect procedure and is disturbing to the mental outlook of the individual, but surely at this point after our having considered God's great exhibition of love, in the propitiation made by His Son upon the Cross, and the wonders of grace available to us by faith, in our death and resurrection with Christ, we are ready for a consideration of the sovereign grace of God. Be not troubled by this doctrine of predestination, but praise God for it.

I. The Purpose of God.

"We know that all things work together for good to them that love God, to them who are the called according to his purpose." This statement of the Divine purpose in all things that take place brings us into a head on collision with the mass of modern thinking. Here we have the doctrine of Divine providence, that there is a hand which controls the affairs of men, ruling and overruling them, turning and overturning in the midst of them, weaving a strand of Divine purpose into the web of human destiny. There is a resurgence of interest in providence during this second World War. Lincoln O'Brien, a famous Boston editor, has stated that the present revolutionary war is a blow at the church, especially at Protestantism because of its doctrine of providence, which teaches that an Almighty God superintends and controls the events of history. According to Mr. O'Brien the overrunning of Protestant countries by a mighty war machine with suffering foisted upon innocent peoples and Protestant ones at that, impinges upon the doctrine of Providence and sets up a conflict in the minds of those who formerly trusted in Almighty God.

Much discussion in magazines and sermon form has come forth as to why God permits war. Men have been shocked by this spectacle and they feel the necessity to reconcile the presence of evil with the control of the world by God. In fact, some atheists have even gone so far as to assume that this triumph of force in Europe proves that there is no God. May we or must we admit that they are right?

Can even such events as this mighty upheaval be permitted by God for a purpose? Certainly the Bible teaches that Providence controls all events in spite of the presence of sufferings in the lives of believers. This same passage says, "Who shall separate us from the love of Christ? Shall tribulation, or distress, or persecution, or famine, or nakedness, or peril, or sword? As it is written, for thy sake we are killed all the day long; we are counted as sheep for the slaughter." This does not describe a world in which there is never an upheaval, a catastrophe or a holocaust, but this describes those great events as working together for the good of believers, even the believers who suffer in the midst of them. This is a wicked world under the power of the prince of the air, who controls the children of disobedience, and the normal condition of a world, in which a fallen spirit is instigating universal rebellion against a sovereign God, is one of persecution and suffering for believers. A Biblical view never promises us in this age freedom from suffering. Truly God will care for His own in the midst of these things, but He has never promised to keep His people from these things. The very scroll of the heroes of the faith describes them as such because "they were tortured, not accepting deliverance; that they might obtain a better resurrection: and others had trial of cruel mockings and scourgings, yea, moreover of bonds and imprisonment: they were stoned, they were sawn asunder, were tempted, were slain with the sword: they wandered about in sheepskins and goat skins; being destitute, afflicted, tormented; they wandered in deserts, and in mountains, and in dens and caves of the earth." Yes, they suffered and as these heroes of the faith suffered so the early Christians suffered in tortures but received Divine consolation in the midst of their torture and agony. War or the temporary triumph of evil never disproves the doctrine of Divine Providence.

Here we have the declaration that all things work together for good to them that love God, to them who are the called. This declaration is conditioned. It never says that all things are good. It never calls war, murder, torture, hunger, pain, sorrow, good, but it does say that even these things may be the means of good. Some people can never see the good in war. They can never realize that wars have often been the means of bringing some of the greatest benefits to mankind. The enlightenment followed the Crusades and was caused partially by the Crusades. Directly connected

THE REACHES OF CHRISTIAN DOCTRINE 131

with the movement stated in the Crusades was also the Reformation and the new economic era. It was this great war or series of wars that broke the inertia of the Middle Ages and the bondage of feudalism, bringing forth in its birth pangs the modern era. Who is there that will say that no good came out of the wars of liberty in the Netherlands or from the Puritan conflicts in England? Who is there that will say that this present conflict may not be the means of doing away with communism in the world and the opening of the Gospel privileges to more than one hundred fifty million people who have lived in darkness for a quarter of a century? Who knows but what an era of cooperation in economics and politics will emerge from the present war? War is evil, but we are confident that even war can work together for good.

Moreover, this passage never says that all things work together for good to all men. It says to the called, to the lovers of God, to the redeemed and they alone are spoken of. Who is the man who loves God? It is he who recognizes that God first loved him and gave His only begotten Son for him on the Cross, one who has met God at the Cross through his repentance, his converting and his believing that God has provided salvation for him. Who is the called? He is not only one who is invited by the Gospel, but one who accepts the Gospel and thus reveals that he is chosen in Christ. In other words, all things work together for good for the redeemed.

This Scripture does not say that all things are now good. It only says that they work together for good in the loving plan of God for the benefit of the saved, that is, in the ultimate purposes of God. One should note here that this text really should be connected with the two verses preceding it, namely, that all things work together for good when the Spirit of the living God is praying in the redeemed according to the will of God that the Divine purpose may take place. There is also a condition in this great common Scripture.

We hold that this declares the most infinitesimal and the most gigantic part in the history of events in this universe are interconnected with Divine benevolence for the people of God. Infinite intelligence and power are back of all things for good for the saints. The inanimate world, the forces of nature, the energies of mankind, the desires of Satan with his principalities and powers, all may be in opposition to us, but God says they are working for us. They are submerged to a great purpose under a fixed and vast will. All things are subordinated to this end. Paul declares this to be "the purpose of him who worketh all things after the counsel of his own will." Surely God's plan or purpose includes lesser wills or lesser first causes, but they are so limited as to their activity that the Divine will may know the end from the beginning. Thus the Shunamite woman, after hurrying from her home because of her burden in the death of her child, fell at the feet of Elijah and made a confident reply to his question. "Is it well with the child," said he. She answered even while the child was dead, "It is well." Only a confidence in the purpose of God can so speak in the presence of death. Only such a confidence could enable servants of God, Paul and Silas, to sing in a Philippian dungeon when their wounds from scourging kept them awake during the night. Only such a confidence could enable us to fulfil the Scriptural command, "In all things give thanks."

This confidence is affirmed in the words, "We know." This describes a revealed knowledge from God's Word to the soul, something promised, tried and proven. It is an experiential knowledge coming from the art of living. Paul was writing out of a full experience, but it is even more than that. It really describes that inner apriori knowledge such as the knowledge God has of us, namely, immediate knowledge. Another word is used to speak of knowledge gained from learning. Hence, the Christian has an inner heart assurance that his Almighty Father is working things out for his good, even in the midst of his trials and tribulations. Here is the comfort wherewith we are comforted of God.

The concept of purpose involves the Divine decrees. Purpose is that which one sets before his mind as an object to be obtained through the will. Purpose in relation to man is something which he is incapable of fulfilling as the purpose of the mariners who took Paul to Rome, to winter at Phenice, was frustrated. So the purposes of any of us may be frustrated. In relation to Christians, purpose may only be fulfilled by Divine grace. Thus we are exhorted with purpose of heart to cleave unto the Lord. Even Christians sometime fail in their purposes, but in relation to God's purpose there are no contingencies. What God purposes He is able to perform and there is nothing which is able to hinder the purpose of God. With God there is no lack of wisdom or of power, neither is there any variation nor shadow of turning. Therefore what He wills He also performs.

Paul described God's purpose as eternal, saying, "According to the eternal purpose which he purposed in Christ Jesus our Lord." In eternity God decreed certain objectives which would be brought to pass according to His will. These decrees constitute a glorious and intelligent plan for all of His creatures, so that, the whole earth will ultimately be filled with the glory of God. Hence, the Scripture declares that all things are foreordained according to the counsel of God's own will. In making a statement such as this we must be careful not to confuse God's infiniteness and timelessness with our own subjection to finitude and to succession.

Some of the objects embraced in the Divine purpose declared to us in the Scripture are: the fall of man, the death of Christ upon the Cross (foreordained before the foundation of the world) the salvation of His people (who hath saved us and called us . . . according to His own purpose and grace, which was given us in Christ Jesus before the world began) and the ultimate triumph of His church with Christ over all hierarchies of beings in the ages to come. Nothing can alter this purpose of God.

There is great comfort in this doctrine of the Divine purpose determining that all things shall work together for good to the believers, for in the midst of terrible events, in the midst of the worst that Satan or evil men can do, this brings peace and rest to the soul of the believer. God's sovereign plan and purpose is for the good of the believer. The very hairs of his head are numbered. A little sparrow can not fall to the ground without the knowledge of the Father and we are confident that this heavenly Father in His divine will and power will care for us.

II. THE PREDESTINATION OF GOD.

Predestination deals with soul salvation, a subject more detailed than the events of Providence. The Bible tells us that predestination is based on foreknowledge. We read, "Whom he foreknew, he did also predestinate." That the Bible always connects predestination with the foreknowledge ought to be the clue to the reconciliation of predestination with man's freedom. Peter said, "Elect according to the foreknowledge of God the Father." If God has elected and predestinated us because He foreknew something, what is the meaning of this foreknowledge? An answer is given when Paul said, "God hath not cast away His people which he foreknew." This is a quotation, a reference to the words of the prophet Amos, "You only have I known of all the families of the earth." We take the sense to be that of preacquaintanceship, that is, that

God foreknew or was fully acquainted with what we now are long before we ever existed as persons. Though we now are only becoming acquainted with Him, He foreknew us or had preacquaintanceship with us back in eternity, through His infinite knowledge. Thus if predestination is a deciding beforehand, it is based on a preacquaintanceship of God with men.

What it is that God foreknows in us is never stated. We simply know that He is acquainted with us. He is acquainted with the fact that we are all fallen and depraved, that we are unprofitable servants. He declares also that it is not by any works of ours that we are saved, for all is of sovereign grace. Nevertheless, God has conditioned our salvation upon our repentance, our converting and our believing, which are not works of salvation, but only works of obedience. Unquestionably God has predestined those to be saved whom He knew would respond to His grace. Thus foreknowledge, predestination and purpose are interchangeably connected. This is better stated in another place, "According as He hath chosen us in Him before the foundation of the world, that we should be holy and without blame before Him in love." Be assured that the purpose of God is good, holy, just and inscrutable. It is also beyond any appeal from us. We have no evidence or statement in the Scripture that God ever wills any man to perish, but we have much to the contrary.

Therefore, we accept both predestination and free agency of man. These very same books of the Scripture which tell of this "Appointing before" by God of men to be saved, also most strongly emphasize the freedom of action or agency on the part of men. In Joel, in Acts and in Romans are repeated the words, "Whosoever will call upon the name of the Lord shall be saved." Many Scriptures ask for the consent of man's will, saying, "Why will ye die?" And again, "Turn ye, turn ye." And again, "Except ye convert." God commands all men everywhere to repent, to convert, to believe. He invites men to accept the free gift of salvation, salvation not dependent upon any works of man, provided by God through Christ upon the Cross, but dependent in its application upon man's repentance. These facts we can not and we must not overlook.

These facts we hold to be utterly reconcilable with the presence of the teaching in the Scripture concerning the Divine purpose, foreordination and predestination according to His good pleasure. It is possible, of course, to press the philosophical presuppositions of this until we are in water that is too deep for us. Our finite minds

THE REACHES OF CHRISTIAN DOCTRINE 135

can not sound the depths of this subject. We stoutly affirm on the basis of the Scripture that God has foreordained all events, that God predestines the salvation of those who will be saved, according to His preacquaintanceship with people and events, and that God has given to man free agency which He commands to act according to certain principles. This is sufficient to place the responsibility for salvation upon ourselves and to give us confidence in God's goodness. We may live as James describes the life of a believer, "If the Lord will, we shall live, and do this or that." What we determine to do must be in accordance with God's will.

Our Scripture goes on to declare the progress and the end of predestination. "Whom he did foreknow, he did also predestinate to be conformed to the image of his son, that he might be the first one among many brethren." The object of predestination is that the believer shall be like Christ. This statement presents the limitless reach of the Divine work of redemption. What it fully means to be like Christ our minds can not even grasp. Christ is the only begotten son of God. He was made lower than the angels but is a being higher than the angels. By Him were all things made and for Him were all things made. He is the heir of all things. He is the center of the Divine councils. He is the object of the Father's love. He is the king of the kingdom and He shall rule forever and ever. We shall be like Him. We shall bear the impress of His glory, of His holiness, of His grace, of His purity, of His beauty, of His love and of His tenderness. "Now are we the sons of God, but it doth not yet appear what we shall be, but we know that we shall be like Him for we shall see Him as He is." Let therefore the song of our hearts be, "oh to be like Thee, oh to be like Thee, blessed Redeemer, pure as thou art."

To this end certain steps are the means. "Whom he did predestinate, them he also called: and whom he called, them he also justified: and whom he justified, them he also glorified." To be called means to be chosen or elected or designated. It is an act of God and not a mere invitation and it applies most certainly to those who have accepted the invitation of the Gospel. To be justified goes beyond being called, beyond even justification by faith as an experience. It is a word that reaches back into the eternal councils of God where Christ agreed to die for His people and the Father justified them. "He glorified" reaches both forward into eternity and back into eternity. Though believers are waiting for their glorification they are in the purpose and decree of God already glorified. Thus God looks upon us as already in purpose conformed to the image of His Son, though we are being more and more sanctified in practice day by day.

The fulfillment of predestination shall take place in what is called the regeneration. Christ was the first-born of many brethren. We the brethren shall also rise from the dead. We now hold a resurrected position by faith, having been identified with him, but we shall also hold a resurrection position in fact, for we shall also be born from the dead. This position will be higher than that granted to angels for, believers will be exalted to heaven and presented in the family of God.

III. PRESERVATION BY GOD.

Here we come to the great conclusion of the matter. Paul cries, "What shall we say then to these things? If God be for us, who can be against us?" Some might speak against the great truths of the Divine purpose and predestination, but why? It merely shows that God is for us in spite of all that we are in our finitude, our sinfulness and our failures, and because God is for us certain other matters follow.

If God is for us, no man can touch us. The entire epistle shows us that God is for us. It declares that man is sinful and condemned, but that God sent His Son to die for man. "While we were yet without strength Christ died for the ungodly." It declares that God spared not His own Son, but offered Him up on the Cross to show the infinite, frightful, awful cost of redemption. The only begotten Son of God was delivered to suffering and wrath for us sinners that we might be reconciled to God.

Since God was for us sufficiently to deliver up His own Son on our behalf, Paul declares that he will freely give us all things. There can be no logic in withholding the lesser gifts when God has given us the greatest. This very fact gives us courage to ask God in the time of need, for we know that He has already given Christ for us. The "all things" include the created universe as well as spiritual blessings. "Ask and ye shall receive."

With this confidence that God is for us we can challenge Satan, hell and the world as did Paul. The persecuting activity of Satan was ever against Paul, but it never succeeded. No accusation can be laid against God's elect, for when Christ is for us no man can be against us. If God justifies who can condemn? It is declared that there is no condemnation for those who are in Christ Jesus, for He

THE REACHES OF CHRISTIAN DOCTRINE 137

died and rose again for our justification. We remember this fact and also the fact that Christ is at the right hand of God making intercession for us, that if any man sin we have an advocate with the Father and that the Holy Spirit helpeth our infirmities. We have the full source of Divine assurance against the accusations of Satan or the world.

When God is for us no danger can defeat us. Then we are "more than conquerors through him that loved us." The rhetorical question, "Who shall separate us from the love of Christ" is a direct reference to Satan and his attacks for he is the great opposer of God. He is the great seducer of souls. He is the accuser of the brethren. Many are the devices of the devil against which we must stand. Paul enumerates some of them here, these possible things which might separate us from the love of God.

Shall tribulation separate us? This tribulation is affliction which comes because of the Gospel. Some afflictions come to all men in the world, but some come to the saints as directly instigated by Satan. The sufferings of Job are an illustration of this. Do not think in your tribulations that you are always being chastened of God. You may be tempted by the devil in them. Shall distress separate us? That is, anguish of heart and mind? Paul himself was pressed beyond measure so that he passed the sentence of death in himself that he might trust in a God Who raised him from the dead. But distress did not separate him from God. Shall persecution separate us? The Lord Jesus has announced that we would be persecuted, that the world would hate us, but it hated Him also. Shall famine separate us? Many are hungry in this unregenerate world. Literally tens if not hundreds of millions of people at this very moment are experiencing the pains of hunger and of famine, but famine can not separate us from God. Shall nakedness, that is the lack of good clothing or a sufficiency of clothing separate us from God? Never! Shall peril separate us? Paul spoke of being in "jeopardy every hour" and of "dying daily" and of being in "peril," but though all these perils were round about him every hour and every day they did not separate him from God. Shall the sword separate us from God or His love? Never, for the sword can only bring death, and we are counted as sheep for the slaughter. Many have been the times of slaughter of the saints and there is yet the greatest persecution of all to come, but this will never separate us from God nor His love.

Yes, "V" stands for victory and the Christian is more than conqueror through Christ Jesus. He may have to pass through all these things for the love of Christ. His victory may never be apparent to the world. The unconverted may think that he is the most miserable of men, but angels will rejoice at his integrity, at his security and at the victory of his soul in all these struggles. Every victory and conquest must be won by the Cross, that is, through Him Who loved us and Who died for us. That was the manifestation of the Divine love which Satan hates and it is through that love that we become more than victors in every affliction.

No wonder Paul cried out this paean of praise, that nothing can separate us from the love of Christ. This glorious persuasion of the soul was the source of such security as to provide comfort in every contingency of life. Many are the possible enemies. There is death, but death is emptied of its fear. There is life and all its temptations, but that will not be too much for us. There are angels, namely, fallen ones who oppose us, but Christ made a triumph openly of them. There are principalities, that is the mystery of the invisible powers or energies that affect the world, but these are subordinate to His will. There are things present like unemployment, or bereavement or need, but they have lost their bitterness. There are things future like our fear of what may come, but a God of the future conquers fear. There are created things which are innumerable, but the individual with God is a majority against them. None of these things can separate us from the love of God which is in Christ Jesus our Lord. This is the assurance given to the saved. This is declared for the elect, for the redeemed, for the called according to God's purpose. That it is for us we may know by receiving Christ in faith according to the teachings of this epistle.

What more can we add? Here are the heights and the depths of wisdom and love. Here is God's offer of salvation, righteousness and life. Here is the truth by which you may be saved. Now is the moment in which you may be installed in the place which has been yours from eternity. Remember God is for you and has demonstrated His favor in the giving of Christ for you. Therefore no man and nothing can be against you.

XIV
THE POTTER AND THE CLAY
OR
GOD'S REJECTION OF THE JEW

TEXT: *"Hath not the potter power over the clay, of the same lump to make one vessel unto honor, and another vessel unto dishonor?"*
—ROM. 9:1-33.

THE clay on the wheel molded by the hands of the potter is a familiar figure in Biblical literature. Once I visited such a potter in Hebron, the dwelling place of Abraham and the site of David's first capital of the kingdom. In a room joining his home, this Semitic potter revolved a wheel with one of his bare feet, while the clay fastened on the other end of the cylinder was molded by merely a touch from his finger as it whirled around in harmony with the wheel moved by his foot. From the common clay thus used came beautiful pieces of pottery and even some bottles. In fact, everything used by the natives of that section! Humanity is considered the clay, Providence the wheel and the touch of the Divine hand the potter who molds that clay into the kind of vessel which He desires. It is a beautiful example of the Divine influence over man.

The potter and the clay are a representation of the sovereign grace and activity of God in reference to men and nations. The human mind, however, constantly rebels against such independence of Divine action. Man believes that there must be something in him which becomes the basis of Divine molding. Not so, however, with the potter, for he has an idea in mind, and he molds the clay in conformity with his idea. This chapter of Scripture shows that God acts in accordance with justice, love and mercy which are the attributes of His nature, but that He molds the vessel according to His will. The question of the sovereign will of the potter is raised by the offering of the Gospel to the Jew and Gentile alike under the same conditions which necessitated the setting aside of the Jew as a special object of God's favor when he in turn possessed all the promises of God. This raises the question, "Does God act in an arbitrary manner or is He faithful to His promises?" There could be no doubt when Paul wrote the Roman epistle that the Jew was rejecting Christ and was being set aside by God because of this action. Was this process due to predestination or to the action of the Jew? The answer is, to both. Here we behold the truth of predestination and freedom brought into play in all of its perfection and in its nature of a stumbling stone to some minds.

The subject opens with the expression of Paul's great burden for his brethren according to the flesh. "For I could wish that myself were accursed from Christ for my brethren, my kinsmen according to the flesh: who are the Israelites." This burden of Paul expressed in his willingness to have his own salvation blotted out for the sake of his brethren stands on a level with that great height in the Old Testament reached by Moses when he prayed, "Oh, this people have sinned a great sin, and have made them gods of gold. Yet now, if thou wilt, forgive their sin—; and if not, blot me, I pray thee, out of thy book which thou hast written." A burden such as this can only be given by the Holy Spirit. Lewis Browne, in telling of the great revival which swept thousands into the church in the Congo in 1938 and 1939, described the burden which first descended upon him and on the other missionaries. There were times when they could not sleep nor eat nor even pray, when they felt in all earnestness that they, too, could pray this prayer of Moses and of Paul. Such a burden can only be given by the Holy Spirit. The proof that Paul had this burden lay in his attempt to win his brethren to Christ. In every city in which he labored Paul first preached to the Jews and continued to preach unto them until they either were converted or rejected his gospel. Paul invariably went to the Jew first. That burden for the Jews ought to still rest upon those who know the gospel during this dispensation. Any contemplation of the condition of Israel today as rejected of God should sadden and burden the heart of a true believer.

Paul dealt with this problem of the Jews in their partial and temporary rejection because there were numerable Jews in the church at Rome who would raise the question. When they read the message in the third chapter, stating that there was no difference between Jew and Gentile for all have sinned, they would be unable to reconcile this with the knowledge of the wonderful privilege which God had given to the Jews as a people. The astounding change from God's former ways in dealing with this people made it hard for the Jews to grasp the new way. Hence, Paul repeated often that there is no difference and that this "no difference" state exists

THE POTTER AND THE CLAY

between the Jew and the Gentile now. For this purpose the problem is dealt with fully by the great apostle to the Gentiles in these chapters of Romans. They constitute a vindication of God's past dealings with Israel, a reason for His present dealings with Israel and a prophecy of His future dealings with this chosen people.

I. THE SOVEREIGN CHOICE OF ISRAEL BY GOD.

Israel is God's chosen people. Paul described them, "My brethren, my kinsmen according to the flesh: who are the Israelites." A strange new teaching has arisen in the world in the last century which is called Anglo-Israelism. It advocates that the Anglo-Saxon peoples of the world are identical with ancient Israel, that is, the ten northern tribes as distinguished from Judah and Simeon. The claim is that the throne of Britain is the throne of David, that England is Ephraim, a multitude of nations, and America is Manasseh and that all the promises made unto ancient Israel apply unto these two great peoples today. We are told by these teachers that the Jew and the Israelite are utterly distinct, that none of the promises made to Israel apply to the Jew, that Jesus Christ was not a Jew, and that England is God's battle-ax which will crush the nations.

Without attempting to enter in to a detailed refutation of this particular theory we wish to suggest that there are two kinds of race pride rampant in the world today. One kind is the anti-Semitism of Aryan peoples if there be such, for certainly the Germanic peoples are not pure Aryan. Many are the terrors which have been initiated in the name of this race purity and anti-Semitism, one effect of which is to cast out the Bible and Christianity as being Jewish. Any true Christian will have nothing to do with this type of race pride.

The second type of race pride is this Anglo-Israelism which sets up the Anglo-Saxons, of whom I happen to be one, as *the* people, the chosen ones, the elect of God. A sufficient answer to it is that Israel was punished for its unbelief in the dispersion of 722 B.C. and that if it were possible to identify ancient Israel with the Anglo-Saxons, there has been no time when the nation as such has repented and turned to God. We brand this theory as absurd and foolish, straining the credulity of mankind.

It is necessary to stay close to the Bible in order to avoid these tangents so hurtful to Christianity. The roots of Christianity are in the same revelation as served Judaism. The Lord Jesus Christ was a Jew in tribe and in religion. He who despises the Jews is far from the apostle Paul as revealed here and he is far from the basic conceptions of Christianity.

We do not believe that there are any lost tribes. Rather we believe that during the captivity at Babylon the Jews and the Israelites intermingled, so that those who were called Jews were found in the entire sweep of the provinces of Persia, that when the remnant returned it was made up of the twelve tribes and that in the post captivity books the words "Israel" and "Jews" were used interchangeably. Thus also Jesus and Paul used them. In the thirty-first verse of this chapter Paul speaks of Israel which followed after the law of righteousness, but had not attained to the law of righteousness because they stumbled at that stumbling stone which was Christ. Did the Anglo-Saxons stumble at the preaching of Christ? Was it not the Jews and does not this word "Israel" here refer to the Jews? It is clear that in these chapters Paul is using the word "Israel" to be synonymous with the posterity of Jacob and he had to designate whether it was the natural posterity, that is, after the flesh, or the spiritual posterity, that is, regenerated Israel. Find a way of distinguishing between Jew and Israel in these three chapters if you can. We declare that it is impossible.

In defining who are the Israelites Paul refers to the eight fold privilege which was given to them. First was the adoption. This adoption does not have to do with the new birth of individuals which usually goes under that technical name, but with the adoption of a nation, a people to be God's people. Moses was commanded by Jehovah to say unto Pharaoh when he asked for the liberation of his people, "Thus saith the Lord, Israel is my son, even my first-born: and I say unto thee, let my son go, that he may serve me." Later in Moses' farewell address to the Israelites summarizing God's dealings with them, he said, "The Lord thy God hath chosen thee to be a special people unto himself, above all people that are upon the face of the earth." Amos added to this in the crisis period of the pre-captivity "You only have I known of all the families of the earth." These statements describe the Divine adoption of a special people. That action on the part of God was permanent and was compared with the permanence of the seasons. Said Jeremiah, "If those ordinances (that is, of the sun, moon, stars and sea) depart from me, saith the Lord, then the seed of Israel shall also cease from being a nation before me forever." This adoption was a free act by God to serve His own purposes, namely, that of revelation

THE POTTER AND THE CLAY

and redemption. God has only one people. He elected them sovereignly, which is the clue to the understanding of this chapter. God's election was dispensational.

To the Israelites pertained the glory. This word refers to the Shekinah, the ineffable effulgence of Divine excellence which sinful man cannot behold. It is the word describing the vision of Isaiah when he saw the cherubim covering their faces and crying before the triune God, "Holy, holy, holy is the Lord of hosts." It was the vision that caused Daniel to fall upon his face as dead, that overcame Peter, James and John on the Mount of Transfiguration and that smote John on the isle of Patmos with a sense of his own finitude. It is this glory which, being revealed when Christ comes again, will so overwhelm men that their eyes will rot away in their sockets. When that glory appeared upon the mount of Sinai it was a fatal act for a man to touch the mount for a breach would be made upon him and he would die.

This word describes the presence of God with Israel. Sometimes it was manifested in the pillar of fire and of cloud. On another time it was manifested as Moses saw God from the cleft in the rock where the Lord had hidden him. It was manifested in the symbolism of the mercy-seat where God declared he dwelt among the people. None ever saw the Divine glory as did Israel. All the symbolism of the temple pointed to the presence of the glory of God in the midst of His people.

To Israel pertained the covenant. Of the numerous covenants we single out first the Abrahamic covenant made by God with Abraham that his seed should be as numerous as the stars in the heavens and that unto Abraham's seed God gave the land of Palestine from the river of Egypt unto the great river, the river Euphrates. Of this covenant promise, by which all the nations of the earth should be blessed, circumcision was a sign and seal. Abraham was counted as righteous because he believed this covenant given to him and his descendants.

To David the covenant was narrowed in the promise of an eternal kingdom for his seed. The Lord said, "I will set up thy seed after thee, it shall proceed out of thy bowels, and I will establish his kingdom ... forever ... Thy throne shall be established forever."

Later through Jeremiah and Ezekiel God promised to make a new covenant with the house of Israel, and with the home of Judah: "not according to the covenant that I made with their fathers in the day that I took them by the hand to bring them out of the land of Egypt; which my covenant they break, although I was an husband unto them, saith the Lord: but this shall be the covenant that I will make with the house of Israel; after those days, saith the Lord, I will put my law in their inward parts, and write it in their heart; and I will be their God, and they shall be my people." Jesus said concerning his sacrifice on the cross, "This is the blood of the new covenant shed for many for the remission of their sins." We, therefore, have reason to believe that though this covenant is made with Israel that the Lord has introduced into it the Gentiles, by His redemption upon the cross.

To the Israelites pertain the giving of the law. Familiar to us all is that great experience by which God revealed His law, inscripturated it through Moses and submitted it to the people for their acceptance. It is true that all men have a work of the law written on their hearts, manifesting itself in the form of conscience, but only to Israel was God's external law given. This law holds sway over all men as they come to know it, but it was Israel's privilege to know God's way and to walk in it by revelation. The chief blessings of the law rest in its being a schoolmaster to lead us to Christ, an instrument of salvation. To the Israelites pertained this law.

The Israelites also had the service or the liturgy of God. By this Paul referred to the ritual in the tabernacle and in the temple, all the details of which proclaimed the gospel. Here God's good news of salvation was preached in symbolism. Grace, forgiveness and righteousness were provided by God for those who lived under the law. Once men lived as Abraham did in pure faith concerning God's word, but when the law came they needed the ritual as a means of forgiveness and of worship of God. Now our service of God is utterly different, namely, the presenting of our bodies a living sacrifice or offering unto God which is our reasonable liturgy, but we are indebted to Israel for much teaching even on this.

To Israel pertained the promises. Recall the great promises Israel had of the Messiah, of the kingdom, of blessing to the world. We do not believe that these promises made to Israel can be literally transferred to the church or to individuals. We do believe, however, that the principles which underlie those promises can be taken out of the context, reapplied in similar situations in the New Testament period. The Church of Jesus Christ has been founded on the fact of the Cross and the promises for the Church are in a new dispensation, through Christ and His nature, and we are existing in Him. Thus when we make our prayer it is in the name of Christ and abiding in Him as members of His church, but the promises which have been made to Israel shall yet be fulfilled.

To Israel pertained the fathers. These fathers are the heroes of of the faith and they all came from Israel. With a possible exception of Luke every book in the Bible was written by an Israelite. We Christians are dependent for our knowledge of God upon the individuals of this chosen people and in a real sense every Christian is a child of Abraham whatever his racial background. Whosoever is born of faith is a child of Abraham.

Of the Israelites as pertaining to the flesh, Jesus Christ came. Here is another refutation of Anglo-Israelism. If the ten tribes were lost at this time, how was Jesus Christ an Israelite? He was in fact a descendant of Judah and a Jew by religion and is called an Israelite. From the human standpoint this was the greatest privilege which Israel could receive and for the giving of Jesus Christ according to the flesh we are forever indebted to this despised race, regardless of what men may say. Reject the Jews and you inevitably reject Jesus Christ who is "over all, God blessed forever." This is one of the highest statements of His deity, which He shares with the Father. Thus it was that in Mary, descendant of the tribe of Judah, there was born "the holy thing" called the Son of God. A Jewish maiden was the mother of Jesus.

The principle applied in the choice of Israel is sovereign grace. God chose Israel and bestowed these blessings upon the people not because of their worthiness but in spite of their unworthiness. He had a purpose to accomplish something through this peculiar people and thus all of the blessings enjoyed by Israel were of grace alone. Hence, Paul declared "They are not all Israel, which are of Israel." Because a person was a child of Abraham and an Israelite did not mean that he was saved. John the Baptist proclaimed "Think not to say within yourselves, we have Abraham to our father . . . Now also the ax is laid to the root of the tree: therefore every tree which bringeth not forth good fruit is hewn down and cast into the fire." Jesus said to those who claimed to be the children of Abraham, "ye are of your father the devil." Only those who assume the position of Isaac, that is, the children of faith, who are supernaturally born are God's children. This is the teaching both of the Old Testament and of the New. For this reason Jesus could say to Nicodemus who was a rabbi of the Jews when He was talking about the new birth, "Art thou a master in Israel and knowest not these things?"

Hence we conclude that the privileges of physical Israel were for this world only, unless they apprehended the great spiritual truths in them. The children of the flesh are not the children of God. This teaching strikes a blow at the brotherhood of man and at universal sonship of God. Only the children of promise are God's children and all Israelites were not saved.

Now Paul advances certain illustrations of the truth of Divine grace and sovereignty. He shows that all individuals who enjoyed God's blessing did so by grace alone. First is the case of Isaac rather than Ishmael. The promise was "In Isaac shall thy seed be called." Abraham wondered why Ishmael would not do. Only sovereign grace can answer that question. From Ishmael came a great people, the Arabians who are Moslems. From Isaac came the Israelites, Judaism and Christianity. Why? Only God can answer that question.

The second illustration pertained to Jacob and Esau. Of them it says "the children being not yet born, neither having done any good or evil, that the purpose of God according to election might stand, not of works, but of him that calleth; it was said unto her, the elder shall serve the younger." We hold it is a mistake to apply this to the predestination of individuals, whether to heaven or hell. Rather it applies to the choosing of a people, namely, Israel. We are not told in the Bible that God predestinates children to hell before they are born. Here one is chosen by sovereign grace to be the progenitor of Israel, the people. The very name "Israel" comes from him. God's purpose was that the seed should come from Jacob and that the Edomites should come from Esau. As to the quotation, "Jacob have I loved and Esau have I hated," we must observe that it came from the prophet Malachi almost fifteen hundred years after Jacob and Esau had lived and died. It merely describes the fact that Jacob's descendants had privileges which Esau's never knew. The Edomites had no prophets and no oracles and none of the privileges which pertained to Israel.

Next Paul refers to Israel itself, in the promise given to Moses, "I will have mercy on whom I will have mercy, and I will have compassion on whom I will have compassion." This is a quotation from Exodus regarding Israel's sin by which the people had forfeited all right to the favor of God and the claim to blessing on the basis of law and righteousness. Apart from grace only doom awaited them. God was ready to "blot them out," but at this point Moses stepped in as a mediator with the prayer, "Blot me out of thy book of life."

Then came the promise concerning mercy. God again in His sovereign right and grace showed mercy and withheld His judgment. Thus it is with all men. We all deserve to be condemned, but by God's mercy we are saved. No Jew and no Israelite could ever claim salvation by righteousness, only by God's mercy.

The last illustration advanced is that of Pharaoh. Here is the case of a man whom God apparently left in his natural state with a rebellious, wicked heart, untouched by grace. God has a perfect right to leave all in this condition and the narration concerning Pharaoh leaves the suggestion that it was because Pharaoh had hardened his own heart. God knows the human heart and, though God was not the author of Pharaoh's sin, He made Pharaoh's heart hard in his chosen way of rebellion. It was this man who cried, "Who is the Lord?" Therefore in the Divine purposes Pharaoh was given power for a season to be an example to all the earth of God's power and God's sovereignty. Throughout the history of the Old Testament the Lord was always known as Jehovah who delivered His people from the hand of Pharaoh. One wonders if God did not have some similar purpose in the permitting of the careers of Alexander, Caesar, Hannibal, Napoleon and Hitler, namely, to show His own glory.

All this, Paul said, is to reveal that "it is not of him that willeth, nor of him that runneth, but of God that showeth mercy." We are commanded to repent, to convert and to believe, that is, to run and to will, but all this running and willing on our part without God's mercy would be meaningless. Nevertheless, we should not pass by this important factor, "Whosoever will call upon the name of the Lord shall be saved"; "He delighteth in mercy"; "I have no pleasure in the death of the wicked"; "Why will ye die?" and Christ was the "propitiation for the whole world." We hold that in the general teaching of Scripture there is no reprobation or predestination to death here suggested but only God's infinite mercy. Now we must mention Israel's rejection.

II. THE REJECTION OF ISRAEL BECAUSE OF UNBELIEF.

Paul declares that God manifests His glory on the vessels of mercy whom He called not of the Jews only but also of the Gentiles. These Gentiles had not been called God's people, but now they received the mercy of salvation, being included in the saving plan of God by the teaching of Paul and of every apostle. Wherever Paul went preaching the Gentiles thronged to hear the message of salvation while the Jews often were hardened and rejected. The Jew met this fact with universal hostility. He wanted the Gentile to come to salvation by way of Judaism and because of this he rejected the message of Paul and of the gospel so that ultimately the Christian message went primarily to the Gentiles.

Israel as such is rejected today from being the privileged people of God. Paul applies to them the words of Hosea, "I will call them my people, which were not my people; and her beloved which was not beloved, and it shall come to pass, that in the place where it was said unto them, ye are not my people; there they shall be called the children of the living God." At the present time Israel is not God's people. Through Hosea we have this prophecy, "Then said God, call his name Lo-ammi: for ye are not my people, and I will not be your God." During this period of rejection the Israelites have no claim upon God's mercy other than the same claim which the Gentiles have. "Now in Christ ye who sometimes were far off are made nigh by the blood of Christ, for he is our peace, who hath made both one, and hath broken down the middle wall of partition between us; having abolished in his flesh the enmity, even the law of commandment contained in ordinances." Thus for those who are saved there is no distinction for they are all in Christ.

God is specifically calling out the Gentiles and the Israelites who would be saved and take their places with the Gentiles. Though the Jews considered that the Gentiles were not the people of God during this age they are called the sons of God and Israel must be saved like as they are.

Though most Israelites are rejected, that is, as a nation, a remnant of them shall be saved. The nation after the flesh is apostate, but a remnant even now is being saved and is the object of the loving-kindness of God, even after the national rejection. At the best in any one given era God is only saving a remnant of Israel. That was true in Moses' day, in Elijah's day, in Daniel's day and in the day of Paul. It will also be true in the end of the age in which we live. Paul said, "Though the number of the children of Israel be as the sand of the sea, a remnant shall be saved: for he will finish the work, and cut it short in righteousness: because a short work will the Lord make upon the earth." Jesus spoke of days that would be shortened for the elect's sake, days of tribulation called the days of Jacob's trouble, but only a remnant of Israel will be saved out of tribulation. This saved remnant, both individually and at the end of the age nationally, is a fruit of grace. If God had

THE POTTER AND THE CLAY

not intervened in sovereign grace, their end, Paul said, would have been as Sodom and Gomorrah. Those who put off their salvation till the time of the coming of the Messiah know not their jeopardy for only a few shall live to acknowledge their glorious Messiah in His coming.

Israel, therefore, missed out in righteousness because they sought righteousness after the flesh and omitted the righteousness which is of faith. The Gentiles which followed not after righteousness, have attained to righteousness, even the righteousness which is of faith. The faith-righteousness is righteousness through the Cross of Christ bestowed as the free gift of God's grace on all those who will commit themselves to Him. The Gentiles know that they are lost and condemned and thus they believe. They gladly accept the gospel of a Saviour and by faith they are saved through grace. But Israel sought a law of righteousness by which to gain salvation and because they trusted in works failed to attain to righteousness. That God should set forth Christ as a propitiation for the sins of men, became a stumbling stone to Israel and was the cause of their falling and rejection, because they would not believe. It was the rejection of Christ which caused the rejection of the Jew, but whosoever within Israel believeth on Him shall not be ashamed.

III. THE QUESTION OF FATALISM.

We would return for a moment to the 19th to the 22nd verses on which the argument has been based that God's will is unchangeable and irresistable and that man is a puppet, either dammed or saved before his birth. We must admit that if we were forced to that belief it would compel us to Atheism. If, however, we accept that this chapter teaches God's dispensational dealings with a people and does not pertain to personal salvation, the objection is removed. God certainly grants privileges to some which He does not grant to others. If we ask why, the answer must be that of the potter and the clay. God has the power and the wisdom to do as He pleases with His creatures in accordance with His plans. Moreover, this choosing of and rejecting of the Israelites is altogether just in the light of their rebellious history.

That eternal issues grow out of such temporal elections we cannot doubt, but we must accept the fact that in every realm God is absolutely sovereign. God endures vessels fit for destruction until the time of their destruction. It is possible that God could bring judgment on all now, but He will not and He does not till all who shall be saved will be saved, for it is not the will of God that any should perish, but that all should come to the knowledge of the truth, but the time of destruction and of wrath will come in what is called the great tribulation.

If some insist that this teaching applies to personal election, we must admit that God has the sovereign right to do so if He chooses to use it, but we believe that God has given to us a sense of justice which is qualitatively like unto His own and that He would not do anything which would violate the innate sense of justice implanted in man. God has placed great responsibility on the will of man to repent, to convert, to believe and to commit himself to Christ. If man refuses to do this, God is certainly just at the end of the period of probation in condemning such a person to destruction. No true Christian will ever deny to God the right to save whom He will or to allow to perish whom He will in accordance with His justice and mercy.

In this chapter we have seen the great wisdom of God in action in the history of a people. First, Israel was chosen in grace. Then it was rejected because of unbelief. That rejection was not complete nor was it final, for Israel is still being saved in remnant form and will be saved in national form. Thus the Israelites or the Jews continue to exist in the world as the evidence of the truth of God's word.

XV
THE PREACHER AND THE WORD
OR
THE INTERIM RELATION OF THE JEW TO GOD

TEXT: *"Whosoever believeth on him shall not be ashamed. For there is no difference between the Jew and the Greek: for the same Lord over all is rich unto all that call upon him."*—ROM. 10:1-21.

WE WISH to speak about the Jew as an individual. In our last discussion, based on chapter nine, we came to the conclusion that the Jew nationally was rejected. Does this mean that every individual Jew is also rejected?

Chapter nine revealed God's sovereign choice of Israel, manifested in the bestowing of wonderful privileges upon them which singled Israel out as a nation above all other nations. This choice of Israel was not because of any merit in the nation, but because of the purposes of God to bring blessing unto the world. In fact, the illustrations produced by Paul reveal that this sovereign grace was manifested unto Israel in spite of its demerit, on the basis of which it forfeited all right for favor and privilege.

Due to unbelief, Israel as such is now rejected by God. The teaching in the twenty-eighth chapter of the Book of Acts in which Paul says, "Be it known therefore unto you, that the salvation of God is sent unto the Gentiles, and that they will hear it," means that Israel as a nation was rejected. God was so speaking through the Holy Ghost. The means of salvation, revealed in Christ the stumbling stone, became an offense unto Israel who rejected Him and crucified Him, thus taking the final step in their moral degradation. God has a perfect right to reject Israel entirely, but out of His great mercy in every period He has saved a remnant. This remnant of Israel today is made up of individual Jews who are saved.

Paul quotes Isaiah as saying that without grace Israel would have been as Sodom and Gomorrah who are examples of the Divine judgment, but there was a remnant, a seed left unto Israel in the time of Isaiah and there was a remnant left in the time of Paul. This remnant consisted of those who sought righteousness by faith and not by works, which was the error of the nation. Though Israel as a nation is rejected this does not in the least exclude any individual Israelite from salvation. It merely emphasizes the statement of Paul, "There is no difference."

It would be well for us to summarize the truths about the Jew and the Gentile today as revealed in the Bible. Paul says concerning the Gentiles and the Jews, "Now in Christ Jesus ye who sometimes were afar off are made nigh by the blood of Christ. For He is our peace, who hath made both one, and hath broken down the middle wall of partition between us; having abolished in His flesh the enmity, even the law of commandments contained in ordinances; for to make in Himself of twain one new man, so making peace; and that he might reconcile both unto God in one body by the Cross, having slain the enmity thereby." Today there is no difference between the Jew and the Gentile in reference to God. The only righteousness which exists for any man, whether Jew or Gentile, is righteousness received through faith in the propitiation which has been made by Christ. Christ alone is the righteousness of God to any man today. That the Jews still seek righteousness by the law is due to their ignorance of God's righteousness and of the teaching of their own Scriptures. Paul said, "I bear them record that they have a zeal of God, but not according to knowledge. For they, being ignorant of God's righteousness, and going about to establish their own righteousness, have not submitted themselves unto the righteousness of God." There could be no question concerning their zeal, but it was a zeal of ignorance. That there are many Gentiles of Christendom who seek righteousness by the law today reveals that they are in an even worse bondage than the Jew. They are making futile efforts to develop a character under the law which is acceptable unto God. This is worse ignorance of the requirements of God than that found in Israel. That sinners should be justified in the Presence of God, before such moral men are, is altogether proper on the standard of faith which is God's requirement. The harlots and the publicans shall enter the kingdom of God before the Pharisees who trust in their own righteousness, whether they are ancient or modern Pharisees.

Zeal in seeking righteousness in my way can never substitute for submitting to righteousness in God's way. God's way of righteousness has been clearly declared to us in this Book of Romans. Almighty God is righteous or just in forgiving the sins of wicked men because of the death of Christ upon the Cross, which made a complete satisfaction to the demands of righteousness. Therefore righteousness is given by imputation from Christ to all who believe upon Christ, so that Christ becomes the righteousness of God to the believer. Thereinafter, the righteousness of the law is fulfilled in us by Christ, through our walk after the Spirit and not after the flesh. Christ is the end of the law, Paul says. This can only mean one thing, that the law has no longer any authority over the believer, not even as a rule. It remains only a revelation of what is right and of what is wrong, a standard of judgment. The believer is already righteous in the sight of God and the indwelling Spirit is fulfilling God's righteousness in him.

What then should be the Christian's attitude toward the Jew? Paul says, "Brethren, my heart's desire and prayer to God for Israel is, that they might be saved." Surely, like as Paul, Christians should pray and labor for the salvation of the Jew as well as for the salvation of the Gentile. A Christian must be free from all hate and all prejudice of race. It appears from this, that Israel's salvation was a delight for Paul to contemplate. We shall see in the next chapter of this great treatise that Israel's salvation shall bring a tremendous blessing to the world. It shall be the beginning of a season of blessing beyond anything we have ever contemplated.

Meanwhile, there is no special place which should be given to the Jew in this age. God has rejected Israel nationally. We are not to place the Jew first and the Gentile second. They stand together before God as sinners with no difference. If ever there was a need for strong messages of condemnation and repentance to individual Jews in order that they might be saved that day is today. Instead of approaching them intellectually or on a literary plane, it is time for the church of Jesus Christ to speak to the Jew as a common, ordinary sinner who is not the child of God, whose nation is not the people of God and who needs to be saved or he will pass into eternal judgment of hell. In fact, the judgment of the Jew who has had the knowledge of the Old Testament, with all of its righteousness, will be more terrible than the judgment of any heathen who did not know this revelation.

The Christian, then, must recognize that God is preserving the Jews indestructible, as a nation, until His world purposes are fulfilled through them, but the individual Jews must be saved exactly as the Gentiles must be saved. One prophecy is sufficient to show us the future purposes of God in connection with Israel. "As I live, saith the Lord God, surely with a mighty hand and with a stretched out arm, and fury poured out, will I rule over you: and I will bring you out from the people, and will gather you out of the countries wherein ye are scattered, with a mighty hand, and with a stretched out arm, and with fury poured out. And I will bring you into the wilderness of the people, and there will I plead with you face to face." The warning of this tribulation has been given by the prophets, Daniel, Jeremiah and John the beloved. It will be a time of such suffering as will far over-shadow anything which the world sees at the present time and out of which only a remnant of the Jews and of the Gentiles shall be saved, but meanwhile, the appeal of the Christian preacher must be to Jew and Gentile alike, on the basis of the truth which is involved in this great passage of Scripture. Although it is primarily addressed to the Jew and is reenforced by many quotations from the Old Testament, it is the one and only means of salvation for the Gentile today. How wonderful that God said, "There is no difference (between men), for all have sinned, and come short of the glory of God!" Jew and Gentile have been included under sin. Now He declares that there is no difference in His offer of mercy, "for the same Lord over all is rich unto all that call upon Him."

This chapter suggests to us two main subjects of discourse. First, What God Offers The Jews and Gentiles Alike. Second, What God Requires of Jews and Gentiles Alike, during this interim relationship of the Jew to God.

I. WHAT GOD OFFERS TO JEWS AND GENTILES ALIKE.

The first topic of this chapter is righteousness. The Jews sought righteousness by works, but Paul speaks of the righteousness which is of faith. This we hold to be God's offer to Jew and Gentile alike, righteousness of faith. The righteousness of faith demands the utter abandonment of all works and rules as a way of righteousness and the acceptance of righteousness in Christ and Him alone. Paul quotes the Old Testament to show that the use of the law as a means of righteousness compels its use in judgment. "The man which doeth those things shall live by them." As soon as the individual judges himself according to God's law, he finds that he falls short and if he must live by it or be judged by it he is condemned. The Jew found that the law only ministered death, for all failed to measure up to God's great standard. Every mouth was stopped by the law so that God might be just in condemnation of all men. This is the burden of the teaching in the third chapter of Romans. The law may be considered as an instrument which shut every man up under sin, in order that God might offer to every man righteousness through Christ. Thus this same third chapter of Romans gave the alternate method of righteousness being the gift of God. "Being justified freely by His grace through the redemption that is in Christ Jesus: Whom God hath set forth to be a propitiation through faith in His blood, to declare His righteousness for the remission of sins that are past, through the forbearance of God." The marvelous benefits of this great justification or righteousness are then brought forth by Paul in reference to the individual life.

In spite of this means of righteousness which was inherent in the Jewish Scriptures, the Jews themselves continued to seek with zeal a righteousness by works and they spurned Christ, as multitudes do today. What men need is not a standard or an example of righteousness, but a Saviour from their sin and a means of obtaining righteousness before God. Paul said, "Say not, in thine heart, Who shall ascend into heaven? Or, who shall descend into the deep? (that is to bring the means of righteousness). But what saith it? The Word is nigh thee, even in thy mouth, and in thy heart: that is, the word of faith which we preach." Placing a new meaning into these words of Moses, taken from Deuteronomy 30:11-14, Paul showed that there was no need for some one to come from heaven to show the way, for Christ already has come by the Incarnation and has fulfilled all righteousness. There was no need to talk about bringing Christ back from the dead after He died, for He is already resurrected, and declared to be so by infallible proofs; thus, justifying in God's sight the new life given unto men. Exactly as the Israelites under Moses knew the Word of God, so those of Paul's day knew the facts about Christ. Christ was then and is today a living Person to be dealt with. The word of faith is in thy heart and in thy mouth.

This offer of righteousness is made universally unto men. Paul said, "Whosoever believeth on him shall not be ashamed." This likewise was based on a promise of God taken from Isaiah 28:16, "I lay in Zion for a foundation a stone, a tried stone, a precious corner-stone, a sure foundation." In this great passage pronouncing judgment upon wicked Israel, Isaiah gave God's promise that a refuge should be found in this precious corner-stone. "Judgment also will I lay to the line, and righteousness to the plummet: and the hail shall sweep away the refuge of lies, and the waters shall overflow the hiding place." There shall be no refuge in self-righteousness before God's inquisition. Self-righteousness or righteousness by works will be like the bed which is too short for a man to stretch himself on and the covering which is too narrow for a man to wrap himself in. It shall never be sufficient. There is only one righteousness by which a man can stand. One will never need to be ashamed before God when he stands in the perfect righteousness of Christ. To such there is no condemnation, for all righteousness is fulfilled. We need not be ashamed of the Gospel of Christ. Thus whosoever believeth is established in God's sight as righteous and unashamed forever.

This whosoever is reenforced by another which says, "Whosoever shall call upon the Name of the Lord shall be saved." This is a quotation from Joel who manifests that the Gospel shall reach out beyond the Jew unto every one. It is not limited to Jew or Gentile, to elect or non-elect. There is no difference between men. The Gospel message is to be to all and any, to every one who will call upon the Name which is above every Name. Paul and Joel make known a "whosoever" in the righteousness of God which is not too narrow for any one.

On the other hand, whosoever will not believe and obey is lost. This is the reason the Jews are rejected; not because they are Jews. They will not believe and call upon the Name of the Lord in faith. Therefore, they are not saved. There is no mystery about the hardening of Israel. It is the result of unbelief and there is no mystery about the rejection of an individual who will not believe on the corner-stone, the Lord Jesus Christ. There is a uniform doctrine of righteousness in Romans. In the abstract, righteousness as applied to God is an attribute of His Being. God is righteous whether He deals with men in condemnation or in justification. It is the groundwork of His very Being, the basis of love, mercy and justice. God's concrete righteousness is applied in Christ, manifested on the Cross in condemning sin and demanding the just penalty therefor. The Cross is the exhibition of the righteousness of God in dealing with sin. The applied righteousness of God in believers, whether Jew or Gentile, is their justification through the act of faith in what Christ has done for them. Thus God is just and the justifier of those who believe in Christ Jesus. This righteousness which is offered by God is offered to all and it is called Justification by Faith.

The second object which God offers both to Jew and Gentile alike is salvation. Salvation is a larger word than justification or righteousness. These deal with the believer's standing before God. Salvation deals with the believer's experience of deliverance and of

THE PREACHER AND THE WORD

safety. Deliverance is from sin's penalty, power and presence. Safety is the eternal state of the soul.

Think of the meaning of salvation as deliverance. What a joy it is to know deliverance from the penalty of one's sins. Sins in their guilt are not only forgiven but they are forgotten by God. The figure is used of burying them in the deepest sea, of removing them as far as the east is from the west and of blotting them out. No wonder the church sings:

> "I'm saved, saved, saved. This is my story.
> Glory to Jesus, He set me free."

Yet a greater joy than this is to be delivered from the sin of one's nature by sanctification through the indwelling Spirit. This means the breaking of the power of sin. Sin has no more dominion over the believer. This deliverance is a present salvation from the power of evil in the individual life. But greatest of all, will be that salvation from the very presence of sin which will occur at the second coming of Christ. Thus Paul says, "Now is our salvation nearer than when we believed." This is complete salvation manifested in the restoration of body and of soul. It is for this phase of salvation that "the earnest expectation of the creature waiteth," and it is for this that "the whole creation groaneth and travaileth together in pain until now. And not only they, but we ourselves also, which have the first-fruits of the Spirit, even we ourselves groan within ourselves, waiting for the adoption, to wit, the redemption of our body." With such a view of salvation, is it any wonder that Zacchaeus rejoiced when Jesus said to him, "This day salvation is come to thy house?"

Salvation is not only deliverance but it is a state of eternal safety or security for the soul. This security is against sin, death, and judgment, guaranteed by God in an irrevocable covenant of blood, the blood of Jesus Christ our Lord. A believer is eternally secure and is in God's keeping. Safety is a work of God alone and not of the individual. One of our verses says, "Whosoever shall call upon the Name of the Lord shall be saved." This is in the passive. It always speaks about being saved. No man can save himself or make himself secure. He is only secured in salvation when he is in the keeping of Almighty God. Christ said, "No man shall pluck them out of my hands." The new life implanted in the believer is salvation in the germ, so that every believer is a saved man. During the Christian life, salvation is worked out by the Spirit Who dwells in us by faith. Thus Paul says, "Work out your own salvation with fear and trembling, for it is God which worketh in you."

Salvation is the Good News of the Gospel. It is the great message of the preacher which has been wrought out by God and freely offered to all. It is called the gospel of peace, the glad tidings of good things. Yes, truly here is good news offered to men by Almighty God. The means of presenting this salvation unto men is preaching. Paul says, "It pleased God by the foolishness of preaching to save them that believe." The word, "preaching" really means "a thing preached," that is, Christ crucified. This is the means of salvation. When Cornelius had prayed for a long time concerning the way of salvation, God sent an angel to instruct him to send for Peter by whom he should hear words whereby he should be saved. God always uses preaching as a means of salvation. Hence, we have here the succession of steps brought about by preaching, so as to save men. Paul said, "How then shall they call on him in whom they have not believed? And how shall they believe in him of whom they have not heard? And how shall they hear without a preacher? And how shall they preach, except they be sent?" If we omit any one of these steps, there will be no means of salvation. First, the preacher must be sent by Almighty God. Then he must proclaim the Word so that men can hear; and, when they hear, they must believe; and, when they believe, they must call upon the Lord for salvation. Thus, we receive the high estimate in which God holds those who preach salvation. Paul quoted the words of Isaiah who said, "How beautiful are the feet of them that preach the Gospel of peace, and bring glad tidings of good news!" He who directs his footsteps in the preaching of the Gospel is beautiful unto the Lord. It is the common Christian belief of all branches of the Church that there is no salvation without Christ, although acceptance of Christ may be in other terms than those of the organized church (Cf. Jh. 1:9; Micah 5:2; Rom. 10:18). Hence, this missionary command of the Lord Jesus Christ and the missionary implication of this passage of the Scripture. The Church is to go and to preach the Word. This preached Word is the Gospel of salvation without the knowledge of which man can not be saved. Thus, when Paul was preaching in Antioch in Psidia he said, "Men and brethren, children of the stock of Abraham, and whosover among you feareth God, to you is the word of this salvation sent." The word of salvation is sent unto the peoples of the world, Jew and Gentile alike.

THE PREACHER AND THE WORD 159

Third, God offers the riches of His grace. "The same Lord over all is rich unto all who call upon Him." The riches of grace offered by Almighty God to man are the riches of mercy in our forgiveness and our acceptance in the beloved. "Let the wicked forsake his way, and the unrighteous man his thoughts: and let him return unto the Lord, and He will have mercy upon him; and to our God, for He will abundantly pardon." His riches of mercy are inexhaustible. Second, there are the riches of power provided in the Holy Spirit Who indwells the believer bringing illumination, encouragement and comfort. God has provided a wealth of power so that there need be no weakness in the Christian. Third, there are the riches of life in the new creation, made after the image of Christ, the second Adam. This life is eternal life, abundant life, manifested in new motives, new impulses, new virtues and new power. Here then we see something of the inexhaustible wealth of God which is available to all believers. Such is God's three-fold offer, riches of grace, salvation and righteousness through faith. It is made to all men.

II. WHAT GOD REQUIRES OF THE JEW AND GENTILE ALIKE.

The above blessings, though offered by God to all, are not enjoyed by all, because they are conditioned. These conditions are faith, confession and obedience as they are revealed in this chapter of Romans.

Faith is first emphasized. Righteousness itself is called, "The righteousness of faith." Listen to these statements about faith. "The word of faith," "believe in thine heart," "believe unto righteousness," "righteousness of faith." Yes, faith is an inextricable condition of the blessings God offers. Christ died for all, but all are not saved. The difference between the saved and the lost, whether for Jew or Gentile, rests in the matter of faith. Paul has made very evident in this great treatise what we must believe. First, that Jesus was the Christ, that the Christ had come, had died for sin, been buried, had been raised, and had been seen by many witnesses. This is the Gospel as it is explained in Corinthians. Many of the Jews sought a sign that Jesus was the Christ. It is not by a sign that faith is stimulated; we are to believe the naked Word of God as we know the truth. Abraham walked by faith because he believed God, but the Jews of Jesus' day insisted upon a sign. If one is to have righteousness before God it must be a righteousness of faith.

There is a justification for faith, however, in the resurrection of

Christ. The resurrection was an attested fact of history firmly established on the intellectual plane, demonstrating the Deity of Christ. Historically, He appeared unto people who witnessed to it in writings which are authentic. Psychologically, disheartened men were encouraged. Logically, there was the open tomb which the enemies of Christ could not gainsay. The heart belief in the resurrection of Christ is an essential of righteousness. "With the heart man believeth unto righteousness." Inasmuch as righteousness pertains to God only, it may remain a matter of heart and still be discerned by God. This faith Paul says comes by hearing and hearing by the Word of God. If a man is willing to hear God's message concerning Christ and righteousness, that man will find faith stimulated in his heart. He will believe. That is God's work in his own heart. God will take care of his faith, but the Jews would not hear, nor will many hear today. Paul quoted the words of Isaiah which said, "Go, and tell this people, Hear ye indeed, but understand not; and see ye indeed, but perceive not. Make the heart of this people fat, and make their ears heavy, and shut their eyes; lest they see with their eyes, and hear with their ears, and understand with their hearts, and convert, and be healed." How any one can hear about Christ, His goodness, His mercy and His love and yet not believe is a mystery.

The result of faith is justification before God, righteousness and salvation. A man's faith is reckoned to him as righteousness. In self, he is sinful, fallen and wicked, but God accepts him as righteous, gives him the gift of the Spirit which will fulfill righteousness in him. God declares him to be righteous. All the individual has to do is to believe, only believe. Then faith becomes the principle by which the righteous live, following the great example of Abraham. God's Word and God's will are supreme in their lives as they walk by faith.

The second requirement of God is confession. Paul said, "If thou wilt confess with thy mouth Jesus as Lord thou shalt be saved, for with the mouth confession is made unto salvation." The object of this confession is Jesus as Lord. To confess Jesus as Lord was for the Jews blasphemy. It was a violation of monotheism. It was this claim to Deity which so stirred the antipathy of the Jews to Jesus Christ. It was the primary cause for their rejection of Him. Nevertheless, each one of the disciples came to the position where he called Jesus Lord. First, there was Nathaniel. He said, "Rabbi, thou art the son of God." Second, there was Peter. He said, "Thou art the Christ, the Son of the living God." Third, there was Thomas. He said, "My Lord and my God." No man is able to call Jesus Lord with sincerity without the Holy Spirit, and he who has the Holy Spirit is a born-again child of God.

There was a great difficulty in Jesus' day for a Jew to confess Jesus as Lord. It was the hardest thing he had to do. It meant persecution, ostracism and perhaps death. Saul the persecutor drove men from town to town, persecuted them and cast them in prison, and sometimes gave his voice against them, when they were put to death, simply because they worshiped Jesus as God. There is still a great persecution against any one who accepts Christ as God today. One ought to count the cost before confessing Jesus Christ as his Lord lest he bring shame upon the Lord and upon himself. This confession is primarily unto God Who saves the individual, but secondarily unto men. It is necessary for every believer to make a confession with his lips of Christ as his Saviour if he would be saved.

The reward of this confession is salvation. Paul said, "With the mouth confession is made unto salvation." There are those who believe in Christ as the Lord, who rejoice in their own salvation and yet who fall away. They are like the seed which fell on the rocky and thorny soil and sprang up, and then either it was scorched, or it was choked out, and it did not bear any fruit. They were not saved. Hebrews says that it is possible for those who once were enlightened, and have tasted the heavenly gift, and were made partakers of the Holy Ghost, to fall away, and warns against such falling away. Paul tells us that one may believe unto righteousness, without confessing unto salvation. Follow the process through to its logical conclusion. Burn the bridges behind you and you will not fall away. The Lord Jesus said that if we confess Him before men, He will confess us before His Father and the angels which are in heaven. There is no assurance given that until a man, whether Jew or Gentile, confesses Christ as his Lord, that he will be saved. Confession is required by God.

The third requirement by the Lord is obedience to the Gospel. Paul cried, "They have not all obeyed the Gospel. For Isaiah said, Lord, who hath received our report?" Here is a quotation of a prediction from that great prophet that all would not believe on a suffering Messiah, as revealed in the fifty-third chapter of Isaiah. As soon as Christ was revealed as one who must be bruised for our iniquities, upon whom the chastisement of our peace is laid, and

Who was to be put to death, He became a stumbling block for the Jews and also for many others. The atonement in Christianity continues to be an offense to multitudes today. Some have called it a slaughter house religion. Others have utterly rejected it. Jew and Gentile alike, men have hardened their hearts against this message of the Gospel. They have not obeyed it.

Israel actually disobeyed the Gospel which was given to them. Paul said, "Have they not heard?" He replies to this question in the words of the nineteenth Psalm to describe the way that they had heard and had been called, saying, "Yea, verily, their sound went into all the earth, and their words unto the ends of the world." Israel actually had an opportunity to accept Christ and actually rejected. Then he quoted the prophetic warning given by Moses, that God would reject Israel and would choose another people who in comparison with the privileges that Israel had received were no people at all, in order that He might utterly provoke them to faith. The only way that Israel shall ever be saved as a nation is to see the blessing of the Gentiles in Christ and to be provoked to faith in Him by jealousy. When the Church is taken out of the world and Israel realizes that Christ was the true Messiah Whom she has rejected, she will then turn to Him in mourning and in faith, realizing that she missed what was really hers. Paul here describes God's longsuffering with which He treated the Jewish nation before rejecting them. "All day long have I stretched forth My hands unto a disobedient and a gainsaying people." The Lord in the fathers, such as Abraham, Isaac and Jacob, in the prophets such as Isaiah, Ezekiel and Daniel, and ultimately in Christ and in the Apostles offered salvation unto the Jews and the Jews rejected. Is is any wonder that they are no longer God's people today? And yet in mercy God is calling both Jew and Gentile today to a personal, individual salvation, for Paul says, "I was found of them that sought me not. I was made manifest unto them that asked not after me." This describes the Gentile period of salvation in which God is seeking, reaching, discovering, through preaching of His servants, and bringing men into the kingdom of God. What we must do is to hear, and hearing believe, and in believing trust Him as our Saviour, and to this means of salvation the Jew may come as well as the Gentile today. It is God's interim relationship for the Jew, no place of privilege for him now.

The invitation will remain the same throughout this age until Christ comes again. If you will come to Him whether you are a

THE PREACHER AND THE WORD 163

Jew or a Gentile you may be saved. Does not this Christ giving Himself as the righteousness of God, bearing the penalty of your sin and delivering you from the power thereof, stimulate your faith? There is a grand "whosoever" which includes you. Believe in your heart that God has raised Him from the dead and confess Jesus as Lord with your lips and you shall be saved. This is the Divine promise. Yes, today Paul and the preacher stand in the place of God to you. We are His ambassadors calling you through the Word of faith to be saved. "We beseech you in God's stead, be ye reconciled to God." Reject this message and you reject Him, for by the foolishness of preaching it pleased God to save those who believe. There is no other way. There is only one Name given under heaven whereby men may be saved. It is the Name of the Lord Jesus Christ. "Whosoever believeth on Him shall not be ashamed. For there is no difference between the Jew and the Greek; for the same Lord over all is rich unto all who call upon Him."

XVI

THE OLIVE TREE AND THE BRANCHES
OR
GOD'S PLAN THROUGH THE JEW

TEXT: *"And if some of the branches be broken off, and thou, being a wild olive tree, wert grafted in among them, and with them partakest of the root and fastness of the olive tree; boast not against the branches. For if thou boast, thou bearest not the root, but the root thee,"* ROM. 11:1-36.

THE importance of getting the correct knowledge of the division of the Word of God is inestimable. To be unable to rightly divide the Word of truth has a very grave and serious effect upon one's understanding of Christianity. Paul said to Timothy, "Study to show thyself approved unto God, a workman that needeth not to be ashamed, rightly dividing the Word of truth." We are to study, to make application to the Word, to show diligence in our attention and not to neglect the Word of God. Inconceivable mental peace and blessing and wisdom result from study of the Word. Nevertheless, many Christians have so neglected this study that their understanding of the principles of the Word of God is childish. The Bible was meant to be understood, not to be a book of enigmas. Any man who will reasonably approach it, seeking the guidance of the Holy Spirit can understand it.

This chapter of Scripture is so important to a correct understanding of the Bible and the principles of redemption that we would place it foremost as an essential. It proclaims the covenant of grace, the sovereignty of God and the continuity of grace in the different dispensations. This chapter tells us of the place of the Jew and the Gentile in God's plan for mankind. It is truly the climax of the doctrinal teaching in the book of Romans. The main subject is not church truth or individual salvation, but that of God's dispensational and race dealings with mankind.

Our attention is now to be given to the future of Israel and to the future of the Gentiles in connection with Israel and to God's dealings with this people. Chapter nine revealed God's sovereign choice of Israel, the privileges extended to it and the rejection of

THE OLIVE TREE AND THE BRANCHES 165

Israel through its unbelief. We have declared that nationally Israel is not now the people of God. Chapter ten showed that at present there is no difference between the Jew and the Gentile. Both are out of Christ and lost. Both must be saved in the same way, by faith, confession and obedience to God's Word. The Jew has no special place in God's program during the present age. The present chapter will reconcile this rejection of the Jew with God's previous promises and His eternal plan, showing what He intends to do through this nation which He has miraculously preserved in spite of all attacks made upon it. Probably there was never a day in history when the Israelites were more universally persecuted than they are at the present time. Even in America oft repeated tirades against the Jews are being uttered on a wide front.

The picture drawn for us in this chapter is of the olive tree and its branches and it is intended to be an illustration of the truth of God's great redemptive plan. The tree itself represents the redeemed people of God of all ages, of whom Israel is a branch. This great tree includes all of the saved from Adam and Abel unto the last soul who will be saved in time. Remember this is not a figure of the church or of Israel but of all the redeemed of the ages. The illustration consists of an horticultural lesson typifying the breaking off of the Jews from God's redemptive plan, the ingrafting of the Gentiles temporarily and the ultimate restoration of the Jews to that redemptive plan. That the process as Paul writes of it is contrary to nature emphasizes the Divine mercy and grace in redemption. Paul tells us that the good branches of the olive tree were broken off by the husbandman and that wild branches were grafted in. This is not the natural process. Any one who tends roses knows that often he is swindled in purchases of rose bushes, for the bushes are wild roots into which good branches have been grafted so that they temporarily bear beautiful roses, but when the root puts forth new shoots and the old branches die the amateur gardener soon discovers that what he has purchased is a wild rose bush instead of a highly bred bush. What we never do in grafting, Paul declares that God did in the case of the salvation of the Gentiles. He took wild branches and grafted them into a good tree. Let us consider this more in detail.

I. THE BRANCHES WHICH WERE BROKEN OFF—ISRAEL.

Unequivocably Paul declares that the natural good branches of the olive tree were Israel. This nation had a place of privilege through the sovereign grace and goodness of God. Chapter nine, verses one to six declared that truth. It was through Israel that the blessing promised to Abraham was to come to the whole world. God intended that through Israel His revelation and His Saviour should come to men. Through them God intended to make Himself known unto men. This accounts for the wonders which He did for and through Israel, such as the mighty deliverance from Egypt, the paternal care in the wilderness by the pillar of fire and the pillar of cloud, by the feeding with manna and with quails and by the innumerable wonders that God did during the wilderness journey, such as the triumphal entry into Canaan, the sending of the judges, the giving of the tabernacle, the institution of the kings and the sending of the prophets as well as the periodical mighty deliverances which God gave to Israel from her enemies.

This special people chosen as the apple of God's eye is here described as branches upon the olive tree to which God gave close attention and extreme care that they might bear fruit. Under another figure in the Old Testament Isaiah tells the parable of the vineyard in which the husbandman came seeking luscious grapes and found that it brought forth wild grapes. To this vineyard, on which he had spent much and from which he gathered out the stones and planted with choicest vines, and built a tower in the midst of it, and a winepress therein, he now did what was perfectly logical. He took away the hedge thereof, broke down the wall and let the vineyard be trodden down and lie waste, without pruning, or digging or taking away the briers and the thorns. In other words, he appointed it to destruction. These two figures represent God's care of Israel, as He purged it, pruned it, chastened it and rebuked it in a series of Providential blessings, calamities, disasters and captivity. When these branches namely, Israel, should have been a testimony to all the world of holiness, justice and grace, in reality the name of God was blasphemed among the heathen by them, as declared the prophet Ezekiel and also Paul.

The condition of these branches, or Israel, was ultimately revealed when Christ came to this earth. The moral perception of the nation was dulled and blinded. Jesus Christ called them stiff-necked, rebellious, murderers of the prophets and guilty before God of a broken covenant. Reread the terrible denunciation of this nation by Stephen, as well as the words spoken by Jesus Christ in Matthew 23. Isaiah and Paul depict the nation as resisting God's entreaty. All through the age God stretched out His arms to a disobedient and a gainsaying people. They would not reason concerning righteousness but argued back and, though the righteousness of faith through Christ was shown unto them by the Apostles, they sought the righteousness of works. They rejected Christ and then after the resurrection of Christ they rejected His Apostles.

Ultimately, therefore, these branches were broken off. Time came when God no longer would wait for Israel, as the time came when He would no longer wait for repentance with the antediluvians. Therefore, a transition came, in which the Gospel was sent to the Gentiles, for the Jews rejected it. The church was first Jewish in its leadership and its constituency, but now it became Gentile. Paul at Rome, after quoting the prophecy of Isaiah that the eyes of this people should be blinded and their hearts wax gross, said, "Be it known unto you, that the salvation of God is sent unto the Gentiles, and that they will hear it." Shortly after this, Jerusalem was destroyed and the chosen people, being completely rejected as a nation, were sent into dispersion. The Gospel was placed in the keeping of the Gentiles. Racial connection with national Israel today means that one is not in God's olive tree of redemption. He is broken off. He must be regenerated and brought into the olive tree through the new branches grafted in by the husbandmen. All who die with merely a racial connection with Israel are unquestionably lost. It is upon natural Israel that Paul here bespeaks the imprecation, "God hath given them the spirit of slumber, eyes that they should not see, and ears that they should not hear; unto this day. And David said, let their table be made a snare, and a trap, and a stumbling-block, and a recompense unto them: let their eyes be darkened, that they may not see, and bow down their backs alway." All this had been foreseen in prophecy, for it is merely a quotation of the words of Isaiah and the words of David, but it is terrible in its implication and in its fulfillment, for Israel was broken off from God's olive tree or redemptive plan.

A qualification must here be made, however. Not all the branches were broken off. Israel was rejected as a nation, but no one was rejected as an individual. Paul asked the question, "Hath God cast away His people?" And he answers, "God hath not cast away His people which He foreknew." Are all the irrevocable promises of God to Israel to be set aside, to be invalidated, to be revoked? God made an irrevocable covenant with Abraham that his seed should possess the land. God made a covenant with David concerning the kingdom over which he would establish him. God through the prophets called attention to the fact that Israel would not cease from being a people before Him forever. If these then were revoked, is it possible that we can depend upon any of God's promises? The answer is clear. God has not finished with His people Israel. He has a purpose of salvation for the nation and He has a present offer of salvation for the individuals. This is simply the truth of the remnant of grace which is declared in this great chapter. God always reserves a remnant of grace. Elijah thought that he alone remained of those faithful to God in the days of Ahab, but the Lord soon declared unto him that he had seven thousand who had not bowed the knee to Baal and just as He had reserved a remnant in Elijah's day and in Daniel's day and in Paul's day, He has reserved a remnant unto Himself today. The rejection of Israel is not complete and it is not final.

All the branches were not cut off then nor are they all cut off now. We must not forget that there was a remnant of Israel and of grace who believed on the Lord Jesus Christ and who were saved. Jesus came unto His own, and His own received Him not, but to as many as received him, to them gave he power to be the sons of God. It was no inconsiderable number who believed upon Jesus Christ when He was here upon earth and immediately following His crucifixion and resurrection. These also were all Jews. Moreover, Paul was saved and Paul was an Israelite, of the tribe of Benjamin, which was largely identified with Judah after the division between the northern and the southern kingdoms. Just as multitudes of Jews accepted Christ and believed on Him then, so many of them are accepting and believing on Christ now. These multitudes constitute God's remnant of Israel. That the opportunity is given to the Jews to be saved exactly as the Gentiles are saved in this age has been clearly declared in our exposition of chapter ten.

Even the nation which at present is broken off will in remnant form be reinstated in God's favor. "They also, if they abide not still in unbelief, shall be grafted in: for God is able to graft them in again. For if thou wert cut out of the olive tree which is wild by nature, and wert grafted in contrary to nature into a good olive tree: how much more shall these, which be the natural branches, be grafted in to their own olive tree." The promises which God made to Abraham, and David, will be fulfilled. "For the gifts and calling of God are without repentance." God still has a glorious purpose for Israel through which the whole world will be blessed. It is apparent from Scripture (Zechariah 13:8 and 9) that only one third of living Israel will be saved nationally at the end of the age, because of the intense

THE OLIVE TREE AND THE BRANCHES

tribulation called "Jacob's trouble," through which Israel must pass. It is also apparent from Scripture that this remnant will be the instrument of Divine blessing to the nations during the millennium. It is Zion, Jerusalem and Israel of which God speaks as the source of blessing, yes, Pentecostal blessing in the golden era to come. Yet we are convinced that the privilege of even this remnant which shall be a blessing to the world will not equal the glorious destiny of the church, which is being called out as Christ's bride during the present age. Israelites converted during this age will be members of the church and will have a higher privilege than those participating in what is called the national salvation. Paul contrasts the blessings which flowed from the rejection of Israel by the crucifixion of Christ and the blessings which shall flow from the national conversion of Israel and their acceptance of Christ. "If the fall of them be the riches of the world, and the diminishing of them the riches of the Gentiles; how much more their fulness." If the Gospel is going to the ends of the earth in the great missionary enterprise through the Gentile Church in this dispensation, during the rejection of Israel nationally, then all that is described as millennial blessing will come to pass through conversion and the fullness of Israel.

It is time now to call attention to the purpose which was revealed in this rejection of Israel. "Have they stumbled that they should fall? God forbid: but rather through their fall salvation is come to the Gentiles, for to provoke them to jealousy." That this salvation was to come unto the Gentiles without the mediation of Israel was a mystery unforeseen by the prophets and revealed through the Apostle Paul. He called it, "The mystery, which was kept secret, since the world began, but now is made manifest, and by the Scriptures of the prophets, according to the commandment of the everlasting God, made known unto all nations for the obedience of faith." The Divine purpose in Israel's hardening and rejection and crucifixion of Christ was the salvation of the Gentiles. By the process of moral hardening which occurred in Israel and culminated in Calvary for Christ, the riches of grace extended beyond Israel unto the nations of the world. Therefore, we contend that it is not logical to say that the church age is merely a parenthesis in God's plan. It was no afterthought of God, but it was part of His great plan to reach the whole wide world with the Gospel of redemption.

Let us repeat it. The purpose in Israel's stumbling was not that it might fall, for God takes no pleasure in the fall of any one. Christ Jesus was not sent to condemn Israel, but to save Israel. That Israel did not see God's purpose and understand and believe is a great tragedy, but it has been overruled for the good of both Israel and the Gentiles in the wisdom and purpose of God. Through this rejection by Israel came the Saviour and the propitiation for the sins of the world. Moreover, every Israelite may share in God's great purpose today. He may by faith in Christ be saved and he may participate in being the bride of Christ and therefore in being exalted with Him through eternity. The fact that the nation of Israel is rejected from its privileged position is no hardship on any individual Jew. God simply commands that every man whether Jew or Gentile should now repent and believe on the Lord Jesus Christ.

II. THE BRANCHES WHICH WERE GRAFTED IN.

The attention of Paul is then turned to the Gentiles. He said, "I speak to you Gentiles, inasmuch as I am the apostle of the Gentiles." The branches which were grafted in represent the Gentile church. When God rejected Israel nationally in part it was to substitute the Church for Israel as His witness on the earth. Note from this that the Church is not Israel and Israel is not the Church. This illustration of the olive tree makes this clear. The Church is composed of the saints of God, the redeemed ones in this age. Jesus said, "I will build my church." The Church as the bride of Christ was initiated at Pentecost. The promises of Israel do not transfer to the Church which has specific blessings and privileges of its own. These promises no more apply to the Church than they apply to the Anglo-Saxons of our day, but if Abraham, through whom all the families of the earth are to be blessed, is the root then the Abrahamic promises extend to those who are of faith, "the sons of Abraham." Paul declares, "Know ye therefore that they which are of faith, the same are the children of Abraham." We conclude then that the gift of the Holy Spirit is "the blessing of Abraham . . . on the Gentiles through Jesus Christ; that we might receive the promise of the Spirit through faith." Unquestionably every believer today is a child of Abraham spiritually, but he is not part of Israel.

Since we Gentiles were merely grafted in to God's olive tree in place of the Israelites, there is great need for humility among us, for as Paul said, "Thou bearest not the root, but the root thee." Race pride manifested in the persecution of the Jews by the Gentiles would seem to say, "The branches were broken off, that I might be grafted in." This was the attitude taken by the Church when it instituted the inquisition against the Jews. Let us remember that it

THE OLIVE TREE AND THE BRANCHES

is only by faith that a Gentile Christian stands in the redemptive line, not by any superiority of race or other considerations. Therefore we are warned of the severity of God as it was shown in His dealings with Israel. Let us fear lest the privileges which have been extended to us Gentiles be removed because of unbelief. "If God spared not the natural branches, take heed lest He spare not you. Behold, therefore the goodness and severity of God: on them which fell, severity; but toward thee, goodness, if thou continue in His goodness: otherwise thou also shall be cut off."

All Gentile blessings of redemption are of grace and not by nature. We are wild olive branches grafted in to the good olive tree. No discipline, no morality and no righteousness of any kind was found by God among the Gentiles. The description given in Romans, chapter one verses eighteen to thirty-two, adequately describes the wildness, uselessness and merited destruction of the Gentile nations. Over against this Jewry was monotheistic and to a large degree moral. If, therefore, Jewry was cut off and we were grafted in, so that being joined to Christ we should share His fatness, life, strength and position, it is not any matter for boasting.

At this point we must recognize that not all Gentiles are ingrafted, just as not all Jews are broken off, and though all Gentiles now stand in a place of privilege which they formerly did not have, they are not all redeemed. Once it was necessary for the Gentiles to come to God by proselytism of Jewry. Once they were described as afar off and as aliens to the commonwealth of Israel, but now they have been made nigh by the blood of His Cross. Once they were called dogs in contrast with Israel, but now the Gentile is placed in the privilege which Israel once enjoyed, but the individual Gentile who would be redeemed or joined to the Church as an engrafted branch must be born again, born of water and of the Spirit, that is, totally regenerated. For this reason, Jesus said, "Except a man be born again he can not see the kingdom of God." At present the Gentile church is accepted in the place of the Israelite nation but this does not designate individuals to salvation any more than the national rejection of Israel designates individuals to rejection.

There is an implication given in this Scripture that due to the unbelief of the Gentiles the time is coming when they should be cut off. "If thou continue in his goodness: otherwise thou also shall be cut off." There is a time coming when Gentile privilege shall come to an end. Paul declares "The fulness of the Gentiles shall come in." Gentile privilege called Christendom is now failing. We have not assumed our full responsibility of evangelizing the world, but rather we have substituted character salvation, works, liturgical processes, a priestcraft and rituals for the spiritual priesthood of the believer, the atonement, the presence of Christ, and the responsibility for world evangelism. God has extended such Divine goodness to the Gentiles that when our day of reckoning comes His judgment upon us will be far worse than it was upon Israel. The day will come when the Divine goodness toward the Gentiles in receiving them through a crucified Saviour and bestowing upon them the gift of the Holy Spirit will be exchanged for severity surpassing that manifested to the Jews. One need only read of the destruction of Jerusalem and of the awful suffering of the Jews from that day to this to know what it means to be out of Divine favor.

What is this fullness of the Gentiles which shall come in? This means the completion of the Church of Christ, the number of the elect, those who are to be saved and to become the members of the bride of Christ. Some day this event will happen, namely, the last sinner from among the Gentiles will respond to the Spirit of God. He will repent. He will convert. He will believe the Gospel and he will be saved. That last one will conclude the history of the Church on the earth. In that moment, it will be caught away. "In a moment, in the twinkling of an eye, at the last trump: for the trumpet shall sound and the dead shall be raised incorruptible, and we shall be changed." "The Lord himself shall descend from heaven with a shout, with the voice of an archangel, and with the trump of God: and the dead in Christ shall rise first: then we which are alive and remain, shall be caught up together with them in the clouds, to meet the Lord in the air." This we hold to describe the glorious deliverance for the saints of the Church, whether Jew or Gentile, who have come to God by faith in the Gospel preached in this book of Romans. They shall be delivered from what is described as the wrath to come.

The times of the Gentiles will go on for some period after the fullness of the Gentiles has come in and the Church has been taken away. The description of this awful period of Gentile terror and of Jacob's trouble, called the tribulation, is beyond any possible exposition here. It shall be such a time upon the earth as never existed before, a time when the wrath of God will be poured out upon men. At its conclusion all Israel left alive "shall be saved: as it is written, there shall come out of Zion the deliverer, and shall turn away ungodliness from Jacob."

THE OLIVE TREE AND THE BRANCHES 173

III. THE INGRAFTING OF THE NATURAL BRANCHES.

This national conversion of Israel is described as the ingrafting of the natural branches. It is connected with the fullness of the Gentiles. Three things, declared in the Scripture, will occur at the end time. First, is the rapture or the taking away of the Church before the awful tribulation and time of Jacob's trouble. This is the great event which is the object of expectation in the Church and that for which Christ commands the believers to lift up their heads and to look when their redemption draweth nigh. The second event is the judgment of the nations in Christ's return at what is called the battle of Armageddon. This is in reality no battle at all, but is a judgment upon the Gentile peoples who have given over their complete allegiance and worship to the Antichrist. The coming is described in this Scripture as "a deliverer shall come out of Zion." The events of that end time we believe are described in the fourteenth chapter of Zechariah and in the nineteenth chapter of Revelation, as well as all Scriptural passages which refer to the day of the Lord. It is a day of judgment. The third event is the conversion of Israel. "Ungodliness shall be turned from Jacob." It is a time when all Israel shall be saved. Every Israelite living when Jesus comes shall be converted. Zechariah said, "I will pour upon the house of David, and upon the inhabitants of Jerusalem, the spirit of grace and of supplications: and they shall look upon me whom they have pierced, and they shall mourn for him, as one mourneth for his only son, and shall be in bitterness for him, as one that is in bitterness for the first-born." Zechariah goes on to tell us that only one-third of all Israel living at the beginning of the tribulation shall come through that awful period of suffering to be converted in the national transformation of this people. Then the veil will be removed from their eyes, the hardness from their hearts, the dullness from their hearing and in sorrow they shall see that He whom they crucified on Calvary is the Messiah, the Lord of glory. Then the new covenant made by God with Israel in which He will write His law upon their hearts shall be fulfilled.

This national conversion of Israel will have a great meaning for the Gentiles, namely, the great blessing to come from the fullness of this nation. Then the nations or the Gentiles shall dwell in peace, in plenty and in prosperity. The representatives of these nations shall "go to the house of God" each year and the kingdom of David shall be rebuilt. Then the knowledge of the Lord shall cover the earth as the waters shall cover the sea. Then the Spirit of the Lord will be poured out upon all men and then the residue of the Gentiles will seek the Lord. Simeon declared at the Apostolic Council how God "at the first did visit the Gentiles, to take out of them a people for His Name . . . after this I will return, and will build again the tabernacle of David, which is fallen down; and I will build again the ruins thereof, and I will set it up; that the residue of men might seek after the Lord, and all the Gentiles, upon whom my name is called, saith the Lord who doth all these things." This will be the spiritual renewal of the whole human race and the world will resemble a veritable resurrection from the dead. It is what is called in prophecy the golden era. Here we catch a glimpse of the power of God to overrule the failures and faults of His saints for the good of the world and also for the good of all men.

Glance then at the means God has used for this fullness of the Gentiles and fullness of the Jews. These Jews "as concerning the gospel, they are enemies for your sakes: but as touching the election, they are beloved for the father's sake." All that God promised unto the Jews will occur. There is no change or transmutation in these callings of God. The blessing to the Gentiles consists in that "as in times past ye have not believed in God, yet have now obtained mercy through their unbelief." The nations have received Divine blessing through the fall of the Jew, but through the blessing of the Gentiles the Jews will be provoked to faith as Paul said, "Even so have these also now not believed that through your mercy they may also obtain mercy." Therefore God included both Jews and Gentiles in condemnation in order that He might show mercy unto both. "God hath concluded them all in unbelief, that He might have mercy upon all." This, of course, refers only to classes. Individuals have been dealt with earlier.

Then comes the mighty verse of sublime spontaneous doxology upon this thought. Oh, the riches of the gospel of grace with which God has met a sinful and needy world! Oh, the salvation for all who will believe! Oh, the unsearchable judgments, the wonderful ways in the thinking of God! How far above man's ways and how far beyond man's tracing are they! No counsel can ever be added unto God and God's plan, for it is perfect. God is in no man's debt, for any suggestions or any service which he gives. In the finality of doctrine, His own supremacy is asserted, or translating literally, "Out of Him, and through Him, and unto Him be all things." This is the great circle of existence. With this thought we may rest in trust where we can not fully understand.

XVII

A REASONABLE PLEA FOR CHRISTIAN CONDUCT BASED ON DIVINE MERCIES

TEXT: *"I beseech you therefore, brethren, by the mercies of God, that ye present your bodies a living sacrifice, holy, acceptable unto God, which is your reasonable service. And be not conformed to this world: but be ye transformed by the renewing of your mind, that ye may prove what is that good, and acceptable, and perfect, will of God."*—ROM. 12:1, 2.

THE absolutely astounding fact about God shown in the Bible is that He pleads with men. The prophet writes: "Come now, and let us reason together, saith the Lord: though your sins be as scarlet, they shall be as white as snow." Again he said, "Let the wicked forsake his way, and the unrighteous man his thoughts: and let him return unto the Lord, and He will have mercy upon him; and to our God, for He will abundantly pardon." So also Jesus said, "Come unto me, all ye that labor and are heavy laden, and I will give you rest. Take my yoke upon you, and learn of me; for I am meek and lowly in heart: and ye shall find rest unto your souls." These are examples of the pleas given by God to men.

Usually God does this by means of ambassadors who are human beings. In our text, the plea is made through the instrumentality of the Apostle Paul. To find God pleading with men instead of commanding them is a great wonder. Think who God is and what He has done, what He can do and what He will do. Think of the creation. Think of the sustaining of this universe. Think of the marvels of redemption. Think of the ultimate goal toward which all things move and the astonishing nature of this activity of God is made manifest. It is evident that God stoops to our weakness, mighty as He is, that He might cause us to love Him. As such an ambassador Paul said, "We are ambassadors for Christ, as though God did beseech you by us: we pray you in Christ's stead, be ye reconciled to God." There is wisdom in this placing of the responsibility of destiny on each man. God does not desire to force men into the mold of His will. Rather He pleads with them concerning salvation. He says, "Turn ye, turn ye . . . Why will ye die?" and "Now is the time."

The only alternative to this offer of God of eternal life is hell and punishment.

An even more wonderful fact about this Divine plea given to the Christian is the basis upon which it is made. Paul said, "I beseech you, therefore." This word, "therefore," connects with two great divisions of the book of Romans. The first half which deals with salvation and the second half which deals with the conduct of a Christian in the church and in the world! There is no book in the Bible which reveals God as He is revealed in the book of Romans, as a God of love, of forgiveness, of compassion and of holiness. The mighty mercies of this God are clearly defined for us in the doctrinal section of the book of Romans. It is true that there are other mercies such as the gifts of sunshine and rain, of the beauties of nature and of all that we love and need in life, yet these gifts and mercies go far beyond that. They include the grace of justification, which gives us a new standing as redeemed men in the sight of God, of identification with Christ in new life instead of with Adam in the old, of sanctification by the indwelling of His Holy Spirit which He has given unto us, of election to redemption in which we are transformed into the image of Christ and of preservation in love by God's grace. These are great truths and are the mercies of God.

Paul addresses those who know these great truths with the words, "I beseech you, therefore." If you do not know these truths go back and study the first eleven chapters of the book of Romans. Learn them and make them yours. The Divine plea is based upon this logical standard.

What God then asks from the believer who has been the recipient of His Divine mercies and blessings is the norm for every Christian life. Remember that if I hold up a high standard for this congregation, God's standard is higher. Let us never be satisfied with our own state of spiritual attainment. It is easy to rest back on what is past, on a former revival, on attainments in missionary giving and support, on a long history of faithfulness to orthodoxy, but this is not enough. God wants us to go on, on to constitute ourselves soul-winners, to sanctify ourselves from sin and to win new spiritual victories. The standard which God gives to us is in this plea for Christian conduct. It is a plea for worship, for life and for character upon a higher plane than we have been accustomed to live.

A PLEA FOR CHRISTIAN CONDUCT

I. The High Service or Liturgy for Which God Asks.

From the very earliest times in religion, men used liturgies by which they were to worship God. A liturgy is a service of worship. These have been constituted by the presentation of offerings, of prayers, of incense and the enactment of certain forms. The Old Testament prescribed a definite liturgy for the worship of God. There were, to summarize them, four kinds of sacrifices; two which were offered before redemption and two offered after redemption. The first two concerned themselves with sin and trespasses and the second two with consecration and fellowship. The first two correspond with the first section of the book of Romans, in which Christ is presented to us as the victim for our sin and trespass offering. The last two correspond with the second half of the book of Romans, in which we present ourselves as victims unto God in consecration and fellowship. These Old Testament levitical sacrifices were very meaningful. They were only a shadow of things to come. They merely represented the reality which should occur in the Christian life. All the Old Testament liturgies of form were fulfilled and put away when Christ made propitiation for our sin. God thereinafter required them no longer and now He desires worship in Spirit and in truth, not in form. It would behoove us to beware of any emphasis upon liturgy or a service of worship unto God. Beautiful as these may be as presented by our churches, they can never substitute for the kind of worship which God now requires from the believer.

The liturgy which is acceptable unto God today is here defined as "our acceptable service." This is constituted by the making of an offering to God of ourselves, not of the bodies of animals. "I beseech you that ye present your bodies a living victim or sacrifice unto God." The body carries with it the implication of the whole person. This presentation or yielding or giving in worship of one's body can only take place after the person has been redeemed. Worship, then, or spiritual service, or a liturgy for a believer, is the presentation of himself to God as a living victim. Let us note what Paul says about this spiritual service.

First, this is to be a holy sacrifice. God said, "Without holiness no man shall see the Lord." Anything which is unholy is unacceptable to God. Every sacrifice presented to Him had to be without blemish and without defect. Even the Lord Jesus Christ was of value as an offering to God because of the perfection of His character and His perfect fulfillment of the law. Thus Peter says, "Ye were redeemed . . . with the precious blood of Christ, as of a lamb without blemish and without spot." The holiness in which the believer presents his body unto God is a holiness provided by the cleansing of the blood of Christ and by the indwelling Spirit of the living God Who sanctifies us. If we know by experience the mercies of God, as defined in the book of Romans, we are then holy and may present ourselves unto Him. However, our holiness of practice comes from sanctifying ourselves through the process of separation and avoidance of all appearance of evil. Even the Lord Jesus prayed unto the Father, "For their sakes I sanctify myself . . . sanctify Thou them through thy truth: thy word is truth." It is absolutely essential for us to yield our bodies in holiness unto God if we are to be acceptable unto Him.

This worship of God, this liturgy, means the presentation of a living sacrifice. This is a paradox. Whenever a sacrifice was offered in the Old Testament times it was first killed and then burned upon the altar or cooked and ate as a peace offering of fellowship. Sacrifice usually meant unto death. How then can we present our bodies unto God when they are still alive? The thought is very simple and the contrast brings it out. The believer is to be a living martyr for the Lord. God has saved him to live, to do things, to perform God's will upon earth. Hence the value of coming unto the Lord and presenting ourselves a living sacrifice to Him in the days of our youth. What right do we have to throw a worn out body upon God when we can do His will no longer upon earth? How much better to come and remember our Creator in the days of our youth, before the evil days come nigh!

Thirdly, Paul says this is a reasonable sacrifice. The word used is logikos. It is a word which means spiritual, divine and reasonable service. Peter contrasts it with the carnal ordinances. God does not ask for a carnal service. He wants a spiritual, a reasonable service. Moreover, He is not asking any more from us than He has done for us. The hymn writer puts it:

> "I gave my life for thee,
> My precious blood I shed,
> That thou might ransomed be,
> And quickened from the dead;
> I gave, I gave My life for thee,
> What hast thou given for me?"

This giving of our bodies unto God in response to what He has done for us is the highest kind of human action.

This might be called a liturgy of love. I have said that God did not command this. He asked us to give it. God could have commanded, but He does not command us to give ourselves to Him. The whole action is left to voluntary choice. Duty or law has no part in this plea. God simply relies upon our gratitude and our love because of what He has done for us. His grace and His mercy are free gifts. There is nothing we can do to merit them. We may merely accept them. God will never drive us to accept them and God will never drive us after we accept them to do His will. Our worship and service must be motivated by the fact that God loved us and redeemed us by sending His only-begotten Son as a propitiation for our sins. This is the only logical, reasonable and expected liturgy or service of God. When I stood at the altar with the lovely girl who became my wife, I said, "Forsaking all others I will cleave unto thee as long as I live." There I not only accepted her, but I gave myself unto her. It is this that God expects of us. If we receive Him, then we in turn must give ourselves back to Him. Anything less is base ingratitude and reveals an illogical mind. Just as all I have and all I am belongs unto my wife, so all the believer has and is should be God's.

II. THE HIGH LIFE FOR WHICH GOD ASKS.

The second part of the plea, based on this logical reason, is that we be not conformed to this present world, but transformed by the renewing of our minds. We are not to be conformed. The word "conformity" means "to fashion" or "to mold," according to an external show or appearance, a scheme of things. It is the adaptation to some custom, tradition or standard easily performed even when our hearts are opposed to the matter. To be conformed to the world means to scheme together with the world. The scheme of things as they exist in the world is not the standard for the Christian. Wherever and whenever he adopts the worldly practices and becomes fashioned according to their customs, he is walking in forbidden ground whether it be in a religious organization or in the external contacts of life. For a Christian to conform to the world is as hypocritical as for an unbeliever to conform to Christian standards. God looks upon the heart and God knows our condition. Christianity is not a way of conformity, but of individuality. Herein lies a basic distinction between the Christian way of life and the regimented way of life of Nazism, Fascism, Communism and Statism. There one has a forced conformity unto a standard. In Christianity, it is not conformity at all. Conformity may be a good or a bad thing in itself. We may conform toward high standards or low standards. There is a struggle occurring in Korea and Japan at the present time which illustrates what conformity to the world means. The command has gone forth that all schools must force their pupils to attend the shrines of Shintoism for worship. This means the deserting of the standards of Christ for the Kami of Shintoism. As a result, scores of missionaries have resigned from their mission fields, the mission schools have been turned over to the natives and the mission work is receiving a great setback in Japanese territories and in Japan itself. Nevertheless, some missionaries have been willing to conform unto the Japanese standard. This conformity means the renunciation of Jesus Christ as clearly as burning incense to the emperor of Rome meant the renunciation of Christ for the early Christians. That is conformity in a bad sense.

It is this conformity to the world which is forbidden for the Christian. The world is the scheme of things among unregenerate man, or as the world is without regeneration. It is a world without God and without hope, or even a world in opposition to God. This world, John says, "lieth in wickedness," and Paul says is "evil." It is the world which is in contrast to the Messianic age, that is, the world which embraces everything effected by the fall of Adam without the redeeming influence of Christ. This world pays its respect and gives its obedience to the god of this world, who is the devil. Friendship to this world is enmity to God. This does not mean that inventions and instruments of this world are evil in themselves, but only that when they are used in the service of the god of this world they are evil. Thus an automobile or radio or any other invention might be a good thing or a bad thing depending upon that to which it is devoted. The believer must not be conformed to the unregenerate scheme of things.

In contrast to this, Paul urges transformation. He says, "Be ye transformed by the renewing of your mind." This word, "transformation" means metamorphosis. Some one may object that the word, "conform" is used in Rom. 8:29 where Paul said, "Whom . . . he also did predestinate to be conformed to the image of his Son," but the root of the word, "conform" in this passage is "morpho" which is the same as in metamorphosis or transformation in the text. It is merely a difference in translation. The picture is that of a butterfly emerging from the house which it constructed for itself as an ugly caterpillar after a season of hibernation, and then beginning to exercise itself toward the yearnings which are within. It sees the beauty of the blossoms and the trees. It feels the loveliness of the wind sweeping over it and longs to fly, and then with a sudden effort it finds that it can fly. It is no longer an ugly caterpillar. It is now a beautiful butterfly. It is such a transformation from within about which Paul is here speaking, a complete metamorphosis.

The greatest illustration of this is that of the metamorphosis or transfiguration of Christ. There He reflected heaven's glory. There He was a being utterly different from the kind of being which men looked upon in ordinary intercourse with Him. In fact, His faithful disciples could not even look upon Him. This glory of transformation was merely a foretaste of what will take place at His second coming, for Peter later referred to it in the following words, "We have not followed cunningly devised fables, when we made known unto you the power and coming of our Lord Jesus Christ, but were eye witnesses of His majesty. For He received from God the Father honor and glory, when there came such a voice to Him from the excellent glory, This is my beloved Son, in Whom I am well pleased, . . . which we heard when we were with Him in the holy mount." It is to this image of Christ that we are more and more to be transformed, for, "We all, with open face beholding as in a glass the glory of the Lord, are changed into the same image from glory to glory." That blessed privilege of being like the Son of God which will ultimately occur at His coming for every believer may be partially experienced now.

The power of this process of transformation of the believer is the Holy Spirit. Paul said, "By the renewing of your mind." God does not command us to do this, to transform ourselves, by our own power, but He gives us an inner power through the indwelling Holy Spirit to perform this great work. There are two works of the Spirit of God for the believer. The first work is the applying of the redemption of Jesus Christ to the sinful soul that the value of the blood may cleanse that soul from all sin. The second aspect of the work of the Spirit is the renewing aspect of the person of the believer. Paul said to Titus, "He saved us by the washing of regeneration and renewing of the Holy Ghost." This renewing work is wrought for us by the Spirit. The passive voice is used. "Be ye transformed." All the affections, the tastes, the memories and the desires of the believer are renewed. Those faculties of the mind which are so often corrupt are now made new. Here is regeneration or the new birth viewed mentally. Man becomes a new creature as God makes him over. He puts off the old man and puts on a new, being renewed in his mind. The whole mind of the individual man is the object of this renewing. God Himself is working in us to will and to do of His good pleasure. The Person of the Holy Spirit Whom God gives to the regenerate believer is God Himself.

The degree of the renewal of the believer depends upon his surrender and his consecration to God. It is true that many believers live in the midst of their old tastes, habits, desires, affections and memories. They have not been thoroughly cleansed of them. The reason is simple. They have not yielded their bodies a living sacrifice unto God which is their reasonable service. Our freedom from sin and our love of righteousness entirely depend upon our relation to the Holy Spirit. If we are to be transformed into the likeness of His image, from glory to glory, it is by the Spirit of the Lord and in no other way. Every believer to have an acceptable life before God must not only believe in Christ, for the salvation of his soul from sin and sin's guilt, but he must be baptized and filled with God's Holy Spirit in order that he might live holily and righteously in this present world.

The standard has been referred to on several occasions. It is the image of Christ. This is the goal ever held before us, the mark toward which we are pressing in our more and more being sanctified. It is the work of the Spirit of God to testify to Christ, to tell of Him and to mold our persons and minds unto His own image. The Spirit's guidance is final in this transforming process. Our actions will follow in holiness as the Spirit dominates our lives. Remembering that we are sanctified by Christ, when we accept Him as our Saviour and are redeemed by His blood, we must also emphasize that the Spirit of God must bring every thought into captivity to Christ before this sanctification becomes fully practical and applicable in our lives. Thus Paul pleads with us to live a high life, sanctified in holiness before our God.

III. THE HIGH ACTION FOR WHICH GOD ASKS.

Paul urges us to "prove what is that good, and acceptable, and perfect, will of God." Proof here, according to several authorities, is the evidence in one's experience. Thus it is proof to ourselves, proof to others and proof to God. It is the working out in experience of God's will for us. As one is transformed by the Holy Spirit by the renewing of his mind, he will discover that God has a will or a plan for each one of us. That plan of God is far better than anything we can plan or will for ourselves. We may outline what we consider an ambitious and perfect program, but it can never be comparable to the program which God has planned for us. God's will is good, acceptable and perfect and is leading to our own perfection. Nothing can be higher for any man. This will of God can only be known in experience by surrendered saints. He who wills to do his own will as a Christian can never know the plan of God. It requires obedience, following the Divine guidance which reveals God's will to us. John quoted Jesus as saying, "He who will do the will of God shall know the doctrine." If you make your willingness to do His will, your surrender to Him, a beginning point, your transformation into the likeness of the plan will have begun.

Only a surrendered will will be able to follow God's plan step by step. Fear not to follow it or to prove it, for it will be the very best. There are some who hesitate to submit themselves unto God, to abandon their pleasure for God's good pleasure, to lay aside their plans for the plans of God for their lives, fearing that God will make them walk a hard road, will bring chastenment and discipline into their lives. What kind of God have you? Do you have a loving Father who is all wise, all powerful and all good? If your earthly father would plan only for the best for you, how much more will your heavenly Father? Self-will can only mean sorrow. A surrendered will means happiness, means transformation into the Divine image according to the will of God. You can only find this out by experience. Prove God's will to be good and acceptable and perfect to yourself.

Second, we are to prove God's will as good, perfect and acceptable to others. Talk of regeneration, of transformation and of sanctification on the part of believers, while they go along as formerly, with the manifestations of corruption in their conversation and habit, is to give the lie to the word of God. It invalidates His testimony concerning us. The world simply must see a change in us if we are to prove to the world that God's will is good, acceptable and perfect. When the Divine fruits and gifts and attributes are evident in the life of a believer, as God will put them there and bring them to pass, the world will believe that His will is good and acceptable and perfect. If God has done a supernatural work in us as we sometimes testify, it should be evident by our conduct before men. We have far too many dishonest, prejudiced, envious, greedy Christians to convince the world that God's plan is worth anything. Jesus said, "When he (the Holy Spirit) is come (unto you), He will reprove the world of sin, and of righteousness, and of judgment." The only way to bring any conviction on the world is to demonstrate by our actions that God's will is good.

Lastly, I think we must prove it to God. It is only by this kind of action that we can prove unto the Lord that we are His faithful servants. Are you in the position, doing the work which God has asked you to do? God knows what He has asked you and called you to and you know it. Are you doing it? Are you faithful to Him and to His cause? Are you a teacher, if He has called you to teach? Are you a missionary, if He called you to that? Are you a faithful steward in business, if He has called you to business? Is God able to depend upon you? Are you proving His will in the world to Him? Yes, if we do not walk according to God's will He will judge us or chasten us. Therefore, let us judge ourselves lest we be chastened of the Lord. Let us remove all self-will and self-confidence and, because of His great mercy which He has demonstrated to us in a series of redemptive acts, show that we have yielded ourselves, living sacrifices, holy and acceptable unto God, that we are transformed by the renewing of our mind, and that we are proving His perfect work. Then the unfolding of our lives will be a demonstration of God's plan, good, acceptable and perfect.

Is this too much for God to ask? After all that God has given to you, after all the resources, the powers and the blessings which you have received from Him, is it too much to ask that your life be like the plan? I submit to you that this is your only logical or reasonable, spiritual service. You must do His will.

Years ago, I had a roommate who was a beautiful soloist on constant call from many churches to sing at their morning services. I remember two lines of one song which he used to sing beautifully in public and often in the halls of our dormitory as he went to and from his work. These lines were:

> "To do Thy will, yes that is all,
> To do Thy will, obey Thy call."

Pastorates and musical positions opened for that young man on the right and on the left in this country. But before him was the object of doing the will of God, of making his life like the plan. For ten years he has been serving in interior China, oftentimes separated for six months at a time from his family and his children, but singing his way into the hearts of the Chinese, the poor whom he has fed and kept from starvation, and others to whom he has pointed the way to life. Whenever I think of that young friend, I think of what God will some day say as He makes an evaluation of his life. With satisfaction and joy, He will say, "Just like My plan."

Not empty words or vain thoughts or silent meditation is the liturgy God desires of you. He wants a life which is like the plan. Let this be your worship of God.

XVIII
GOD'S PLAN FOR THE UNITY AND LIFE OF THE CHURCH

TEXT: *"Prove what is that good, and acceptable, and perfect, will of God."*—ROM. 12:2-21.

THERE is a similarity between the teaching of Paul and of Jesus, especially in this chapter of the book of Romans.

We often hear the argument that Paul taught a different Gospel from Jesus. We are told that we must disregard Paul and return to the teaching of Jesus. This is effectively refuted by the fact that every word of this passage of Paul is found in the teaching of Jesus. One would almost think that Paul had the Gospel of Matthew before him when he wrote this epistle to the Romans. There is a wonderful parallel between the teaching of verses three to eight and the teaching in John 15:1-8. Both passages deal with abiding in Christ and the fruitfulness that results therefrom. Likewise, there is a close parallel between the ninth to the twenty-first verses of the twelfth chapter of Romans and the latter part of the fifth chapter of Matthew. This section might be called Paul's sermon on the mount. Herein we have the irrefutable argument that the sermon on the mount is for serious application to Christians in this age and is not only for some millennial age which is to come. Any accurate student rereading this chapter will be impressed by the close similarity to the teaching of Jesus.

The entire argument of Paul is based on the foundation experience of verses one and two, namely, a complete presentation of our bodies unto God as a living sacrifice, holy and acceptable unto Him which is our reasonable service. These subsequent teachings are rules and principles of Christian conduct in the church and in civil society. They assume that the doctrinal truths presented in the first half of the epistle have been apprehended by the reader. We observe, however, that the division into doctrinal and practical sections of this great epistle is entirely artificial. Paul's dogmatic teaching is constantly suggestive of practical consequences and his moral and spiritual exhortations are continually based upon dogma. There is an inevitable practical manifestation of the truth contained in the first twelve chapters and there is a full doctrinal basis for the exhortations of the last five chapters. The presentation of ourselves as living sacrifices to be transformed by the Holy Spirit is the beginning of the life and unity of the church and is also the necessary condition of proving God's will to be good, acceptable and perfect. Therefore, unless we have made such an absolute surrender of self unto God in Christ, it is necessary for us to reconsider Paul's great plea for that act based upon the mercies of God as revealed in the epistle to the Romans.

The argument here is that God has a plan for His Church and for every individual in it, both as to his service and life. More and more as I study this epistle I am impressed with the great gulf which separates the actual condition of the Church from God's plan for it. It reminds one of the Washington Cathedral where Woodrow Wilson and other notables lie buried. Magnificent as the transepts and choir and crypt are in that cathedral they are still insignificant when compared with the projected nave of the main church building. No one would think that the present structure is like the cathedral plan. It is only like it in part, for the cathedral is very incomplete. Remember that in speaking of the Church we are not thinking of a tangible, worldly organization of priests, hierarchies, buildings and offices. We are thinking of a spiritual organism made up of redeemed individuals. Wisdom dictates that in considering the rules of life for the Church we should follow God's revealed plan of action.

I. THOUGHTS CONCERNING OUR PLACE AND USEFULNESS IN THE CHURCH.

The first six verses of this Scripture deal with what is called Church truth. Paul says, "We, being many, are one body in Christ." The illustration, drawn from the human body to represent the Church, is often used in the New Testament. The human hand is invaluable to the body for all work which it wishes to perform. It is also a most beautiful part of the physical body and it is revelatory of character. A Biblical scholar in reading a recent literary anthology of New England writers came across a reference to a cast of Browning's hands. He spent considerable time looking for a reproduction of this famous figure. The day on which he discovered it, he returned to my office greatly disappointed, exclaiming, "there is no romance there. They simply express death." Yes, the hands are very expressive. Every one is acquainted with Leo-

THE UNITY AND LIFE OF THE CHURCH

nardo da Vinci's "Last Supper" which distinguishes itself from all others by attempting to portray the individual attitude of the disciples in their reaction to Jesus' statement, "One of you shall betray me," in the expression of the hands. But the hand does not think, love, hate, see or taste and to exalt it into the chief member of the body would be to unbalance the whole functional structure of the body.

The mind, in turn, can think, but it can not feel. It plans, spins its theories, solves its problems, but it can not win the object of the desire of the heart. This demands the voice, the lips, the eyes, the arms and the whole body if necessary. Nevertheless the mind is most important. At least those of us in the English-American tradition would prefer the enslavement of the body to the enslavement of the mind.

The loss of the use of an eye, a hand, an ear or any member of the body causes the realization of the interdependence of the body. Once I was compelled to keep utter silence over a period of four months, being compelled to write every desire or communication which I had. Never shall I forget the sense of dependency upon the vocal cords. The incapacitation of one member of the body brings hurt to the whole organism and perhaps incapacitates the organism.

The application of this simile is plain. The Church is Christ's body, the only instrument which He has on earth to do His will. Every believer is a member of this body. That member is only living when it is associated directly with Christ through the Holy Spirit. Christ is the head of that body. Paul said, "God hath put all things under His feet, and gave him to be the head over all things to the church, which is His body, the fullness of him that filleth all in all." According to Paul, Christians "speaking the truth in love, may grow up to him in all things, which is the head, even Christ: from whom the whole body fitly joined together and compacted by that which every joint supplieth, according to the effectual working in the measure of every part, maketh increase of the body unto the edifying of itself in love." Believers are members of the body of Christ which is adequate reason for their separation from all sin. But believers are also members one of another, "Every one members one of another." Therefore loss to one believer is to all believers, hurt to one is hurt to all, infection in one member of the body is infection in all the body. Herein is the great mutual responsibility of Christians one for another, for one backsliding believer affects the whole organism. In a real sense the Church is a true incarnation of God today as Jesus was during His earthly life. What a sober realization this is of our responsibility before the world for conduct and life.

From this idea of the body we can gain a true conception of the unity of the Church. It is utterly erroneous to conceive of local organizations as independent churches and to plan or talk about promoting organizational unity with other groups. Unity in Christianity is not something to be obtained. It is something which already exists. When Jesus prayed in His high priestly prayer, "Make them one that the world may believe" He prayed a prayer which God answered. On the day of Pentecost the body known as the church was formed and into this body every individual member was baptized, so that the unity was formed. This not only fulfilled Jesus' prayer but it also fulfilled Jesus' promise that He would build His church. External unity of organization forced upon us by undesirable means will only culminate in the Antichristian false prophet who will persecute true believers. Emphasis is needed today on body-truth, which will make for unity in diversification.

Turn now to God's plan for each believer in this church. There is a work for every member of the body, a different function. Paul was given grace to be an Apostle, but to others other gifts were made. "God hath given to every man the measure of faith." This measure of faith is not the faith which justifies us before God, but it is the grace of faith measured out by the Holy Spirit to the individual Christian. It will differ in quality and in intensity with different Christians. Therefore a man's measure of faith is generally the true measure of his general spiritual capacity.

The practical gift made to each Christian to exercise is in proportion to the measure of his faith. If you believe that God would have you preach, then go to preaching, or if you believe God would have you teach, go to teaching and thus also with exhorting or ministering. As Paul says, "Having then gifts differing according to the grace that is given to us, whether prophecy, let us prophesy according to the proportion of faith; or ministry, let us wait on our ministering; or he that teacheth, on teaching; etc." Only a man who believes in himself can make others believe in him. This is the measure of his faith. Such a belief in himself was the secret of the personal magnetism for soldiers held by General George B. McClellan or by Napoleon. Whenever McClellan rode into the midst of retreating or fleeing troops they were galvanized into action so as to be able to turn and charge the enemy. The measure of your faith will be evident by the gift which you exercise. If you are unable to exercise the gift you do not have the measure of faith for that gift.

The gifts which God bestows upon believers are different, but they are all according to grace. Grace is the vital force of the body of Christ flowing from Him to all its living members and manifesting itself in the ability of a particular member to do his part toward the whole body. I think of women who are gifted in teaching children, of business men who are gifted in governing a church, of individuals who have been given the gift of vision for missionary enterprise and of innumberable other gifts manifested in churches I have served.

These gifts are enumerated for us here and again in the twelfth chapter of I Corinthians and in the fourth chapter of Ephesians. They may be summarized under the following head. First, prophesying, that is, forth telling the truth. There was a day in the time of the apostles when the gift of prophecy also included foretelling events which were future. That gift ceased and prophecy continued to be forth telling the truths of God to the people. Next is the gift of ministering. This does not mean preaching, but it is the capacity of deacons and deaconesses and of elders to serve in the church, such as the seven men full of the Holy Ghost and faith sought out by the apostles. Next is the gift of teaching. What a gift that God should raise up men who are a bulwark against error, who have an intuitive sense of evangelical truth and who are able to present it to their students! Yet another gift is exhortation. Once in the Methodist Church there was an order of men called Exhorters who, after the preacher had concluded his sermon, pressed the people for decisions for Christ or who made particular application of the truth. The practice of exhortation is largely lost from the church. Another gift is that of Christian liberality. Paul said, "He that giveth let him do it with simplicity." Great riches in this world if gotten in an honest way are a gift of God and should be used accordingly. Giving may be a ministry. Next Paul mentions ruling. He who has the gift of government, being a true elder or ruler in the church, may often save his preacher and teacher from being a glorified business man immersed in the details of church affairs. Paul speaks of mercy, here summarizing the work of cheerful servants, of Christians assisting their neighbors and I suppose also what was called in another place the gift of healing. Sometimes God even gives the gift of tongues, the means of glorifying Him in other languages. We must say that this is not a qualification, however, for the Spirit-filled life and since it may only be given, it often is not given to all men.

Thus every one has some gift. The apostle addresses this "to every man that is among you." The highest and the lowest and all that come between should expect some gift of God to serve in His church, to be functional members of the body.

In the midst of this teaching concerning the gifts of God to believers is an injunction concerning Christian humility or the means by which they should be exercised. "I say . . . to every man that is among you, not to think of himself more highly than he ought to think." Each believer should form an accurate and therefor humble estimate of his own importance to the Church. The great antidote for pride concerning the standard of gifts which God provides is the measure of our faith. Some men think themselves capable of or aspire to offices which are higher than the measure of faith which God gave them warrants. Too often we Christians think too much of ourselves. We think we should be doing something that God never intends us to do, or we think that people are talking about us or are avoiding us when in reality we are far from their thought. Some of us preachers think that we can manage a better pulpit. Some laymen think they could have a better job. Some political men, a better office! As a result of this personal pride there come slights to personality and to our false dignity. Aaron Burr and Benedict Arnold were led to their detestable actions because the former wanted to be President of the United States and was only elected vice-president and the latter could not stand the advance of subordinates over him in the army. False pride led them to their actions. In a lesser way Christians often do similar things.

The positive precept of Paul is "to think soberly." Let us have no flights of imagination, no ecstasies concerning our own abilities whether they be in music, art, athletics, speaking, or any other field. It is one thing to have a talent given by God and it is another thing to keep telling the world we have that talent. Think soberly about yourself.

The regulative standard of what you ought to think about yourself is "according as God hath dealt to every man the measure

THE UNITY AND LIFE OF THE CHURCH

of faith." Do not falsely take a reticent, self derogatory, self despising attitude which belittles your gifts, but in honesty, humility and service utilize your gift for the good of the Church. Only the pressing home of this responsibility will provide the needed laborers within the Church organism.

II. THOUGHTS CONCERNING OUR LIFE AND CONDUCT AS MEMBERS OF THE CHURCH.

The above rules in a large part apply to those having specific gifts which have been mentioned, but the following rules are for every Christian. They are rules for his personal life and conduct within the church. The first concerns love. "Let love be without dissimulation." This love is a Divine affection to God and man implanted in man who is a believer by God. It manifests itself in many ways. It is in reality what it professes to be in the words of Paul, namely, unfeigned or without hypocrisy. This love is called agape and is the love given in the person of the Holy Spirit. Only God can inspire this love as the result of Christian faith in the redeemed heart. It is the same word which expresses the love of God to man, the love of redeemed men to God and the love of Christians toward Christians. Depraved man knows nothing of this love. It is this love which John uses as a test of our salvation and new birth, saying, "Beloved, let us love one another: for love is of God; and every one that loveth is born of God, and knoweth God." For this reason when Jesus asked Peter by the lake of Galilee, "Simon, son of Jona, lovest thou me" and used the word agape in its verb form Peter refused to respond with that word but merely said, I am fond of you, using a word for human love. He knew that he had no right to use this Divine love unless it were implanted in him by God.

This love implies the hatred of and shrinking from moral evil and adhesion to the moral good. "Abhor that which is evil; cleave to that which is good." The word actually means "separate from" evil. It implies a horror with which evil is viewed resulting from the Christian practice of the separated life. "Cleave" means to attach oneself to a leader or to a master. It is in this way that men cleave to dictators calling them their leaders or in which they become slaves of drink and drink is their master. This good to which we are to cleave is God, God's will and everything that contributes to promoting God's will.

Love implies the same relation existing between Christians as exists in a family, namely, brotherly love. Love in a friendly, fond, pleasureable way lies within the capability of all men, but love in a Christian sense is that which is derived from relationship. This love is described "in honor preferring one another; not slothful in business; fervent in spirit; serving the Lord." The first phrase must be connected with each of these phrases and it really means that in brotherly love and honor we are to go before or to surpass others or to show the way, to blaze the trail. It means that in acknowledging merit in others we are to take the lead and thus set the example. Christians ought to express honor and affection and respect to one another, especially to those whom God honors with great gifts.

This love is synonymous with enthusiasm. The literal translation would be "As to zeal, not slothful" meaning that we should be spiritually fervent in God's service. We are to seize every opportunity to do good, not missing one chance.

The next rule concerns hope. "Rejoicing in hope." The essence of this hope, or better the object of it, is the coming of the Lord and the attendant Christian's reward, namely, a body redeemed, a crown of rejoicing and glory. The effect of such hope upon the soul must be joy. The passive effect of this hope upon the soul is patience in tribulation. When hope and joy are combined they make patience easy and the practical result of hope, joy and patience is perseverance in prayer, by which these former characteristics are mutually strengthened.

The next rule concerns works which are the practical outworking of love. They are described "distributing to the necessity of the saints; given to hospitality." We must have a communion with the wants and needs of God's people. This is most difficult because so many of God's people are needy, but each one of us must do what we can as unto the Lord and to satisfy Him alone. The phrase "given to hospitality" actually means pursuing human kindness to strangers and hence referred to the unbefriended of those days. Today we are willing to be hospitable to our friends, but few of us go out of the way to be hospitable to strangers. Yet this is the practice repeatedly enjoined upon us in the New Testament.

The above rules were enjoined upon the Christian in relationship to other Christians. Now we have certain rules for the Christian in relationship to the society round about him, which is chiefly pagan. First is his attitude in persecution. Paul says, "Bless them which persecute you: bless, and curse not." This is merely an

THE UNITY AND LIFE OF THE CHURCH

echo of the teaching of Jesus in the Sermon on the Mount. It is a high standard for the believer but we must strive to fulfill it by His grace. It is not easy to love those who hate us, to bless them and pray for them, yet the Christians who were persecuted and killed by the heathen emperors and proconsuls prayed for their persecutors. Thus Stephen prayed for his persecutors and the Lord Jesus Christ prayed for His. This precept and practice may become the means of winning them to the Lord. Peter in speaking of such persecution even said, "Ye should inherit a blessing." Christians actually ought to glorify God on behalf of persecution because it works for them a greater inheritance.

Secondly, Christians are to be sympathetic in joyful or sad circumstances. "Rejoice with them that do rejoice, and weep with them that do weep." It is necessary for us to enter into the experience of others, bearing their burdens and sharing their joys. This, too, is a high standard of self-forgetfulness.

Then Paul quotes for us the Golden Rule. Says he, "Be ye of the same mind one to another." Christians above all people should strive to be harmonious, to do unto others as they would that they should do unto them.

Christians also must transcend the lines of class distinction. "Mind not high things, but condescend to men of low estate." The Christian is not to be self-confident or pompous in his opinions. "Be not wise in your own conceits."

Next comes a rule which is absolutely startling in its implications. Paul said, "Recompense to no man evil for evil. Provide things honest in the sight of all men." The last clause should be translated, "being preoccupied with the beautiful." This statement does not mean pacifism for Paul specifically states that the magistrate bears not the sword in vain and that he is the minister of God, but it enjoins upon us in our private practices non-retaliation for evil. It means the practice of turning the other cheek which only a regenerate heart can do. The Christian standard is, render good for evil. The only way this can be done practically is by "being preoccupied with the beautiful." The word "beautiful" comes from a Greek word, kala (plural), meaning the honorable, the pure, the wholesome, the estimable, the good in itself. This was one of the Greek triumvirate of ultimates called the good, the true and the beautiful. Whenever one is occupied with the kala, the evil that men may do to us is inconsequential. With the praiseworthy things occupying the human mind the picayune things will affect one slightly.

This is the greatest defense and insolation against little people. No great scientist, musician, artist or engineer can leave what he is doing to engage in little acts of revenge. Thus also a busy Christian engaged and preoccupied with the lovely things of life will not be affected by the little things.

"If it be possible, as much as lieth in you, live peaceably with all men." Before general heathen society, if it be possible at all, live peaceably. This is not absolute as the text says, for some things we can not control, for there are those who would persecute us and who would seek a quarrel. But in so far as the cause of dissension lies in ourselves we may live at peace with all men. We believe that the majority of disputes would never occur if one party to the dispute were preoccupied with the good and the beautiful.

Finally, Paul gives us rules of conduct under a sense of injury. These are probably the most interesting of all. First, he tells us what we are not to do. "Dearly beloved, avenge not yourselves." The primary meaning of this is to vindicate your rights. In spite of the fact that justice must be done in the universe, we are not to take vengeance for ourselves. We are not to place ourselves in the position of a judge. God is judge and God alone can take vengeance. Only a truly regenerate man will leave the vindication of his rights to God because only such a man can trust God. The phrase, "Give place unto wrath" means something utterly different from what the average man takes it to mean. It actually means "Give place to God, or make room for wrath, or step aside and commit your injury to God." Leave it in His hands. Once we take the vengeance in our own hands we are assuming the Divine prerogative and we hinder His terrible justice and wrath. Woe unto the man who falls under the wrath of God even in this world. When an unbeliever touches a Christian he touches the apple of God's eye and he will fall under God's wrath. "Vengeance is mine. I will repay, saith the Lord." God will deal with evil-doers in His own time and in His own way. Step aside. Give place to wrath. God will undertake for you. This is a truth which will bring perfect peace to a wronged and troubled soul. Instead of fretting about the way to vindicate yourself, turn these wrongs over to the Lord. If God does not vindicate you immediately it is because he has some good to give you through this suffering for Christ's sake, but He will repay. Whatsoever we sow we shall also reap. This is true in every relationship of life.

THE UNITY AND LIFE OF THE CHURCH 195

If this is what we are not to do, then what are we to do? We are to be energetically kind to the one who has done us wrong. "If thine enemy hunger, feed him; if he thirst, give him drink; for in so doing thou shalt heap coals of fire on his head." This is a challenge, a challenge to give food and drink to our enemy to keep him alive so that he can do us more harm if he will. Human wisdom would repudiate this, saying, "I was burnt once. Now I will stay away." But God says, "Go the second mile. Turn the other cheek." Thus the Sermon on the Mount is shown by Paul to apply to today. This attitude will have a twofold result. Either it will produce remorse in the evil-doer and a change of heart or it will increase his judgment, damnation and the wrath of God upon him. Certainly if he does more harm his punishment will be the greater. But if we win the evil-doer we shall save a soul from death and shall shine as the stars in the firmament forever.

The purpose of God in this rule is that we shall not be vanquished by evil but shall overcome evil with good. To return evil for evil is to let evil reign in the world. Thus all good would be overcome. To return good for evil is to make evil the instrument of greater good. This would be love's triumph. In this teaching there is enough philosophy, sociology and religion to transform the world.

In the light of this teaching let me raise some important questions. Is this teaching to be applied to nations or only to individuals? Should nations resist aggression when cities are bombed as we have seen them bombed, countries are invaded as they have recently been invaded, when people are thrown in concentration camps as they are being today? Should we turn the other cheek? Is Gandhi right when he says that it would be better for Britain to be overrun by the Germans and to choose the Jesus way? Does the Bible teach a slave psychology for the world? If this is our duty in personal life, what is our duty to the State? Must we be pacifists or can we bear arms in war?

XIX
THE CHRISTIAN AS A MEMBER OF THE STATE

TEXT: *"Let every soul be subject unto the higher powers. For there is no power but of God: the powers that be are ordained of God."* —ROM. 13:1-14.

THIS important subject of the Christian's relation to the State marks the transition from our private duties to our civil duties in the life which is an outgrowth of Christian experience.

Other passages in the Scripture bear upon this subject. Jesus said, "Render unto Caesar the things which are Caesar's, and unto God the things which are God's." Certainly the teachings of the Lord Jesus and His willingness to pay tribute, as we have it recorded in the incident of the miracle of the coin found in the mouth of the fish which Peter took and gave to the tax gatherers, reveals that the Christian has obligations in the realm of the State as well as of the Church. Moreover, Paul's appeal to Caesar during his trial before Festus must have necessitated at least some exposition of and reference to the Scripture and to Christian teaching which would place Caesar in judgment upon whether Paul had done evil or not. There are some who believe that Paul should never have appealed unto Caesar but should have taken the consequences of his preaching and that he would probably have been set at liberty. However, there is no question but that God placed his approbation on Paul's conduct and that Paul set the example for a Christian appealing to the law courts of the State. Another great Apostle, namely Peter, presented precepts which are entirely parallel to the present passage of Scripture which we expect to explain. Peter said, "Submit yourself to every ordinance of man for the Lord's sake, whether it be to the king as supreme, or unto governors, as unto them that are sent by him for the punishment of evil doers, and for the praise of them that do well, for so is the will of God that with doing well ye may put to silence the ignorance of foolish men . . . honor all men, love the brotherhood, fear God, honor the king." Here we have the agreement of the foremost of Apostles and also of the Lord Jesus in

CHRISTIAN AS A MEMBER OF THE STATE 197

reference to political matters and this teaching arouses our interest.

There is a general interest in this subject at the present time. Never was there a day when preaching on the relation of the individual Christian to the State was more necessary than in this day of world revolutions and of war. Our age is one of the great transition ages of history like that of the break-up of the Roman Empire, like the rise of nationalism in Europe after the Renaissance and like the period of the Industrial Revolution. Let us make no mistake. This present war is a revolution, a mighty and terrible world revolution which will affect the life of every man in the world, even in the remotest sections of Africa.

There is also the particular interest of individuals in a subject like this just now. We are living in a time when confusion of thought exists among Christian people of all kinds. We have read of clergymen in several parts of the nation refusing to register for the draft on the reasons of conscience and now being faced with severe penalties by the Federal Government. Are they right and should every clergyman act like that? We approach this subject of momentous interest humbly accepting the teaching of the Bible and drawing our conclusions therefrom.

I. THE STATE IS OF DIVINE ORIGIN AND EXERCISES A DIVINE FUNCTION.

Our Scripture says, "There is no power but of God: the powers that be are ordained of God." These are powerful words when speaking of the State and they have great teaching value for our minds.

What then is the place of the State in God's scheme of things? We say unhesitatingly that God established the State. The State was instituted after the Flood as a check upon man's evil deeds and thoughts. Before the Flood, God saw that the wickedness of man was great in the earth and that every imagination of the thoughts of his heart was only evil continually. Then He sent the Flood in punishment upon this type of society and after the Flood God instituted human government. God said, "Surely your blood of your lives will I require. At the hand of every beast will I require it and at the hand of man. At the hand of every man's brother will I require the life of man. Whoso sheddeth man's blood, by man shall his blood be shed, for in the image of God made He man." Before the Flood there was a homogeneous society of men, but of evil men, and this society failed to warrant its continued existence in the form in which it was found at that time. God instituted human government to restrain the evil impulses of man and to give some sense of security unto man.

A note ought to be made here that the ultimate aim of the Marx-Leninist Communism is a governmentless society. The steps in this theory are: first, the violent Revolution of the Proletariat whereby the means of production are seized and put in the hands of the workers; second, the development and working of socialism; and third, the homogeneous classless society in which no government at all will be necessary for men. The Bible here reveals that this Marx-Leninist theory is an error. There can be no homogeneous society without government because man is sinful, depraved and fallen. He needs a restraining influence, a government of his fellow men established by God.

God not only established the State, but it is God's power which governs the world through the State and acts through the civil magistrates. From certain passages in the Scripture which speak of Satan as the god of this world, there was an early tendency in the church to create a dualism and to ascribe the civil power unto the devil or Satan. The author of the Clementine Homily says, "The true prophet says that God the creator of all things assigned two realms to two beings, the one good, the other evil. To the evil being, He gave the lordship of the present world with the proviso that he should punish those who do evil: to the good being, the future, eternal world . . . the children of the future world are, while they remain in this one, in the hostile realm of a foreign king." Liddon says this antagonism enables us to understand Paul's insistence on what seems to be a truism, namely, that there is no authority but from God. This leads us to inquire what is Satan's sphere? The Scripture evidently teaches that Satan's sphere is purely spiritual. He is the god of this world and the prince of this world, but only because the mass of people in the world have accepted his spiritual domain. He governs most men and leads them to do his will, but he does not have kingdoms to give except as he can use other evil men to do his will. In the end time we are told that wickedness shall be so universal that Satan shall appoint the Antichrist who will have both a spiritual power and a political power. Whenever Satan's emissaries act in conflict with God's law, as they do in Russia, Japan and even Germany, the Christian is brought into conflict with the law of the State, but this does not mean that the State itself is evil. Satan's kingdom is only a spiritual

CHRISTIAN AS A MEMBER OF THE STATE

kingdom, a kingdom of darkness, as Christ's kingdom is a kingdom of light.

If Hitler, Mussolini and Stalin are authorities of States today, God established them. It was God who gave to Nebuchadnezzar a kingdom and though Nebuchadnezzar did not acknowledge this truth at first, after he had been humbled as the beasts of the field, he said, "He doeth according to His Will in the army of heaven and among the inhabitants of the earth, and none can stay His Hand or say unto Him, what doest Thou?" Daniel said, "The Most High ruleth in the kingdom of men and giveth it to whomsoever he will." God gives the reins of government to those who fit into His inscrutable purposes either of chastening or of punishment of the people of the world.

Acknowledging this truth that God gives the authority in the State to whom He will, we find the whole range of authorities as providential. We are to be subject to the higher powers. This does not only mean the supreme powers of the State, but the range of authorities which are above the ordinary citizen. The means to the establishment of these authorities, whether the divine right of kings, the result of popular franchise, or the result of revolutionary force, are still providential. For us to resist these authorities is to resist the ordinance of God or the Divine arrangement. Resistance brings judgment through the State itself. I do not understand this passage to mean that God intervenes in judgment upon one who resists the State, but I understand it to mean that the State itself executes the judgment upon the individual when the individual has resisted the authority of the State itself. An exception should be made here, for the believer must not actively cooperate or even passively cooperate with evil. He must distinguish between the authority and the incumbent of the office, so that if an evil incumbent occupies an office and commands something contrary to God's law, though we submit to the office, our firm, religious conduct will itself ultimately break the tyranny even if we suffer for it.

God not only established the State and committed the power unto the rulers thereof, but also sets the bounds of the habitations of nations. Paul said, "He hath made of one blood all nations of men for to dwell on all the face of the earth, and hath determined the times before appointed and the bounds of their habitations." After the incident of Babel when the tongues of men were confused, God established the nations for a purpose. Hence, we may believe that nationalism is natural and supernaturalism in the Christian family is natural, but that internationalism of communism or socialism is not natural and will not succeed. One nation may over-run temporarily many other nations, but it will ultimately recede unto the bounds of its habitation as set by God. Even the rulers and kingdoms are, according to the Scriptures, weighed in the balances and often found wanting. Then when they are judged, it is in this world, not in the world to come and it is judgment wrought out usually by the sword. What we have just said does not militate against some sort of League of Nations or Federation of Nations, if in the providence of God such should ever be proposed and wrought out in the earth.

There is a definite purpose to this civil government which God has instituted. It is to control fallen man in his social relationships. If man is inherently bad, corrupt, depraved and fallen, it is obvious that these bad tendencies will soon come out in his social relationships with his fellow men and that man must be curbed, restricted, ruled and controlled. In fact, this is the great problem of government. The Utilitarians worked out a scheme whereby by the adding of punishments to evil deeds and of rewards to good deeds they could make men, who were inherently selfish and who sought their own greater happiness, to work for the happiness of the greatest number of mankind, for an unsocial act would bring with it more personal pain than a social act. The theory itself is not bad in its operation when we are dealing with man on the natural plane, and it is largely the basis of the theory of modern government.

The purpose of civil government according to this passage is to inspire fear and thus to restrain evil-doers. Paul said, "Rulers are not a terror to good works, but to evil. Wilt thou then not be afraid of the power? Do that which is good and thou shalt have praise of the same, for he is the minister of God to thee for good, but if thou do that which is evil, be afraid for he beareth not the sword in vain: for he is the minister of God, a revenger to execute wrath upon him that doeth evil." It is true that an unjust law or a tyrannical power may make the authority appear evil, but it is a minister for good. Those who have read that very notable and instructive book, *The Tree of Liberty* by Elizabeth Page, will remember the time when Peyton Howard, the Philadelphia lawyer, was seized and accused of sedition, for the new Republic had passed a law of sedition which permitted those who spoke in criticism of the government to be cast into prison and be fined. When the

CHRISTIAN AS A MEMBER OF THE STATE

trial had reached its great climax under the presiding officer Judge Chase, Peyton in his final plea asked the Judge and the Jury and the large assembly of lawyers and auditors, "Is this the kind of thing you want (this limitation on the freedom of speech, the imprisonment of men who declare their convictions), is this what you want?" The reaction to the trial was so strong that, as Peyton foresaw, his own suffering was to do away with the Sedition Law. Thus it is with the Christian. He may suffer under an unjust ruler, but his own suffering will ultimately bring about the change in that law. It is the evil-doer, not the righteous who needs to fear the authorities, for the authorities are established to punish evil-doers.

Let us remember that the sword is not carried in vain. There is much talk about the desirability of doing away with capital punishment, but capital punishment was established and instituted by God and is required to cleanse a land of innocent blood that has been shed therein. Nothing else is able to do that same thing. God reaffirmed through Moses the governmental duty of punishing murderers with death by saying, "Ye shall take no ransom for the life of a murderer that is guilty of death, for blood, it polluteth the land, and no expiation can be made for the land for the blood that is shed therein, but by the blood of him that shed it." There is no other expiation, but by the blood of the man who is a murderer.

The rulers are to reward them that do good. Good works and justice are not merely submission to the rulers, but are active righteousness in social relationships. The authorities are never a terror to such. Well do I remember a government official at Stolpse, Poland, to whom I applied for a visa to go into Russia and when this was refused I then applied to at least go to the border, from which we were thirteen miles away, in order to look into Russia. This also was refused in a high handed fashion until he learned that I was identified with the Evangelical Christians of that city. Then he went out of his way to obtain for me a pass to go to the border and to do anything else which I pleased because, as he said, "These are the best people which exist in this town." They had a good testimony before the magistrate of the Polish Army. Government in general is for the security, the protection, the help and the good of the righteous man.

The Scripture calls the authorities of the State God's ministers at least three times. These men who hold the authority of the State are in a similar relationship to the minister of the church. The very same word "litourgos" is used. Paul often called himself a litourgos of God and the Christian worship is called the liturgy, so that when in inspired language Paul describes the ministers of the State as the litourgos of God he speaks of a Divine institution and Divine power. Nevertheless, this high office is sometimes held by the basest of men. Daniel said to Nebuchadnezzar. "To the intent that the living may know that the Most High ruleth in the kingdom of men, and giveth it to whomsoever He will, and setteth up over it the basest of men." He set up over the kingdom of men such individuals as Nebuchadnezzar, Darius, Cyrus, Nero, Calligula, etc. Often evil authorities are used as God's servants though the men in themselves are giving spiritual allegiance unto the devil himself. They are doing God's will in what they are performing. Thus it is that the Chaldeans were called God's army and that the Assyrians were the rod of His anger. They were performing His will, though they knew it not. How wonderful it is when a good man is a ruler and both grace and providence converge in the administration of the State. We think of the mighty influence of Frederic the Elector of Saxony over Germany during the Protestant Reformation, the great influence of Gladstone in England in the Victorian era and that of Washington and Lincoln in America. These were good men, upright and honorable, and their office was that of Divine minister so that a two-fold source of blessing came to the hearts of men through them. Legion is their number and for them may the common people of the world be grateful.

II. THE CHRISTIAN MUST BE SUBJECT TO THE STATE.

Paul said, "Let every soul be subject unto the powers that be . . . ye must needs be subject . . . render honor to whom honor is due." It is the Christian's duty to submit himself voluntarily unto the State in which he lives. There are, of course, exceptions to this rule which are made in the Scripture and which we must acknowledge, but for the most part the first duty of the Christian is to be an acceptable citizen of the State.

The Christian's duty is one of a dual relationship, for this is written unto "every soul." The Christian is a citizen of the State with all of its privileges and its obligations. With his vote, he has the opportunity of selecting his own governmental representatives who are the ministers of God and through his influence over other men for righteousness he is able to have something to do with the condition of the nation. What an error it is then for these religious

CHRISTIAN AS A MEMBER OF THE STATE

groups to say that they will not vote and will not have anything to do with the State until it acknowledges God or Christ in its fundamental law. Whether it is acknowledged or is not acknowledged, God is the authority and power back of government. As a believer, the Christian is also a citizen of the kingdom of God. To this kingdom his loyalty must be supreme, but for the most part that loyalty should harmonize with his loyalty as a citizen. This arises from the fact that a man who is a Christian lives from the heart in conformity to God's law and since these laws are the foundation also of the State, he ought to make a better citizen of that State. Wherever this conflict is set up between the kingdom of God and the State, the kingdom of God must be supreme in the life of the individual believer. How grateful we should be as Americans that into the fundamental law of the United States of America, such as the Constitution, are written the basic principles of the law of God as contained in the Mosaic code. Thus a Christian is able, especially in America, to be a good citizen. Yet we must remember that the Church, as the manifestation of the kingdom of God, is separate from the State and must not enter into the civil struggle. Its work is with individuals in saving them, transforming their lives, making them Christians. Through these individuals power and influence is given to the Church over the State.

Recently a young man came to me from one of our fine colleges filled with Communism and the desire to utterly transform the whole of the United States under this ideological set up. After talking with him for a long time I made the challenge as to the program of the church, how that the church is reaching out for the individual life, how that the supernatural power of God comes into that individual's life and changes it from one of wickedness to one of justice and righteousness, and how that when the numbers of these individuals are increased the whole nation in its tenor and experience is gradually changed. Suddenly there came a light into the young man's eyes and he saw that here was an effective means of transforming the civilization in which he lived, that it was not necessary to bring about a violent revolution to do this, that it could be done daily and hourly by the power of God upon the hearts and lives of individual men. Yes, Christianity offers a greater challenge in a State such as the American State than any ideology such as Communism, Fascism or its associates.

Paul enjoins obedience to the State by the Christian for two reasons. "Ye must needs be subject not only for wrath but for conscience's sake." Out of obedience to his own conscience the Christian usually will obey the law of the State. If a Christian is not subject to the state's law he must bear the penalty as well as any one else. In the refusal to obey the law of the draft, clergymen are facing five years of imprisonment or ten thousand dollar fines. This wrath is judgment inflicted by the State as God's agent. The Christian has no more right to expect exemption from the State law than any other citizen of the State. What then is the place of conscience in obedience? Conscience should make us obey with more alacrity. There are some who will obey the State laws merely to escape penalty. Christianity should enhance law and order by making men obey from conscience as well as from penalty. What shall we do in the matter of conscience when God's law and the State's law clash? Then we must do exactly as the Apostles did, say, "We ought to obey God rather than men." Then they took the Apostles and beat them and released them, and they departed from the presence of the Sanhedrin rejoicing that they were counted worthy to suffer shame for Christ's Name. Your conscience before God is supreme and it is personal. No one else can tell you what to do, but when you follow your conscience you must prepare to bear the consequences as the early Christians bore the consequences and as the martyrs of the Middle Ages bore the consequences of following their consciences.

Shall I then honor and obey and respect evil magistrates? I shall only in so far as their laws and orders do not conflict with God's laws and orders expressed in nature, conscience and the Bible. When an evil man is on the throne or is in power, what source of redress do we have as believers? First, we obviously have prayer, and prayer changes things more than people sometimes dream. If Christians would pray, they would accomplish far more than in their fighting. Second, we have the recourse to legislation as individuals voting and campaigning for the right type of action. Third, we have the right to revolt which is the last right of man. When our human dignity and rights under God's law are violated, then it falls to some men at last to take the leadership in the founding of a new government which will be dedicated to the rights of man. Thus spoke the Declaration of American Independence. Thus followed the American and French Revolutions. And as long as men love righteousness, freedom and justice, above security, corruption and bondage, they may have it in the earth. That they will ultimately universally yield these for a rule of a wicked dictator the Bible foretells, but it shall be to their shame.

The duties required of the believer in the State are clearly set forth. We are to render to all their due, tribute to whom tribute is due, custom to whom custom, fear to whom fear and honor to whom honor is due. The first command is that we are to pay tribute. Payment of taxes and tribute is for the protection and good received from government. It is a rightful obligation. How gladly should we Americans pay taxes in this last citadel of the free and the home of the brave that we might preserve it as it is now instead of complaining at our required tribute! According to the meaning of these words, tribute is a regular tax which is paid by individuals. Custom is upon certain articles of trade which is paid intermittently. Fear is given to authorities who have the power of life and death and honor unto those who are above us in the range of State authorities. Truly we have no right to enjoy the great American heritage without a willingness to contribute our money and our blood and tears to continue it for our children. When men became soft, effeminate and lovers of luxury in Rome, the barbarians swept in from the north and took away their privileges. These are days calling for strenuous self-discipline of Americans if we are to preserve our heritage.

Is there not in this passage of Scripture the refutation of pacifism? It is true that we abhor war, but wars there will be as long as there are wicked men in the earth and as long as wicked men can organize and combine into great powers. Now if wars must come, as the Bible strictly says that they will come during this dispensation and which any realist recognizes, can we as individuals be pacifists? We have the right to sit in judgment upon whether a war is righteous or unrighteous. Then it is ours to obey or to disobey and to suffer the consequences. If the sword is not given in vain to the magistrate, then it is not only to be used for the preservation of order and righteousness within a State, but also it is to be used to protect the borders and citizens of that State. Conscientious objectors should really study Romans 13. Christianity and patriotism go together. We must abhor war, but because wars will go on, we must be strong. Christ gave the warning that he who taketh the sword shall perish by the sword and we should be very slow in taking up the sword. If we go to war, we shall suffer, bleed and die, but there are times when even death must be preferable to life, times when the light of our minds and our souls is possibly to be quenched.

After the warning has been considered and a nation goes to war, we as citizens have nothing more to do but to obey. Let us remember that Cornelius was a Centurian, a soldier in the Roman army, and when the Holy Ghost fell upon him he was not commanded to leave the army. He continued as a consecrated Christian soldier. Let us remember that John the Baptist preached to the soldiers and did not tell them to leave the army. He told them to do violence to no man and to be content with their wages, that is, to stop their plunder. Some of the greatest generals of the world have been devout Christians. Think of General Havelock, General Chiang Kai Shek of China, General O. O. Howard of Sherman's army, General Stonewall Jackson, Cromwell, William of Orange, and General Allenby. These were men who walked with God, but were soldiers.

Let me give just a brief anecdote of General Howard in Sherman's army. After the great triumph of the army, it was assembled at Washington following the peace and was now to be disbanded. Howard was to ride at the head of his troops in the final parade. Sherman called him in and said, "General Howard, political pressure is being put upon me so that I will not be able to let you ride at the head of your corps tomorrow." Howard replied, "But that is not right. My men love me and I love them and I have led them through this war and it is my right to ride at the head of these men. They will expect it." Sherman agreed and said, "I know that is true, but it is impossible because of political reasons." "But," Howard objected, "I insist that this is my right and I should ride at the head of my men." Sherman quietly said, "Howard, you are a Christian. May I put this to you on a different basis? I appeal to you as a Christian, that you step aside and let some one else take the place which is rightfully yours." Howard said, "If you appeal to me that way I submit." "Well," Sherman replied, "Howard, tomorrow morning when we report for the parade I want you to report to me and you will ride by my side in front of the whole Army," and so he did.

III. THE MOTIVES OF CHRISTIAN CONDUCT AS A MEMBER OF THE STATE.

If a Christian is to conduct himself as a good member of the State he must have inner motives with which to do it. He has. The first is love. Paul says, "Owe no man anything but to love one another, for he that loveth another hath fulfilled the law." In Greek, the word, "Owe" has the same root as "due." Hence all duties are to be fully discharged, but the requirements of love can never be fully discharged. The more we fulfill it, the larger it grows. Paul then quoted the last tablet of the Decalogue dealing with social justice and revealed that the obligations of justice are fulfilled in love. This love is the Divine gift of God, the agape which makes a believer able to be a good citizen because he loves his neighbor. "Love worketh no ill to his neighbor, therefore love is the fulfilling of the law." If we have the Divine love, we can be good citizens of the State.

The second motive is the expectation of Christ's coming in judgment. He said, "And knowing the time that now it is high time to awake out of sleep for now is our salvation nearer than when we believed. The night is far spent, the day is at hand. Let us therefore cast off the works of darkness and let us put on the armor of light." We should know the times in which we live. It is possible to discern the times from the Bible knowledge. Had the Jews known the times when Jesus came they would not have crucified Him. So in our time, important as it is, let us not sink into sleep, but be awake and know what is transpiring. The night of sin and darkness is far spent. The day of His coming is at hand. The Day Star is shining and the Day is soon to dawn. The Sun of righteousness will rise with healing in His wings. That day is the day of Christ and His coming, of which no man or no angel knows, but it is rapidly drawing nigh. In the light of it we should exchange the deeds of darkness for the armor of light, our moral works of righteousness and of light should supplant the unmoral works of darkness and evil. All gluttony, impurity and strife should be put away that we might experience a union with Christ in the new manhood of life, for as it was in the days of Noah so it will be in the days of the coming of the Son of Man.

Thus a righteous life before our fellow men will be greatest influence in winning them to Christ. Let us be moral, patriotic and worthy before the world.

XX

SOME PRINCIPLES OF CHRISTIAN CONDUCT

TEXT: *"Why dost thou judge thy brother? or why dost thou set at nought thy brother? for we shall all stand before the judgment-seat of Christ."*—ROM. 14:1-23.

"BUT I'm doing so many things that are wrong." Thus, ended a conversation after one of these sermons from the earlier sections of Romans. The subject of the sermon dealt with assurance of salvation in Christ. It portrayed the finished work of Christ on the Cross for the salvation of them who believe. When the church was almost empty, one of the faithful members who had lingered behind said, "I needed this sermon today."

"Why?" queried the preacher.

"Because I had begun to doubt that I was a Christian."

"But you believe on the Lord Jesus Christ as your personal Saviour, do you not?"

"Yes," she answered, "but you have said a number of times recently that we may think we are Christians when we are not."

"Quite true," I replied. "Nevertheless if you have come to Him in faith and are obeying Him, He fulfills His promise to save you."

"But I do so many things that are wrong," she answered.

"Then stop doing them." With this the conversation ceased and the friend turned away. But there was something in those glistening eyes of this faithful church member that stayed with me. I could not forget it. The question came, "Why is my friend so confused about right and wrong? Is it because I have failed to make the way of salvation and of Christian living clear?"

You may say that this was a weak person, who, when with one group went one way, and when with another group went a different way. I do not agree with you. This person is strong, has will-power, is educated, and is able to enforce her desires. Something in her expression said that there was more back of her statement than weakness. But you say, How can a Christian vacillate between right and wrong? Wait until you are enmeshed in some net of desire, of environment, or of temptation. Who are you that you should set yourself up in judgment on another person? Remember that pride goeth before a fall and the best of us sooner or later finds himself doing things that are wrong.

To all of us who are in or who sometime will be in that condition, the Scripture has a message. It presents to us certain principles of Christian conduct, which if followed, will be sufficient for the living of a life which will be acceptable unto God. Many times men have wondered what principles of Christian living there are, how far grace frees them from obeying the law, and wherein they can exercise Christian liberty and yet not be judged by others. The Scripture was written for our instruction, comfort and hope. From it in this practical section we gain instruction on the principles of conduct. Paul states the principles here and he applies them in the eighth to the tenth chapters of the first epistle to the Corinthians. These three principles are: Judge not, Offend not, and Follow Christ. In believers whose consciences have begun to be enlightened concerning their walk with God, all states of conscience and progress in the truth will be found. People forget this. And inasmuch as their own belief about things, that is, their own state of conscience, guides them, they almost invariably make their own state the standard for all. This is a most grievous error and a sort of wickedness of pride, in that we make ourselves a standard by which we judge our fellow believers.

I. JUDGE NOT.

When Paul says, "Judge not," he does not mean that the Christian should not exercise judgment on matters which are definitely wrong. There are some things which are unquestionably right, and some which are unquestionably wrong, and there are others as to which the consciences of men differ. C. R. Erdman says, "These questions of conscience arise among Christians and become the sources of serious trouble. Christians who are over-scrupulous are apt to condemn others as lax or inconsistent, while those who feel no scruples as to practices and questions are tempted to despise their fellow Christians as bigoted, or fanatical, or narrow." In order to clear the ground for a discussion of the questions of conscience, let it be said that some things are definitely wrong. There are men who quote the words of Jesus in the Sermon on the Mount, "Judge not that ye be not judged," in order to excuse the looseness of their living. Others say, "To the pure, all things are pure," and thus they excuse themselves for not condemning and ostracizing those who practice wrongs. It is foolishness to say that because a pure man looks upon an impure deed that the deed is pure, or that when an honest man sees somebody steal that the deed is honest. But these are arguments which are often used to excuse filthy movies and plays and obscene sections in realistic novels. Some people take these very words of Paul, concerning the regarding of holy days, to justify their regarding no day as holy. Such people deserve to be judged because they are wrong.

God has given us a revealed law and standard of morals, changeless in its meaning, and He expects us to live up to it. The Ten Commandments are still the essence of the moral law. If anybody is found breaking one of these commandments we have a perfect right to judge him and condemn him. The same is true of the fruits of the flesh, concerning which Paul warned us that they which do such things will not inherit the kingdom of God. Evil doers, wags, contentious men, fornicators, and destroyers of Christian doctrine, are to be condemned. Today, there is a general opinion abroad that it is permissible for people to follow their fleshly desires provided that they are not untrue to some marriage vow. That heathen idea was rampant in the days of Paul. It even invaded the early church so that one of the provisions in the first apostolic decree given at the Jerusalem council was the prohibition of fornication among Christians. The Christian standard has always been against this wickedness because of the truth of the indwelling of the Holy Spirit which makes the body the temple of the Holy Ghost.

On these questions of right and wrong, the answer to which is self-evident, every Christian should take his stand. However, "Some Christians are as spineless as oysters. They are like lollypops to be licked off both sides, worse than an old yellow cat who will only permit his fur to be stroked one way." On matters which are wrong our obligation is to judge and to contend for righteousness.

Obvious is it that the things which are unquestionably right are outside the scope of judgment. Such things are: the right of determining one's occupation, whether he enters business, medicine, teaching, preaching, or any other field, the right to marry or not to marry, contrary to the teachings of the Roman Catholic Church, the right of amusing himself and of using his time as he chooses, provided it is within the law which is laid down by God, etc. With these things and many others no one has the right to interfere.

But when we deal with matters of the conscience, there is a division of opinion in Christian thinking, and often this ends in serious strife and contention. These matters of conscience had a

PRINCIPLES OF CHRISTIAN CONDUCT

large place in the early church. Paul was referring to them in this chapter. He opens his discussion with the words, "Him that is weak in the faith receive ye, but not to doubtful disputations." The weak brother in the early church was the one who had been regenerated by God's Spirit, but who had not as yet been freed from his superstitions, prejudices, theories, and legality. Some of these were Jews. Inasmuch as all meat, before it was sold in the market place, had been sacrificed to idols, some of these refused to eat meat and became vegetarians. They did it because of the Mosaic law which forbade idolatry. It is noticeable that while this problem existed, the apostles also included in the Apostolic decree the exhortation to abstain from meat sacrificed to idols. Some were strong enough to realize that eating meat did not make any difference to faith, and they despised the weak brethren who would not eat the meat. Some who were weak judged those who ate of this meat, thinking that they still worshiped idols. Another problem was that of the Mosaic holy days. Some thought these days ought to be observed in the New Testament times, and some thought they should not be observed. Included in this was the Sabbath. Some observed the first day and some observed the seventh day. But Paul knew that the Sabbath of the Old Testament as the seventh day had been supplanted for believers by the first day. The observation of the first day was not definitely commanded in its place. The first day observance merely grew out of the practice of the early church. It was a matter of proportion that one day in seven belonged unto God. Consequently, it was a matter of indifference whether they observed the first day or the seventh day, for whichever day they observed was regarded unto the Lord. These questions of conscience, along with others, were indifferent to one's salvation, but were the occasions of many misunderstandings.

Matters of conscience have a large part in our thinking and in the church life today. There is a division of opinion upon them. Never has any one heard the speaker denounce deeds in this category or condemn those who practice them. These matters of conscience take up a great deal of our time and energy. They include such things as drinking wine, card-playing, dancing, theater-going, and kindred subjects. Some think they are right, and some think they are wrong. They are not forbidden in the Bible, or in the church law. It is quite true that until 1924, the Methodist Church had laws against them, but they were revoked. These questions of conscience are not dealt with in the Bible as individual rules. They are to be decided according to great laws.

It is wrong to judge anybody who does these things. Paul says, "Who art thou that judgest another man's servant? To his own master he standeth or falleth." Just as we have no right to criticize the servants of another man's household, so we have no right to judge in these matters. Every professing Christian lives unto the Lord. He is the Lord's. If by faith he is unified to Christ and is identified with His death, resurrection and new life, then he is answerable only to Christ. Whatever we do must be regulated by the great principle of the Lordship of Christ. Why then should we judge any one as inconsistent, sinful, or wrong when each of us must answer before the judgment seat of Christ? Every one of us shall give an account of himself to God. God will require of us concerning the things which we have done. Who has the right to set himself on the judgment seat of Christ? Let us therefore not judge one another any more.

Such judgment is due to the fact of our failure to understand the true meaning of salvation. It is not what we do or what we fail to do that makes us acceptable unto God, but it is what Christ has done. We are saved through grace by faith in the merits and work of Christ. As a result of this the law no longer has any dominion over us and we live unto Christ. We are free from the law. "Stand fast, therefore, in the liberty wherewith Christ hath made us free, and be not entangled again in the yoke of bondage . . . for brethren, ye have been called unto liberty; only use not liberty to the occasion of the flesh, but by love serve one another." Paul says, "Am I not free . . . have we not the power to eat and drink, have we not the power to lead about a sister, a wife, as well as the other apostles?" Yes, the gospel of faith in Christ has made us free from the law. We are free to obey our consciences, free to follow the Spirit of Christ who fulfills the law in us. This does not mean that the Christian under grace will turn to anti-legal lawlessness, for though this great truth stands, he has other things which hold him in check. Bear in mind that for a Christian no matter of conscience is in itself sinful, although it may be sinful in peculiar circumstances. We have complete freedom in all things, not in themselves wrong.

II. Offend Not.

The rules of conduct do not end, however, with perfect freedom. Added to this is the principle, "We must not offend another con-

PRINCIPLES OF CHRISTIAN CONDUCT 213

science which is intentionally doing a good thing." Paul urges not to judge one another but rather to judge in another matter, that is, that no man put a stumbling block or an occasion to fall in his brother's way. The essence of this principle is—Offend not.

Assuming that you understand the great truth of redemption and of freedom from the law, that you have perfect freedom to do what you wish, that you are a strong Christian, able without hurt to yourself to enjoy everything that God has placed in this world, yet you still have limiting principles. Under grace Christians have a perfect right to do these things. They are not wrong in themselves and they will not contaminate. Paul says, "I know, and am persuaded by the Lord Jesus, that there is nothing unclean of itself: but to him that esteemeth anything to be unclean, to him it is unclean." The study of higher mathematics is not a good or an evil in itself. It depends upon the use of the knowledge attained. If a physicist uses the knowledge to understand the make-up of the universe and to bring into control forces of nature, higher mathematics may become a good. If a criminal uses it, it becomes an evil. What is true of higher mathematics is true of love, of bread, of wine, of strength, and of everything in life. Seeing this, Spinoza (a Jewish philosopher) made the point of departure in his ethical theory, "Seeing that none of the objects of my fears contained in themselves anything either good or bad, except in so far as the mind is affected by them, I finally resolved to inquire whether there might be some real good, having power to communicate itself." Only as possessions, money, power, are related to our motives and desires are they good or bad.

Add to this the fact that "the kingdom of God is not meat and drink; but righteousness, and peace, and joy in the Holy Ghost." The kingdom of God is within us. It is a very real thing. It is lived in a conscious relation to the Holy Ghost. He is carrying on the kingdom of God here and now in the world in the hearts of Christians. The righteousness of the Christian was fulfilled in Christ before God, but is manifested in the kingdom of God by right-doing in the Christian life. The peace with God was completed by Christ on Calvary when we were reconciled to Him. But the peace of God is shed abroad in our hearts through the Holy Spirit. So also the joy in the Holy Spirit is a mark of the true Christian life. These are the things which matter most. Let not matters of eating and drinking keep us from following after the things which make for peace and edify one another. He that in these things serveth

Christ is acceptable unto God and approved of men. No man can condemn the one who lives in the kingdom of God through the Holy Spirit.

As one who loves his brother, he will have regard to the weak brethren to whom these things mean much. There are some who will be offended and grieved by your exercising your freedom. If you so offend your brother in Christ, you walk not in love. "If thy brother be grieved with thy meat, now walkest thou not charitably. Destroy not him with thy meat, for whom Christ died." By indulging in these questions and by exercising our freedom it may be that we will offend one unto death. If love be the rule of our Christian lives, our brother and his prejudices, weaknesses and former customs, and all to which we had been hitherto subjected in the blindness of unbelief, must be the touchstone of our choices, not our own desires, else we walk in selfishness and the whole truth of the gospel is defeated. While our strong faith enables us to do all things gladly, yet our brother's conscience about these matters must govern our eating or drinking or whatever it might be. "All things indeed are pure; but it is evil for that man who eateth with offense."

As one strong in the faith and living under the principles of grace with perfect freedom, there is still another care which must be exercised by the Christian. The purpose of this precaution is that the Christian hurt not his own spiritual life. Paul says, "Hast thou faith? Have it to thyself before God." Happy are you if you can do all of these things and not condemn yourself by the freedom which you permit yourself. If your faith is so strong that you can do all these things and still are certain of salvation, you may rejoice. Of course, there are limits to that, as James says, "Show me your faith without works, and I will show you my faith by my works." There is a limit to what a man can do and still be a Christian, for faith must translate itself into action. But happier will you be if, when you can do these things, you will refrain from doing them for the sake of the weak brother. There are some who, thinking that they have this liberty, launch out into certain doubtful practices and then they are led into sin because they have doubted. He that doubteth is condemned if he continues in that about which he is in doubt. "For whatsoever is not of faith is sin." There is no broader definition of sin in the Bible. From this broad and marvelous principle of faith, grew the error of antinomianism, that is, the practice of unethical things. Rasputin, the holy devil of Russia, believed that he was saved, but practiced all manner of sin because

PRINCIPLES OF CHRISTIAN CONDUCT

he believed where sin abounds grace does much more abound. Such false Christianity and violation of the laws of faith and grace will end in death. Happy therefore, is the man who knows that he can do all these things, but restrains his right to do them for the sake of the weaker brother to whom they would be an offense and for the sake of his own assurance and security. One has said, "Perhaps you and I have had the fortune to see some deep, quiet saint walking softly but with the light of heaven in his eyes. This is it, it is an inner walk with God which Satan cannot see or accuse before God. If this walk, in view of all God's mercies and of the blood of Christ giving our conscience liberty, be maintained, the believer will be happy in the things he approveth, or which he doeth."

III. Follow Christ.

Add to these negative principles the words—Follow Christ, and we have the true way of living for the Christian. Jesus said, "I am the way, the truth, and the life." If we can take the principles of the life of Jesus and apply them in each situation, if we can measure and judge our actions by Him and by what He would do, we have the perfect principles of action. Paul mentions three of these, and they are quite complete. They show how conversant Paul was with the life of Jesus.

First, "we that are strong ought to bear the infirmities of the weak." These infirmities are burdens on the conscience, prejudices of the mind, wrong personal habits, or incomplete views of the truth. Jesus did not bear with the infirmities of man. He carried those infirmities. He lived with the poor, He ate with the publicans, He fellowshipped with harlots and sinners, and He admitted them into the group of His followers. Sometimes we are willing to bear with people, to permit them to be around, but we are not willing to bear their burdens.

Second, we are "not to please ourselves . . . for even Christ pleased not Himself." Jesus came to do the will of Him that sent Him. Jesus of Nazareth never sought pleasure, ease, power, or comfort. He went about doing good. He was sent to preach the gospel to the poor, to heal the broken-hearted, to preach deliverance to the captives, in short to do the will of God. And He did it. He did not please Himself. It is not our duty to please our neighbors in matters of sin, for we must always be witnesses of what Christ has done. But we will do well to please them in all the things of edification.

Third, Paul says, "Receive ye one another, as Christ also received us to the glory of God." Often, we would like to exclude men who do not act as we would like to have them act, or who do not think as we would like to have them think. But what right have we to be exclusive? Who knows what will happen to these weak brethren in the atmosphere of Christian love? Rather should we love one another. The weak brother may be the hardest of all humans to get along with. He may be full of fear, of prejudice, of ignorance, and of the spirit of quibbling. God says, "receive him unto you, not to doubtful disputations." Try to help him where he is wrong, but bear his infirmities, love him, and in the environment of warming, beautifying love, he will change and grow as he never would under certain corrections.

But why should we receive such weak brethren, such hangers on, such impediments to the progress of the church? We should receive them that we might learn to be of like mind with Christ, that we might discipline ourselves and more and more grow in His image. We should receive them that we may glorify the Father in revealing His perfect love. And we should receive them that they too might see our good works and glorify the Father who is in heaven.

The Scripture instructs us then that weak and strong must grow together in one church, that the strong should not despise the weak, and the weak should not judge the strong. Thus, by judging not, by offending not, and by following Christ, we find the instruction necessary for daily conduct. Then the God of hope will fill us with all joy and peace in believing, that we may abound in hope through the power of the Holy Ghost.

XXI
JOY AND PEACE IN BELIEVING

TEXT: *"Now the God of hope fill you with all joy and peace in believing, that ye abound in hope, through the power of the Holy Ghost."*—ROM. 15:8-13.

JOY, peace, faith, hope and power through the Triune God are all proclaimed in this text. What a precious verse of Scripture. How teeming with truth and consolation! Here is a treasure to lay up in your memory, for life and for eternity.

There was a man in whom joy and peace were incarnate. He lived in the late twelfth and early thirteenth century. Europe in his day was struggling under the burden of incessant war. Russia had been engaged for three centuries in a long struggle against the savage hordes of the Mongols and Tartars which intermittently swept across her borders and ravaged her cities and plains. Constantinople, the capital of the Byzantine Empire, was staggering under the repeated blows from Turks, Arabs and Bulgarians. Spain had been invaded by the Moors across the narrow strait from Africa and the Moslems swept over the sunny plains to maintain a tyranny for centuries. England under Henry II was torn by unrest and civil war. Italy underwent the worst vicissitudes of fortune, for it was the center of the greatest wealth and culture and thus the object of attack by barbarian Normans, Huns, Wends and Czechs who poured in successive waves over the plains of Europe, pillaged its cities and devastated its civilization. Appalling ruin was found everywhere in Europe. Only two centers of security emerged in Europe, one was the feudal castle as the center of brigands and the other the city perched on some height or surrounded by walls for mutual defense. The deterioration which marked the desolate hamlets and villages of Europe also touched the church. The leaders were corrupt, licentious, vicious, while the people were as sheep without a shepherd, living in fear of the clergy and of the feudal nobility. They were sunk in superstition and were ignorant of even the rudiments of the Gosepl. Christ to them was a mysterious figure bound on the Cross, looking down on them from an awful height with eyes that held little knowledge of their needs or sympathy with their sorrows. He needed to be approached by a mediator.

Into an Italian city, overlooking the lovely vale of Umbria with its vines and olives, was born to the family of a prosperous merchant a promising boy. Biographers describe his youth as one of wild exploits in the leadership of his companions, marked by lordly manners and irrepressible gaiety. His father delighted in the expenditures of the boy when they led him to a prominence with the other young men of his class, but one day the excesses of pleasure snatched from him his health and he hovered between life and death. On his recovery his friends enticed him to return to the old life but he could not rid himself of the oppression and restlessness of spirit which clung to him. He began to take long and solitary walks in the country and found no joy in anything but wandering about the fields by himself. He spent hours in the wayside shrines, beseeching God with tears and supplications, to remove the darkness from his mind and the anguish from his heart. Then at last light came. At a wayside chapel dedicated to St. Damian he was kneeling one day in a profound agony of heart crying, "Great and glorious God and thou Lord Jesus, I pray ye shed abroad your light in the darkness of my heart." As he looked up he seemed to see the eyes of Christ fixed upon him in tender love. His spirit leaped to embrace the Saviour and from that hour his heart was transfixed by the love of Christ.

The first manifestation of his change was his resolve to repair the little shrines which had fallen to pieces. It began with that of St. Damian. Now his father opposed his expenditure and when the son continued spending his money upon the poor his wrath knew no bounds. Finally he disinherited him and appealed to the civil magistrates to have him punished. At that moment the son renounced his father, his possessions, his heritage, stripped himself of the clothes which he had received from his father, took an old coat which was given to him by a bishop's gardener and walked out to preach Christ. He became wedded to lady poverty. He continued his work of building shrines, began to preach in the open air and took the words of Christ literally as they guided his life. "As ye go preach, saying, the kingdom of heaven is at hand. Heal the sick, cleanse the lepers, raise the dead, cast out devils: freely ye have received, freely give. Provide neither gold, nor silver, nor brass in your purses, nor scrip for your journey, neither two coats, neither shoes, nor yet staves; for the workman is worthy of his meat." Soon a few disciples gathered about him who also renounced their wealth or gave it entirely to the poor. People were so amazed at the manifestation of love, sympathy and interest by these new mendicants that they listened in great multitudes, renounced their sins, made restitution to those they had wronged and turned to Jesus Christ.

The burden of the preaching of this young man was repentance toward God, faith in the Lord Jesus Christ, a righteous life, the inevitability of judgment and the love of God undergirding them all. Thousands soon took up the work which he was doing and patterned their life after him. The two things which marked every follower of the order were peace and joy. Wherever they went they sang, they laughed, they preached, they made known the love of God and the fervor swept over Europe. During the life of this young man there were no aberrations in the order. It clung to the vow of poverty, chastity and obedience. Instead of being depressed by voluntarily releasing this world's goods, they were filled with utmost joy and marvelous peace which has seldom been equaled in a movement in the history of the church.

This man had an influence which broke the fetters imposed upon the mind as well as those of the spirit. He was the first real precursor of the Renaissance and of the movement which culminated in the Reformation. He was Francis of Assisi, the one man who taught the world that by truly following Jesus Christ one exchanges earthly sources of wealth for an unaccountable new and secret source of Divine riches in peace and joy.

These two characteristics, peace and joy, are largely absent from life today even among believers. Some people grasp the fact of the atonement and then they stop there. We believe the atonement of Christ is a necessary truth and the basis of all Christian life. Concerning the great Manchurian Revival, John R. Mott said, "Those who philosophize sceptically regarding the reality and efficacy of the atonement will find little to support their views in the fact that the refrain epitomizing the central message of this revival was this: There is a fountain filled with blood." Other people accept the atonement and go on to a struggle for victory over sin and they center their life about this struggle, but few enter the state about which the apostle wrote in this text; when he said, "Now the God of hope fill you with all joy and peace in believing." All possible joy and peace may be ours but tragically too many of the things of this world interfere with our belief and remove our joy and peace.

In this text, we have a summary of the book of Romans. It is Paul's conclusion to all these words. This peace, joy and hope arises from our justification or our righteousness, the theme of the book. We must observe that the peace and joy are both objective and subjective. Objective peace and joy exists anterior to any subjective experience which we may feel of them. They are based on truth, on God's promise, on what Christ has done. This emanates from the sayings of the Scripture offering salvation on the Divine oath. They are the result of God's declaration that He has no pleasure in the death of the wicked, that our sins though they are as scarlet may be as white as snow. Ministers are the heralds of these glad tidings. They bring peace and joy.

Subjective peace and joy is not only that of a message of glad tidings, but it is the result of the honest forsaking of all sin and the obeying of God. Orthodox faith in the Cross of Christ may bring the intellectual conception of peace and joy but not the subjective experience of the peace that passeth all understanding and "the rejoicing in all things." For this experience the Cross must become a reality in our lives today. We must seriously believe that if we would be disciples of Jesus we must deny ourselves, take up our cross and follow Him. We must be able to say with Paul, "I live yet not I. Christ liveth in me," and "I am crucified with Christ." In this final summary Paul prays for, pleads for and promises such a life for the believer.

I. THE SOURCE OF JOY AND PEACE—THE GOD OF HOPE.

Our text begins with the words, "The God of hope." There are many other titles by which we know God in the Bible. The Old Testament speaks of Him as Jehovah or the existing One; as Jehovah-Jireh or the Lord will provide; as Jehovah-Nisi or the Lord is my banner; as Jehovah-Shalom or The Lord is my peace; as Jehovah-Tsidkenu or The Lord our righteousness. These are wonderful names for the Lord our God. The New Testament also has many names for God, three of which are mentioned in this very chapter. First, He is the God of patience because God is the author and the foundation of all patience which may come to us. Then He is also called the God of consolation, which comforts and consolations proceed from the Scriptures telling us about God. Lastly He is called the God of peace which is a fundamental conception, for our peace is wrought by the blood of His Cross. It is a good thing

JOY AND PEACE IN BELIEVING 221

as we read these names of God embracing His titles and attributes to fasten upon them in order that they may encourage our faith.

But there is no title given to God greater than the God of hope. Hope and God are interchangeable. In Ephesians we read, concerning the Gentiles who were aliens from the Commonwealth of Israel, "Having no hope, and without God in the world." With God we have hope both for the present and the future, but without God we have no hope. God Himself is the only foundation for hope and in Him all hope rests. He builds the hope in us. Peter said, "Blessed be the God and Father of our Lord Jesus Christ, which according to His abundant mercy hath begotten us again unto a lively hope by the resurrection of Jesus Christ from the dead." Unbelief makes for despair, for the future is only as certain as God and if we have no faith in God we can have no faith in the future. This fact suggests the reason for the hopelessness of our age. It is a Godless age. It is impossible, when evaluating the Europe of today, to forget the degenerate condition of the church in Russia before the revolution, which denied to people the knowledge of the Gospel, the rise of higher criticism and the destruction of the Bible in Germany, which removed people's faith in God, the practical indifference to Christianity in England, which emptied the churches, and the atheism in France. Perhaps Europe's condition may justly be attributed to her Godlessness of the last fifty years. Hope can only rise as it is fastened in God.

Since it is God who fills us with joy and peace in believing, God must come first. Unless God fills us with these attributes we will not be filled.

Paul here summarizes why God is hope to the Jew. He said, "Jesus Christ was a minister of the circumcision for the truth of God, to confirm the promises made to the fathers." Jesus Christ proved the truth of God to the Jew. He came as a minister of the circumcision to His own people, to the lost sheep of the house of Israel. He even commanded that His own disciples should not go to any but to Israel. Truly there were other purposes in Christ's coming. He came to reveal the Father. He came to give His life a ransom for many. He came to be a propitiation for the whole world, but primarily He came to fulfill the promises of God made to the Israelites. In reference to them this was the purpose of His coming. This was for the truth, that is to show that when God makes a promise He fulfills it. He promised a Messiah and He sent Him.

If the first group of promises which pertained to His coming in humiliation and suffering were fulfilled, so will another group of promises be which pertain to His second coming. This is my approach to the Jew. I ask him, "Do you believe the Old Testament?" So do I. "Do you believe the promises of a Messiah?" So do I. I show him that I expect his Messiah just as He does but that I believe more than that, namely, that his Old Testament Scriptures said that the Messiah must first suffer and then enter into His glory. I show him that if he does not first participate in the sufferings of Christ, he will not participate in His Glory. The coming of Jesus in fulfillment of the Old Testament prophecies and promises manifested the truth.

As the minister of the circumcision He perfectly fulfilled the law, lived without blemish and had a right to eternal life. Hence He could become the Saviour from the law. God is the God of hope for the Jew, because He sent Jesus Christ to confirm the promises made to the fathers.

To the Gentiles God is a God of hope for another reason. God deals with the Gentiles not on the basis of promise but in pure mercy. God made no promises to the Gentiles. The Gentiles are mentioned in the Old Testament promises and prophecies but not as a recipient of them. When, however, the Divine oaths to Israel were fulfilled and they had rejected the Messiah and killed him, mercy from God flowed out to the Gentiles. This truth is summarized in the last verse of the prophecy of Micah. He said, "Thou wilt perform the truth to Jacob, and the mercy of Abraham, which thou hast sworn unto our fathers from the days of old." Abraham was a Gentile called out of heathenism in the pure mercy of God, but after the promises were given to him and to Isaac and Jacob, then God was under obligation to fulfill his oath to these fathers.

This extension of mercy to the Gentiles was foreseen and prophesied in the Old Testament in the three great divisions—the Law, the Prophets and the Psalms, examples from each being quoted in this section calling upon the Gentiles to praise God for His mercy and to speak the rule of the Messiah over them. These prophecies are only partially fulfilled in our own age and they stretch on into the millennium, when a root of Jesse shall rise to reign over the nations, even Jesus Christ. The last clause in this series of prophecies says, "In Him will the Gentiles hope." With this hope of the Gentiles do all the Scriptures agree, namely, that he shall first visit the Gentiles to take out of them a people for His Name and after this, He will return and will build again the tabernacle of David that the residue of men might seek after the Lord, and all the Gentiles on whom His Name is called. Thus we recognize that the mercies to the Gentiles rest only in the Cross of the rejected Messiah by which He became a propitiation for the sins of all the world.

II. THE CONDITION OF JOY AND PEACE—IN BELIEVING.

Just as the God of hope is the source of our joy and peace, so believing is the condition of our joy and peace. A syllogism rests upon this text. Let me present it to you with the evidence.

The major premise is "Believing is righteousness." The Scripture says, "Abraham believed God and it was counted unto him for righteousness." God's righteousness is imputed to a man when he believes. Romans has made this plain. The minor premise is: "Righteousness produces peace and joy." The Scripture says, "Being justified by faith we have peace with God through our Lord Jesus Christ . . . and rejoice in hope of the glory of God." Justification is the source of this peace and joy. Believing God, therefore, produces righteousness, for God justified us out of faith. The conclusion then follows from those two statements, which is: "Believing produces peace and joy." But let us remember that the kingdom of God is "righteousness, joy and peace in the Holy Ghost." If therefore believing produces righteousness, peace and joy, believing brings you into the kingdom of God. This is the essence of the Gospel.

But what are we to believe? That has been declared in the Book of Romans. We do not have to assume it. We must believe what God has said: concerning ourselves, that we are lost; concerning sin, that it exiles and excludes one from God; concerning Christ, that He is the Son of God; concerning the Cross, that it was the satisfaction of the broken law; and concerning life, that it is the gift of God to all who believe and trust in Christ. Central to all this is the declaration of Rom. 3:25 that we are "justified freely by His grace through the redemption that is in Christ Jesus: whom God hath set forth to be a propitiation through faith in His blood, to declare His righteousness for the remission of sins." In believing this, we are justified in the presense of a just and righteous God, thus are accepted in Christ, are children of the kingdom and know on the authority of God's Word, objectively, that we have joy and peace.

All this is confirmed by Christ's own teaching in the Gospel. It is also confirmed in the Lord's Supper. He took the bread and blessed it, saying, "This is my body." And He took the cup, saying, "This is my blood of the new testament, which is shed for many for the remission of sins." This exactly confirms Paul's teaching in Romans concerning the death of Christ and the words of the institution of the Lord's Supper as given to us by Paul. If the individual ministers repudiate that teaching today they do it in the face of the continuous teaching of the Christian Church from the time of the Lord Jesus until the present.

III. THE RESULT OF JOY AND PEACE IN BELIEVING—HOPE.

We began with a God of hope. We showed the reason for hope through the death of Christ and now we return to the experience of hope in the Holy Ghost which becomes a subjective experience. Paul said, "That ye may abound in hope, through the power of the Holy Ghost." This is the result of our believing.

The hope of the Christian has its experiential foundation in the power of the indwelling Holy Spirit. The Holy Spirit is the gift of God to the justified believer. Let me quote what Paul said, "Being justified by faith, we have peace with God through our Lord Jesus Christ: by whom also we have access by faith into this grace wherein we stand, and rejoice in the hope of the glory of God. And not only so, but we glory in tribulations also: knowing that tribulation worketh patience; and patience, experience; and experience hope: and hope maketh not ashamed; because the love of God is shed abroad in our hearts by the Holy Ghost which is given unto us." Those words present in inspired language the connection of these blessings about which we are preaching. Remembering then that the kingdom of God is righteousness, joy and peace in the Holy Ghost, we make the connection between our believing, our righteousness, our joy, our peace and our hope, which results from the Holy Spirit which is given to us. Loving and trusting the God of hope we in turn have hope abounding in us.

This Christian hope concerns first our present salvation. We may take knowledge of ourselves that having peace and joy and righteousness through believing, we thus also have a very real hope of our present salvation, for these are the witness thereof. Moreover this hope concerns our future life in glory. When Paul spoke about the redemption of our body at the return of our Lord Jesus Christ, he said: "We are saved by hope: but hope that is seen is not hope: for what a man seeth, why doth he yet hope for? but if we hope for that which we see not, then do we with patience wait for it." It is the hope for the transformation of our body, for the coming of the Lord, for heaven and for glory that we patiently wait. Third, our hope is for the consummation of our present union with Him when, as He promised, in the ages to come he might show the exceeding riches of His grace in His kindness toward us in Jesus Christ.

Hope makes us unashamed. He who is filled and abounds in hope will be unashamed in present tribulation, whether it is disease or poverty or other misfortune, for he knows that the Cross of Christ does not fail. We are unashamed of the Gospel of Christ for it is the power of God unto salvation. We know that we are now the sons of God and we have a real hope that some day we shall be like Him for we shall see Him as He is.

Here we reach the mountain top. This is the "Everest" of redeemed souls. Here nothing can separate us from God and nothing can be laid to our charge and there is no condemnation to our hearts. With this truth we are able to share His passion both figuratively and practically. Let us therefore come, eat and drink the life of the Son of God, in joy and peace and hope.

XXII
THE FULLNESS OF THE BLESSING OF THE GOSPEL OF CHRIST

TEXT: *"I am sure that, when I come unto you, I shall come in the fulness of the blessing of the gospel of Christ."*—ROM. 15:14-33.

CERTAIN Biblical phrases we can never forget, such as "justification by faith," "the riches of grace," "the fruit of the Spirit," "the prayer of faith," and others, but none is more impressive than the phrase "the fulness of the blessing." Often when I have been thinking of accepting an invitation to conduct a series of services, the thought of this text, "I shall come in the fulness of the blessing" rings in my ears. How can we be sure, like Paul was, that we are in the fulness of the Divine blessing and that, when we come unto others, the fulness of the blessing will come unto them through us.

Are you living in the fulness of the blessing of the Gospel of Christ? Ask yourself this important question and I will ask myself the same question. Remember we are not asking "Have I enjoyed the fulness of the blessing?" but we are asking, "Do I enjoy the fulness of the blessing today?" There may come to your mind at at this moment a sharp word you have spoken, an evil thought which passed through your mind, a questionable deed which reproaches your conscience, but let us withhold the answer to the question until we have concluded this precious study taken from the life of Paul. Then I warrant that the answer to the question will do something to us. It will either bring disquietude or great assurance and joy.

We are not talking about a second blessing or about any one blessing which may come in the individual's life. We are at present considering a condition of life available for all believers which is constant and stedfast and present. It is possible to emphasize one experience in our Christian life so as to exclude further Divine undertaking. The specimen of Christian who harkens back in his experience to an event of many years ago but whose present life is barren is quite common in every church. We place a high value in our teaching on certain crisis experiences through which the believer

BLESSING OF THE GOSPEL OF CHRIST

passes, such as his conversion in response to which God gives him the gift of the Holy Ghost, and such as his complete surrender unto God whereby God fills him with the Holy Spirit, but we are also careful to present the great need in the individual life for this constant quality of having the fullness of the blessing. Sometimes our emphasis upon crisis experience may tend to take our attention away from what should be the constant quality of experience. That would be very unfortunate.

This fullness of the blessing is wonderfully illustrated in the rich missionary experience of the Apostle Paul. He could say, "I am sure that, when I come unto you, I shall come in the fulness of the blessing." The words, "I am sure," actually are, "I know." This was one of the matters about which Paul could be certain. On many things he could not be certain. He did not know whether he would come in health or in illness, in bonds or in freedom, with a keen mind or a deteriorated mind, but he did know that as far as his relationship with God was concerned he would come in the fullness of the blessing. What a glorious certainty that is! Paul's past experience of fruitfulness in preaching, of signs and wonders by the Holy Spirit, and of special dispensations of the favor of God was such that it warranted this boldest of all assertions. Now think of what he said. He did not know when he was coming, or whether his coming might be delayed for years, and yet he said, "I know I shall come in the fulness of the Gospel." One emerging from some special season of blessing under the Lord might write about his coming next week with a degree of certainty and boldness, but how can one write in such a tenor concerning the years which are yet in the future? We must look at this text as a whole and at its setting in the Scripture in order to grasp the meaning of this particular phrase "the fulness of the blessing." It is set in an epilogue which is comparable in subject matter with the prologue or the introduction to the Epistle. Both of them speak of Paul's purpose in coming to Rome, of Paul's confidence in his ministry at Rome and of Paul's condition in which he should come to Rome.

I. Paul's Purposed Coming.

The text emphasizes, "When I come to you" as the protasis, the apodosis being "I shall come in the fulness of the blessing." This coming was indefinite with Paul, but it was a long cherished aim. He said, "Having a great desire these many years to come unto you." In the introduction he expressed it, "Without ceasing I make mention of you always in my prayers: making request if by any means I might have a prosperous journey by the will of God to come unto you." It was natural that this Apostle should desire to participate in the life of this much famous church. One notices in church experience that whenever a longing to go to a particular field comes to an individual, resulting in his praying much over it, it usually eventuates in his reaching that field. We have numerous young men in this congregation studying for the ministry. We have other young people studying to be missionaries. But there are two young men in this congregation whose interest in things, which would ordinarily mark the life of a minister of the Gospel, is so keen that for a long time I have believed that they are called to the ministry without their knowing it as yet. At the last prayer meeting one of these young men came to me and said, "I am not certain yet, but I think that God is calling me to the ministry. I would like to have an appointment to talk the matter over with you." Thus it was with Paul. He had longed to see these Roman Christians whose graces had been heralded throughout the Roman world in order that he might also have some spiritual fruit among them and now eventually this was to come to pass.

He described them as "full of goodness, filled with all knowledge, able to admonish one another." What then could Paul add to such an high experience? As the Apostle to the Gentiles, which the majority of the Roman Christians were, it was his office to preach the magnificent truths which we have reviewed from this great book of the Romans, in order to establish them in grace. No church should ever think that it is so established and so sound and so orthodox that other men of God can not minister unto it. The response of the Romans to Paul revealed that this outstanding church was willing to accept and profit by his instructions.

Nevertheless, Paul said, "I have been much hindered from coming to you." Though for years his aim had been to go to Rome something had prevented him. To the Thessalonians he wrote that Satan hindered him from coming on several occasions. That opposition came in the form of physical danger at the hands of those who attempted to frustrate his work. So Satan also in many ways will hinder us from fulfilling our plans which are in accordance with God's will. In this case Paul's multitudinous labors hindered him. It was his desire to thoroughly preach the Gospel from Jerusalem to Illyrium before he went to Rome. How comforting it is to read that even the inspired Apostle Paul could not do everything. Multi-

BLESSING OF THE GOSPEL OF CHRIST

tudinous labors are sometimes sufficient to hinder us from fulfilling high and holy purposes. There is a truth which should be noted here, namely, that Satan not only hinders the church and individual members thereof in their work, but the church also hinders Satan. Paul told the Thessalonians, "The mystery of iniquity doth already work; only he who now hindereth will hinder, until he be taken out of the way; and then shall that wicked be revealed, whom the Lord shall consume with the spirit of His mouth, and shall destroy with the brightness of His coming." The hindering force in the world till the culmination of the mystery of iniquity is the Holy Spirit in the church. In this mighty conflict, our prayer and preaching efforts are hindering Satan, though he may put obstacles in our path also.

Note that this man of God laid plans for the future in the will of God. Paul said that when he had concluded his present great objective of taking the collection, which he was gathering from Macedonia and Greece, to Jerusalem, he intended to come to Rome and then to Spain. Paul was planning for weeks and months and years ahead. When I read these plans of the Apostle, I am ashamed of the paltriness of our own vision which often embraces only days and weeks and months at the most. Here was a man whose vision embraced those who had never heard the Gospel. He was determined to preach not where Christ was known, lest he should build upon another man's foundation. No higher, grander or more Christlike emotion and motive could ever fill and guide a man's life. Even his visit to Rome was to be only for a short season. He intended to be "somewhat filled" with their company, to in a measure assist them, but he contemplated no long visit. He said, "I trust to see you in my journey, and to be brought on my way thitherward by you." Undoubtedly, Paul hoped for their prayer, for perhaps the gift of a travel companion to journey with him and even for the presentation of some support for his work. Here you see was the foundation of this practice of helping missionaries along their way in the great work of preaching to the regions beyond.

The going to Rome and Spain was a part of Paul's Apostolic commission. The grace of God which was given to him was that he should be a minister of Jesus Christ to the Gentiles, that the Gentiles themselves might be acceptable to God. Before this time God had shown in the case of Cornelius that "in every nation he who feareth him, and worketh righteousness, is accepted with him," and may be saved by believing on the Lord Jesus Christ. It was this truth which Paul exemplified in his constant preaching to the Gentiles. He reiterated and offered again and again the free salvation of God to the heathen in this acceptable time, this day of salvation, which this same book makes clear will not continue forever. Freely by the work of the Holy Spirit the heathen may be brought into the family of God, the kingdom of our Lord and Saviour Jesus Christ.

This was the passion of Paul's life. He was not disobedient to the heavenly vision. He was carrying the good news to men, he was not asking men to come to him to receive the news. We in the churches have reversed the processes today. Jesus said, "Go unto all men everywhere and teach them." He instructed His disciples that they were to go into the highways and the hedges to reach the people and bring them in but we in the churches chide the people because they will not come to us. One of the reasons God permits persecution to come to His church is that the members may be scattered abroad and go everyhere preaching the Word.

There is an importance to the words of Paul, "Now having no more place in these parts." Paul did not mean that everybody from Jerusalem to the Adriatic sea was converted nor did he mean that all of the converts were established and perfected in the faith, but he meant that there was no longer any place in all these parts where the Gospel had not been heard and the urge was upon him of reaching the unevangelized regions of the world. Bishop William Taylor closely resembled Paul in this attitude. He went throughout the five continents of the world carrying the Gospel where others had never gone. Not every one can have this urge but what a magnificent thing it is. Our churches are feeding and re-feeding the same people over and over again until they get tired of the staple word of God and want some of the dainties which ministers are expected to provide, yet there are hundreds of millions of people who have never heard our Gospel.

Paul's purpose was also Divinely appointed. The words which he used, "When I take my journey" are the same words which were applied to Christ in pursuing His path to Calvary. We read, "He set His face to proceed to Jerusalem." He said, "I must proceed today and tomorrow" and "The Son of Man proceedeth as it was written of Him." All these represent a Divinely appointed course for an individual to follow. This great appointment to go to Spain had not been fulfilled at the time of Paul's first imprisonment, but at the time of Paul's second imprisonment he was able to say, "I have finished my course." Somewhere between those two periods of writing Paul had done what is not recorded for us in the Bible. He had gone to the regions beyond, in fulfillment of the course which the Father had appointed Him and had placed on his heart.

II. PAUL'S PLENARY CONFIDENCE.

In this text Paul says, "I am sure" or "I know." He also said, "When I have performed this . . . I will come by you into Spain." Determination is expressed here. What is the basis of this confidence of Paul, that he knows he is coming in the fullness of the Spirit? It appears that the basis is what God has already wrought through him. He said, "I will not dare to speak of any of those things which Christ hath not wrought by me to make the Gentiles obedient by word and deed." What had Christ wrought? Think for a moment of those great missionary journeys from Jerusalem to Illyricum. Illyricum was identical with present day Albania and Jugo-Slavia. Beginning then at Jerusalem, Paul had preached in Syria, and in its capital Damascus, in the great city of Antioch, through Cilicia with its great center Tarsus, through Pamphylia and Psidia and Galatia and Macedon, with the great cities thereof, and even into Corinth of Greece and then finally up the coast of the Adriatic. Undoubtedly in all these places, like in Ephesus, it might be said, "All they of the region round about heard the Word of the Lord." Besides all these tireless labors of love Paul was enabled by God to establish churches and to gather the saved out of these multitudes into permanent organizations and a Christian community. Then in connection with these journeys, wonders of grace and redemption had been performed. Paul had suffered terribly, but in response for his sufferings God had given him marvelous fruit. Think of the jailer at Philippi, the noble Christians at Berea, the little band led by Damaris at Athens, the many people of God in Corinth, Philemon at Colossae, Timothy at Lystra, and so we might go on.

Since God had blessed Paul in all these other places, Paul had a right to expect him to bless him in Rome too. For this reason churches vie with one another to invite Divinely used men to minister to them. They base their invitation on the same principle that Paul based his confidence, the message and the ministry of such individuals is tried and proven so that we have a right to expect such results. This is simply a manifestation of the physical law that a body in motion will stay in motion and that a body at rest will remain at rest unless interfered with by some outside force.

Moreover, this rightful confidence of Paul was ultimately fulfilled when he arrived as a prisoner in Rome and sojourned there for two years, preaching the Gospel to all who came and receiving much fruit. Not the least of these converts made by Paul in Rome were Onesimus the slave of Philemon and the saints in Caesar's household of which he speaks in his epistles. Paul was still suffering when he reached Rome from the hindrances of the devil but his epistles and his work are mighty testimonies of the fullness of the blessing.

This confidence of Paul that he was coming in the fullness of the blessing was attested by the power of the Holy Spirit. Paul attributed his previous work to the Holy Spirit and he knew that as long as the Spirit of God had control of life he would have the fullness of the blessing. We submit for your consideration that the Holy Spirit was the one means of confidence in the ministry and life of Jesus, of Peter, of Paul or of any other New Testament character. Each of these characters came into the fullness of the blessing of the power of God through an experience connected with the Holy Spirit. Jesus' miraculous and wonderful ministry began with the baptism of the Holy Ghost at the Jordan River. Peter's ministry of power began with the baptism of the Holy Ghost at Pentecost. Paul's ministry of power began with the filling of the Holy Spirit resulting from the laying on of the hands of Ananias. We reemphasize the fact that if this was so in these mighty men, then we must have the Divine helper, or Paraclete, or Advocate, or Comforter, which is the Holy Spirit, as the resource of our power and life to continue this work of God in the fullness of the blessing today. Our message may be the same as the message of Paul but it must be given in the power of the Spirit and the fullness of the blessing, or it will be arid and dead orthodoxy.

Another evidence of the fullness of the blessing in Paul's life was what God had done through him for the Jerusalem saints. He was now leaving Corinth in the company of a delegation from the churches in Macedonia and Achaia to carry a contribution from the missionary churches to the mother church. What a contrast this is to the customary method of church finance. Here were churches so established in the beginning that they first gave themselves unto the Lord and then they manifested their wonderful love for the mother church and for other Christians by intreating Paul to accept a bountiful and liberal gift made from their own poverty. The cause lay in the fact that Paul had taught them that they were debtors to the Jews at Jerusalem for the spiritual things which they had received therefrom. The gifts which Paul brought were a seal of the fruit which God gave to him in the mission field. They were a witness that these Gentiles were truly converted. Such are our good deeds in the eyes of the world.

III. PAUL'S PROPHECIED CONDITION.

Now we come to this phrase itself, "The fulness of the blessing." This describes the state of the spiritual life lower than which Paul would not permit himself to fall. Nothing else mattered to Paul but that he was in the fullness of the blessing. Paul would not do anything or go anywhere unless he knew that it did not hinder the fullness of the blessing. Here is a great argument which will answer the accusation that when Paul went to Jerusalem, being warned in so many places by the Holy Spirit that bonds and afflictions awaited him, he was disobeying the Spirit of God. Though some prominent Bible teachers affirm this, we declare that Paul was walking his Divinely appointed course, even as Jesus was when he went to Calvary, warned of what was in store for Him. We may be sure from this text, that in all the difficult situations from the riots in Jerusalem to the trials before the Sanhedrin, before Felix, before Festus, before Agrippa, and even on the shipwreck journey to Rome, Paul was walking with God, and, though Satan was hindering, he was to stand before Caesar to testify of the Gospel of God. When Paul wrote this letter he was already being warned by the Spirit that bonds and affliction awaited him in Jerusalem. He did not know how he was going to get to Rome, he did not know when he was going to get to Rome, but all this was not incompatible with the fullness of the blessing. Some of you listening to me are lying on beds of affliction with arthritis or cancer or other terrible diseases. Some of you are smitten by disasters in the economic realm. Some of you are abandoned by loved ones, but all this is not incompatible with the fullness of the blessing in your heart.

What is the meaning of this phrase, the fullness of the blessing? It is the highest blessing which the Gospel of Christ can give. Let us analyze that. First, it includes the knowledge of salvation from sin through the blood of the Cross of Calvary. You can say, "I know my sins are taken away." Second, it includes identification with Christ in a new life. You can say, "I know I am in Christ and Christ is in me." You may even say, "The life which I now live, I live by faith in the son of God." Third, it includes the baptism and the filling of the Holy Spirit. You may say, "I know that I have the witness of the Spirit in my heart for the Spirit beareth witness with my spirit that I am a child of God." Fourth, it means victory over your besetting sin and your temptation in all walks of life. You can say "I know that there is no temptation which will beset me beyond what I am able to bear." Finally, it includes Divine guidance as to the activities of your life in every detail. Now is it any wonder that this fullness of the blessing fills one with joy and peace and faith and hope and power through the Holy Spirit, as our text of last week declared? However, the possession of the fullness of the blessing means that what is available is actually experienced by me. Satisfaction with anything less than the fullness of the blessing is the height of folly, for joy and peace in believing is the will of God for you.

We are thus brought to the consideration of the privilege of the Christian in this matter. If Paul could say, "I am sure or I know" when speaking of next week and next month and next year or the next decade, whether he is exalted or whether he is abased, so should we. This certainty comes from the indwelling Holy Spirit. You or I know whether we have grieved him or not. From past experience Paul knew that he would prefer death to grieving the Holy Spirit and not having the fullness of the blessing. He who has known the fullness of the blessing can not bear a life whence the Spirit of God has departed. His grief would be like that of Samson who having been a mighty man of God was chained to the grist mill of the Philistines when the Spirit of God left him. Paul's constant experience of the fullness of the blessing was dependent on his perfect consecration, his obedience to God. Hence he wrote to us, "I beseech you therefore brethren by the mercies of God that ye present your bodies a living sacrifice, holy, acceptable unto God which is your reasonable service." This book has told us to present ourselves as alive from the dead, being living instruments of righteousness, to present ourselves as living martyrs to prove what is the good and perfect and acceptable will of God, and to present ourselves before the world as incarnating the teachings of the Sermon on the Mount.

By his final word, Paul conditions the fullness of the blessing partly on his own prayers and partly on the prayers of the church at Rome. He said, "I beseech you, brethren, that ye strive together with me in your prayers that I may be delivered . . . and that I may come unto you." Prayer changes things. There were many things awaiting Paul which needed change, if his Divinely guided journey was to succeed. There was the hatred of the Jews. There was the prejudice of the Jewish Christians. There was the corruption of the Roman governor willing to sacrifice him for a political favor. There was the storm at sea and there was the viper that fastened on Paul's hand. Prayer is the Divinely appointed means to bring victory over such obstacles and to accomplish the Divine will. We know that Paul prayed and certainly the church at Rome must have prayed diligently that this purpose should be fulfilled. If a church would have its minister and its members in the fullness of the blessing, then it must strive together with them in prayer that the will of God be done. How strange it is that God's work in the world depends on the prayers of the saints! Yet it is true. Hence I beseech you for the Lord Jesus Christ's sake and for the love of the Spirit that ye pray that we may all be in the fullness of the blessing.

God grant that we shall be able to say, "If I visit, or if I stay at home, if I preach or if I am silent, if I work or if I am idle, if I am well or if I am ill, if I am rich or if I am poor, I am determined to be, and I know that I shall be, in the fullness of the blessing of the Gospel of Christ." This may not bring momentous results to the world, but it will be all that God asks of you and of me.

XXIII
THE RECOGNITION OF THE CHRISTIAN MINISTRY OF WOMEN

TEXT: *"I commend unto you Phebe our sister which is a servant of the church which is at Cenchrea."*—ROM. 16:1-16.

THESE words introduce a wonderful chapter in Scripture which is often passed over with little attention because of the prevalence of unfamiliar names. It is a chapter filled with human relationships demonstrating the harmony of the Christian graces with the ordinary intercourse that takes place in general society.

Here we behold Paul's personal friendship with individual Christians and his continued remembrance of them. What a memory he must have had to have called all these individuals by name when he had never been to Rome and possibly had not seen many of them for years. The place of human love as well as Divine love in existing relationships is here demonstrated. In the eighth verse Paul speaks of "Amplias, my beloved in the Lord." This is somewhat of a contrast with the salutation in the preceding verse which seems to be based more on the human relationship rather than the Christian relationship. Thus Paul could write to Philemon that Onesimus was beloved to him "both in the flesh and in the Lord." It is perfectly possible to love some men in a natural way as well as in a spiritual way. We recognize love of the brethren as a mark of Christian experience. We love these Christians because they are Christians, but we love some men for themselves. It is highly pleasing to read this distinction in Paul because it is so much like our own human experience. On the basis of Divine love we may have a percentage of human fellowship, but if we have agreement in both spiritual and natural things we shall have a higher degree of fellowship.

Another interesting reference in this chapter is Paul's claim of the mother of Rufus as his own. Rufus is quite generally identified with the brother of Alexander and the son of Simon who carried the cross of the Lord Jesus Christ. Some have thought that Simon, being a Cyrenian, was a black man. We would doubt this from the general teaching of the Scripture. Here Paul claims a relationship to the

RECOGNITION OF THE MINISTRY OF WOMEN

wife of Simon and the mother of Rufus which delicately and beautifully tells of the love which he bore to her. He had adopted her as a foster-mother and she had adopted him as a foster-son. This gives us an insight into the human affections of Paul as a lovable man, which is a bit unusual. In many ways Paul resembles each one of us who has at one time or another been befriended by some Godly woman who became to us a foster-mother.

We are also given information here concerning interesting and important individuals in the early church. One is Hermas. We have in Christian literature the epistle of Hermas, concerning his visions, concerning his commands and concerning his similitudes. These were written at a very early time and were identified by such fathers as Irenaeus, Origen, Tertullian, Eusebius and Jerome, with the writings of Hermas, known as the Shepherd. In his vision Hermas refers to Clement who was the first bishop of Rome and also to Jerusalem, which references would reveal that the book was written within fifteen years after Paul's epistle to the Romans. By many of the fathers the writings of Hermas were put on a level with the Scriptures. Irenaeus quotes them under the very name of Scripture. Origen said they were Divinely inspired. And they were even included in some of the ancient manuscripts of the New Testament, the position given to them being next to the book of Hebrews. The epistle was openly read in the churches. However, by others of the fathers they were considered useful but not a part of the canon of the Scriptures. The contents are not heretical and are certainly useful for instruction concerning the way of piety and cover most of the practical aspects of the human life. Undoubtedly the Hermas whom Paul greeted in this chapter was the author of this early Christian writing.

We also learn here that Paul had certain kinsmen in Rome named Andronicus and Junia and Herodion. Whether these were blood kinsmen or not we shall not speculate. It seems that it would have been improbable for Paul to single out three of the Israelites and call them, "my kinsmen," unless they were blood relations to him.

Yet another interesting item is the distinction Paul seems to make in the households to which he was writing. He speaks to the entire household of Aristobulus as if all members were Christians. He addresses in the household of Narcissus only those which are "in the Lord." Undoubtedly, Paul was writing to the Christians a letter to be read in the churches and he was aware of the divisions which existed in these human families, some becoming Christians and some rejecting Christianity. This also reveals that at this time most of the churches or assemblies were meeting in dwelling houses.

The outstanding thing however about this list of persons is that more than a third of the names given are of women. At least nine or ten had gained prominence in the church work, so that they were known by Paul. We note immediatealy that Paul credits them with ministering, with laboring, with helping and with succoring, which ought to suggest to us something of the work which women can do in the churches. These words are hints to us of the place of women in the Christian Church. Paul very honorably gives them full recognition for their indispensable services. Such recognition should be given to them now. One of the greatest women and the most helpful to Paul in his missionary labors was Priscilla the wife of Aquilla. Paul first met this couple at Corinth, whence they had come at the time of the expulsion of the Jews from Rome under Claudius. He lived with them for a year and a half at Corinth and laid the foundations for the Corinthian Church while remaining in their home. Later Paul lived with them at Ephesus and there again they ministered to his needs and there they risked their lives for his sake. Now this couple was back in Rome and Paul dispatched his tender affection to them and to the church which was meeting in their house in Rome. Since the occasion for the writing of this letter was the recommendation of Phebe to the church at Rome, which opportunity Paul seized to present his systematic teachings concerning the Gospel, we are directly indebted to Phebe for this greatest of all epistles. She becomes to us the illustration of the Christian ministry of women.

I. THE PLACE OF WOMEN IN PAUL'S EPISTLES.

We have been much grieved at times to listen to foolish teaching concerning Paul's attitude toward woman. Light, cheap and irresponsible talk accuses Paul of speaking derogatorily of women. Such teaching ought to be forever repudiated by the responsible church. Sometime ago, at a meeting of directors of a certain school, a wealthy individual, who was also a member of the Board, flippantly declared that he would withdraw all support from the school unless women were excluded from its classes and ceased to be trained for Christian service. I felt called upon to withstand him to the face and challenge him to defend his position from the Scripture which he never took the opportunity to do.

This irresponsible attitude is based upon certain sayings of Paul given in particular instances. It is true that Paul wrote to Timothy

RECOGNITION OF THE MINISTRY OF WOMEN 239

saying, "Let the woman learn in silence with all subjection. But I suffer not a woman to teach, nor to usurp authority over the man, but to be in silence." This undoubtedly was given to Timothy as a general rule to be observed by him in reference to women in the Asiatic churches. Moreover, in the first Epistle to the Corinthians, Paul says, "Let your women keep silence in the churches: for it is not permitted unto them to speak; but they are commanded to be under obedience as also saith the law. And if they will learn anything, let them ask their husbands at home: for it is a shame for women to speak in the church." The Bible also generally takes this position concerning women as teachers. When Jesus wished to describe the corrupting influence within the church he said that it was like unto leaven, which a woman took and hid in three measures of meal till the whole was leavened. Meal is made of wheat and wheat in the parables of Jesus represented the good seed of God, the children of the kingdom. Leaven represented corruption and the woman who put the leaven into the church represents apostate teachers, corrupting the church. Whenever a woman is represented in the Bible in the place of teaching, whether it is in Zechariah, the Gospels, the Epistles of Paul, or in Revelation, she takes a forbidden position. Christ even rebuked the church of Thyatira for permitting a woman, who is likened unto Jezebel and who called herself a prophetess, to teach and to seduce his servants.

With this recognition, that a woman's place according to the Bible is forbidden in the authoritative or ordained capacity of teacher in the church, we immediately perceive that Paul was merely teaching in harmony with the entire Bible. This teaching of Paul did not, however, refer to other spheres of intensely important activity on the part of women in the church, which spheres of service we shall refer to in due time. Moreover, we must remember that at least in Corinth there was a serious corruption of heathen society in which women were active for evil and which the church had to guard against most carefully.

Another reservation must be borne in mind. The Pauline teaching concerning the subjection of woman to man is only in the Lord. If the man is a regenerate believer, a member of the body of Christ, loving his wife as Christ loves the church, nourishing her as his own flesh and treating her as the weaker vessel, then his position is the head and the woman must acknowledge it as such. To apply this, however, to unregenerate men, or to hypocritical, unkind and brutal men is soft thinking. The subjection of a woman to the man, in the teaching of Paul, is only in the Lord. No woman should subject herself to any man who does not meet the requirements of a Christian. Even in the Christian home this position may be held only so long as both are obedient to Christ. In this position of mutual, cherished love, honor and respect, happiness reigns.

Now to observe Paul's positive teaching concerning women. In his epistle to the Philippians he addresses an unnamed yokefellow who was probably the bishop of that church, saying, "I intreat thee, also help those women which labored with me in the Gospel, with Clement also, and with other of my fellow laborers, whose names are written in the book of life." We harken back into the book of Acts for some trace of the women to whom Paul may be referring and we remember that his first work in Philippi was among the women who met by the river for prayer, one of whom had her heart opened by the Lord and whose name was Lydia. This woman was upright and worthy and soundly converted. She received Paul, Silas and Timothy into her own home during the period in which they ministered in that Roman colony. Others of the women we do not know. What their labors were, along with Clement and Paul and his fellow servants, we do not know, but Paul says that God wrote a book of remembrance of them and their names are written there. Perhaps even Paul did not remember their names, for if he had he would probably have mentioned them. These women did not preach, but they opened their homes, they prayed, they gave sacrificially, they taught other women and children and they served God in a thousand ways. One tragic thing about Church history, is that it deals with movements and notable individuals, but it passes over the essentials of the making of church history, namely, the individuals who, though they are less spectacular, are none the less heroic and who by prayers, sacrifices and devotion truly build the church of God.

In this great chapter Paul recognizes the sphere of Christian women. He calls the honor roll of the women of Christian works in Rome. Some of these had churches in their houses. Some had risked their necks for Paul. Some had labored with him in the Gospel. Some had labored much in the Lord. Some were ministers and servants of the church. The best illustration is Priscilla who was here first named in her family. We already know that Priscilla along with Aquilla had taken the mighty Apollos, that eloquent Apostle who knew only the baptism of John, and had instructed him in the way of God more perfectly. No doubt she had presented to him that great body of Christian teaching concerning the Church and concerning the Person and work of the Holy Spirit which Apollos had failed to do with his disciples at Ephesus. Priscilla had also helped Paul in temporal things. He acknowledged his indebtedness to her and also the indebtedness of the Gentile Church to her and it would be altogether arbitrary on our part to confine the activity of Priscilla to material ministrations alone. Here was a forerunner of our women missionaries, of our women Sunday-school teachers and of our consecrated women workers and givers who make up the back-bone of the Christian Church. Moreover the description of these other women who were so singled out shows that their work went beyond the mere visiting of the sick or calling upon shut-ins as modern deaconesses.

We are glad to see Paul giving recognition to these women by confessing his indebtedness to them. They had succored him many times. Eunice received him into her home after he had been stoned. Lydia received him into her home after he had been scourged. Priscilla received him into her home after the people had brought him before the seat of Gallio to be beaten. The mother of Rufus, Mary, Persis and others succored him in a time which has not been revealed to us. Paul's mention of their names one by one when he had not seen them for years revealed his fervent love for them and his appreciation for what they had done. Remember that this apostle was homeless, hunted, persecuted, despised and often tortured in one way or another, so that he needed this above all other ministries and he thanked God for it.

The Bible completely re-enforces Paul's teaching. Twice Paul quoted Gen. 3:16 which narrates the Divine punishment upon woman for her disobedience of the Divine command. But Paul suggested that this curse would be substantially lifted during this Church age by saying, "She shall be saved in childbearing, if they continue in faith." We find Peter teaching the same thing at Pentecost, quoting an Old Testament prophecy which said that God would pour out His Holy Spirit upon His sons and His daughters and that they should prophesy. We have witnessed the lifting of the curse in part upon the earth by the ease with which modern cultivation is done through mechanical help. We have seen the lightening of man's work by the introduction of the machine. We have seen the easing of women's pain by modern drugs and we have seen women put on an equality with man in a social world. Progressive liberation but not complete liberation of women has come in the New Testament dispensation. Philip had four daughters who exercised the chief gift of the early church, that of prophesying. With the exception of the ordained capacity of teaching God has placed women in a great ministry and responsibility in the church throughout this age.

II. THE HIGH POSITION OF PHEBE.

Our text introduces a particular individual woman by name Phebe. Here was a woman employed in the business of the church under the inspired apostolic sanction of St. Paul. Paul urged the Roman Christians to assist her in whatsoever business she had need of them. What was the business which drew Phebe to Rome? We have no means of knowing. It may have been some Christian organization of women. It may merely have been some phase of material business concerning property. However, when Paul commanded them to assist her and to receive her as a saint the implication is that it was business of the church. Paul put his sanction on the use of a woman in some phase of Christian endeavor. She was, however, identified with an even greater business in this trip to Rome for she carried this precious and valuable treasure of the Church, the letter to the Romans, the occasion of which was to serve to introduce her to Rome. What a humble agent God used to serve in so great a place! How easy death and danger could have overtaken this woman, but I conceive that God, knowing the purposes He had for this epistle with millions of churches and hundreds of millions of lives, dispatched a legion of angels to protect her on her way. Sometime ago a great diamond was mined in South Africa. The British Company which mined it feared what might happen to it on its journey to London, so they wrapped it carefully, then placed it in a chest, then set a strong guard over it, then dispatched it by a special boat and had it met by an armored train and a strong guard when it reached the English docks to be transferred to the vaults. Strange to say when the package was opened it only contained a lump of coal. The real diamond had been sent by the ordinary mail delivery from South Africa to London as a safer method of carrying it than the use of special guards and precautions. Today ecclesiastical authorities would send a commission of pompous men aware of their importance if they were only transferring the Codex Sinaiticus from the British Museum to New York, but Paul sent Phebe with the epistle to the Romans. Probably Phebe, the humble servant of the church, carried this letter near to her heart where thousands have carried it ever since, not to introduce them to Roman society or to

RECOGNITION OF THE MINISTRY OF WOMEN 243

the church but to the general assembly of the first-born gathered around the throne.

Here was a woman who had succored the chiefest of the apostles. In the Corinthian epistle we read that when he first came from Athens to Corinth he was weak, sick and impotent. Cenchrea was the port of Corinth. Perhaps the refugee, still ill from the scourging at Philippi, persecuted and harassed, found a refuge in her home. At any rate Phebe did a very courageous thing when she took her stand with the hounded Paul. Phebe's name shows that she was converted out of heathenism. We dislike to even read of what these Corinthians were. Paul said, "Neither fornicators, nor adulterers, nor effeminate, nor abusers of themselves with mankind, nor thieves, nor covetous, nor extortioners shall inherit the kingdom of God, and such were some of you." Cenchrea was the port for this wicked city and it certainly was no sheltered spot in which to live for Christ. Some women think that if they are to live for Jesus they must have a conducive environment. They forget that trees grow in the desert sand, that flowers bloom in Alpine heights, that Joseph lived in Egypt, that Daniel lived in Babylon and that there were saints in Caesar's household. If you can not be a Christian where you are there is no place where you could be a Christian.

Paul calls Phebe "our sister." This was no glib terminology, no affected piety. This was the sweetest, purest name which he could choose for a woman who lived like a lily in a fetid swamp and who had succored him daily. She was Paul's own sister in the Lord.

Here was a woman who was called "a minister of the Church." That literally means a deaconess, a servant, a worker in the little church of Cenchrea. What a blessing her service had been to that little group of Christians. I think of the multitudes of noble women with great difficulty serving in the footsteps of Jesus and in their different stations and I remember that Jesus said, "I came not to be ministered unto but to minister, and to give my life a ransom for many." They are following after him. Heaven will ring with their praises and be filled with their glory. Not only the great women, such as Frances Willard, Florence Nightingale and Elizabeth Fry, are servants of God in the church but so are the humblest and most obscure workers in the most difficult places. Chrysostom was called "the silver tongued." Augustine was mentally tempered as a Damascus sword. Luther was fearless as a lion. Tyndale was persevering in holy ambition. The famous personages of Church history were noted for their intellect, their piety and their accomplishments, but at the home coming of some of these faithful women, these mighty teachers of the church will stand silent with awe as the angels sing their praises and conduct them to the throne of the Lamb.

III. The Part God Has Given to You as a Woman.

This Scripture reveals that there are many ministries that a woman may perform. Chief of all is the ministry of motherhood and the giving of noble and righteous children to a decaying world. Perhaps you stand with Helena, with Monica, with Susanna Wesley, with Sarah Edwards and with the other great mothers of the ages. Then thank God for a ministry which is committed to you. It is greater to mother a beautiful Christian child than to paint Raphael's Madonnas, Michael Angelo's Angels or Rembrandt's Soldiers. It is greater than building an empire of Caesar, of Charlemagne or of Napoleon. It is greater than establishing a prospering business. It is greater than speaking with eloquence, and than governing a nation with wisdom. If the ministry of motherhood is yours let it be under heaven's care, near the portals of the church and with the support of prayer.

Your ministry may be the ministry of teaching. Then we think of the stupendous challenge of child evangelism and of the Christless homes which may be reached by consecrated women. One hundred and fifty women are laboring even now in this city to reach the unevangelized children for the Lord Jesus Christ. Seek the children out and teach them. Let us not forget that the Sunday School for more than a century has been carried on largely by women, but the need for consecrated, trained, devoted teachers is greater than ever today. If like Priscilla you know your Bible and you love the Lord, you may yet win a mighty Apollos to a greater grace and usefulness for the Lord.

Perhaps your ministry is to go as a missionary to the foreign field or even to work at home. Remember that the majority of the missionaries of the world are women and that they have gone to far away countries, on dangerous journeys, in great loneliness and with an utter denial of self to carry the name of the Saviour to those who have never heard.

The women gathered in the Upper Room with the disciples for the ten day prayer meeting preceding Pentecost. The women met with the disciples in the early church to pray for Peter when he was in prison. The women have been meeting for prayer and devotional exercises ever since. What would the prayer meetings of the world

RECOGNITION OF THE MINISTRY OF WOMEN

be without women? Perhaps God has called you to this ministry, a ministry of intercession. That is greater than preaching.

Finally, we must confess that the women have exercised the ministry of giving so that every cause of Christ in the world is dependent on them. They have the vision. They see the need. They take of their substance and, as they ministered to the Lord Jesus Christ and to Paul, they continue to minister to God's servants throughout the world.

Paul commended Phebe to the Roman Church. Phebe's character and works were sufficient to commend her in themselves. The life, the character and the works of ministering Christian women commend them to the churches of the modern world. Paul urged Phebe's assistance by the church at Rome and so we call upon the various churches and assemblies to assist women to perform their business, their vision for Christ in the world. Paul constantly held these women up to God in prayer and so we this day commend them to God for His richest blessing, His providential care and a higher and wider ministry.

XXIV
ESTABLISHED IN CHRIST

XXVI—Preaching in Romans

Text: *"Now to him that is of power to stablish you according to my gospel, and the preaching of Jesus Christ, according to the revelation of the mystery, which was kept secret since the world began . . . be glory through Jesus Christ, forever."*—Rom. 16:17-27.

THE epistle to the Romans is recognized by all as the foundation epistle of New Testament doctrine. The other epistles of Paul go on from the foundation laid in this epistle. Thus, though Romans was not the first epistle written by Paul, we believe that the Divine order is followed in placing it first. In Romans Paul presents Christ as God's righteousness for the believer, as a result of which the believer has the witness of the Spirit that he is the child of God. The subject in I Corinthians is not Christ our righteousness, but Christ our wisdom. In II Corinthians we find Christ our sufficiency. In Galatians we have the perfecting of our faith in Christ. In Ephesians the believer on earth is viewed as seated with Christ in the heavenlies. In Philippians Paul himself becomes the example of a believer running the wonderful course toward the goal in the coming day of Christ. In Colossians the believer is represented as a heavenly man on earth. And in I and II Thessalonians the two phases of the Lord's second coming are presented.

Returning to this foundation epistle of Romans, we note that Paul proclaimed his purpose in writing and also in coming to Rome to be the end that they may be established. That a great church existed in Rome was publicized everywhere, but since Paul had never taught them personally, as he had the Christians of other churches, he wrote these foundation truths in an epistle. In the conclusion of this epistle he expressed his delight in the obedience of the Roman Church to the gospel, but he also knew that they needed the Divine revelation which had been made to him in order to be established. For this purpose he wrote to them. We also need this revelation today for there are many Christians who are not instructed in the truth. Paul knew that divisions would threaten the church of Rome as they had already wrought their havoc in the church of Corinth from which he was writing. His epistles to Corinth, completed before this time, reveal a severe upheaval in that church brought to pass by these very divisions. He was exceedingly desirous, therefore, of having a foundation laid in the truth for a unity in the church at Rome which could not be shaken. He desired that the Roman Christians should be established beyond the power of false teachers to unsettle. Thus he said, "Mark them which cause divisions and offenses contrary to the doctrine which you have learned; and avoid them."

The closing scene of this epistle is interesting, for undoubtedly as Paul finished its dictation some of his kinsmen and friends and fellow workers of the church of Corinth were present, not the least of whom was Timothy, his constant companion, his son in the Lord and his true successor in the missionary labors. Among others, Gaius his host was present. According to the Corinthian epistle Gaius was baptized by Paul, and unquestionably was a leading citizen of Corinth. Another leading citizen was Erastus the treasurer of the city. Evidently he later laid down his office and became a companion of Paul. Tertius was the amanuensis to whom Paul dictated his epistle. These Corinthian brethren were dwelling in the finest unity and were an example unto the church at Rome whom they saluted.

Paul seemed to be aware that a shaking would take place in the church of Rome which probably would unsettle the faith of many. If his teaching was an antedote for such unsettling events it ought to be of value to us in this present time of world shaking which is unsettling many men. He foresaw the causes of these experiences in the coming of teachers of error, in divisions between Christians themselves, in suffering caused by external opposition, in sin which remained in the lives of believers and in the Satanic system of the world. The Roman Church certainly passed through that time of shaking. However, even with the record of history of what happened to the Christians in Rome, we believe that there never was a time when the church was being shaken and sifted as it is today. The book of Hebrews says, "Now he hath promised saying, yet once more I shake not the earth only, but also heaven; and this word, yet once more, signifieth the removing of those things that are shaken, as of things that are made, that those things which can not be shaken may remain." In a time such as this only that which is built on the true foundation, which is established by God, will remain.

This brief benediction is the parting blessing of the apostle and in it Paul returned to the power of God which is able to establish men. This power according to Paul's statement is shown in his gospel, that is, the truth which he presents in the book of Romans. Second, it is shown in the Person of Christ who is the center of the gospel and of divine power. Third, it is shown in the revelation of the mystery, which is the church. Here we have a suggestion of future truth which is not revealed in this great epistle, but was yet to be written by the Apostle Paul.

I. THOSE WHO ARE TO BE ESTABLISHED—THE BELIEVERS.

Paul said, "Now to him that is of power to stablish you." Those to be established were the Roman believers or the church. Believers since the Cross are not established individually but collectively, as a Church. On the day of Pentecost, God baptized into Christ by the Holy Spirit those in the upper room and potentially all true believers thereafter. By this experience the Apostles truly knew the mystery of Christ, namely, their union with Him in glory. They realized that Christ had been glorified in heaven and that the gift of the Holy Ghost was the revelation of the glorified Christ to their souls. They entered into a privilege which had been concealed from all creatures until that moment. Nevertheless it was given to the Apostle Paul to expound to God's saints the doctrine of this heavenly mystery or secret. He became the revealer to all men of the glorious things connected with this mystery. These things were called by Paul "my gospel."

The Old Testament Scriptures never spoke of this mystery called the church. They testified of the necessary sufferings of the Messiah, in their types, in their offerings and in the teachings of the Psalms and the Prophets. In fact, Christ said to His disciples, "All things must be fulfilled, which were written in the law of Moses, and in the prophets, and in the psalms, concerning me. . . . Thus it is written, and thus it behooved Christ to suffer, and to rise from the dead on the third day." From Moses to Malachi the Bible told of a suffering Messiah, bruised for our iniquities and upon whose body were laid the stripes of our chastenment. But the Old Testament Scriptures knew nothing of the mystery of the Church, which had been hid from eternity. Though this is still called a mystery, it is now no longer hidden, but is fully revealed. The mystery of the Church may be known to all who take the trouble to read the Scriptures.

What do we mean by this mystery of the Church? The Bible tells us that God had a sovereign purpose to take certain of His creatures into His own glory in order that they might share that glory. He desired also that these creatures should know Him in His nature as Love and be with Him, in that blissful atmosphere of pure love forever. This group of people constitute the Church. Concerning them our Lord's words in the wonderful prayer of John 17 apply. He prayed that they might be kept from the evil one, that they might be sanctified in the truth, that they might be perfected into one, and that they might be with Him in glory forever. It is the desire of Christ that these saved ones shall share His glory forever. Certain creatures were to be brought into Divine glory and manifested with Christ in glory. To this end God manifested Himself in Christ, revealing His infinite love, grace, mercy, tenderness, gentleness and patience. God was seen by His creatures on earth. After revealing fully His gracious love towards sinners, God in the Son went to the Cross, there also revealing His holiness in punishment of sin, combined with His love capable of bearing the sin of a world which rejected the Son. By means of identification with Christ this body of people, chosen in Christ, are cut off from their relationship to the old Adam and begin a new relationship to the Son of God. God said that whom He foreknew He foreordained to be conformed to the image of His Son that He might be the first born among many brethren. The saved become brothers of Christ. The Scripture goes on to declare concerning the saved that in this mystery Christ would be in us dwelling in our hearts by faith in the energy of the Holy Ghost. We are in Christ and He is in us, being energized by the Holy Spirit. This group joined with Christ is to be fashioned anew in the likeness of His glory, and in the ages to come will show forth the exceeding riches of God's grace in Christ Jesus. Moreover, these redeemed ones are, as Christ's bride, to share his dominion in the ages to come. This destiny of the Church is equal to the destiny of Christ Himself.

Now this "mystery," which was hid in the counsels of God from eternity, was manifested through the apostles, and is clearly understood in this age. It is made known by "the writings of the prophets." I take this to mean the New Testament prophets, and the phrase to refer to their inspiration under which God, through St. Paul in particular, made known the nature of this Church as the bride of Christ. God also commanded that this truth is to be "made known to all nations for the obedience of faith." Into this body of Christ, which is the Church, are to go people of all kindreds, tongues and nations who are redeemed by the blood of the Lamb. The call is now going forth to the world by means of evangelism and missions in order to gather out those who will believe and who will be obedient unto the faith. This forming of the body of Christ will continue until God's purpose is complete, until "the fulness of the Gentiles" comes in. When the fullness is come, the bride shall be taken to enter upon her glorious destiny. This mystery of the Church is known by individuals through being baptized into the body of Christ by the new birth. Paul prayed for these saying, "That you may know what is the hope of his calling," that is, that one may utterly know that his sinful history was ended at the Cross, that the resurrected Christ is a heavenly Christ, that he has been joined unto that Christ, and that the life of Christ as a new creature now manifests itself in the believer.

Paul stated that God was of power to establish according to the preaching of Christ. This preaching of Christ is the means of being a member of the Church, is the way to start men on the Christian course. Nothing can be more conducive to awakening a desire in sinners to be participants of this great destiny and in saints to be established than the preaching of Christ according to this mystery of the Church. No one, but those joined to the great apostate spirit Satan, can hear of this and not wish to join in progress toward that end. We remember that faith cometh by hearing, and hearing by the Word of God. Yet, mighty obstacles stand in the way to men being established in this course leading to glory. To these we will give our attention as Paul singled them out and gave the remedies for them in this foundation epistle.

II. THINGS WHICH UNSETTLE BELIEVERS.

J. Coates has used the figure of a steeplechase or of a hurdle race to illustrate these matters which unsettle men in their march toward glory. The sinner, the common, ordinary man, gains a view of this wonderful goal which is the glory of God shared by men for all eternity. As a result he sets out to pursue it and to obtain that goal, but suddenly he is brought to stop by a fence so thick and so high that he must despair of ever getting over it by his own efforts. This fence is nothing else than the sins of which he is personally guilty. One can not go very far toward the glory of God and the image of His Son without finding that he himself is a guilty sinner. This is the difficulty with following the example of Christ as a method of salvation. We can not follow Him because we have the obstacle of sins to overcome, whereas He had none.

ESTABLISHED IN CHRIST 251

As soon as the ordinary man, who starts on the course of glory, comes to this first fence he finds that he is not alone. There he meets three men who are also stopped by the fence. The picture of these men is drawn for us in Romans 1 and 2. First there is the profligate sinner, a corrupt heathen, who has thrown off all the natural restraints of conscience, of the revelation of God in nature and of the evidences of his reason. This corrupt individual is stopped by the fence of his own sins from going on any farther. The second individual is a moralist who is able to tell anybody and everybody what is right and wrong, without himself being any better than they. He too is stopped by his own sins. The third man is a religious man who has a Bible and a knowledge of the true God, but who lets these things be mere external matters instead of a part of his life. These three individuals represent every class of the unsaved and Paul shows them all brought to a standstill before this first great hurdle.

The nature of this fence or barrier is described in Rom. 3:9-23. There we learn of the sins of all men. Every man has sinned and come short of the glory of God; every mouth is stopped before God; no man can justify himself, because he is a sinner in his own right. God's laws have been disobeyed and broken. As a result a sense of condemnation rests upon the individual and he is stopped by the barrier of his guilt. He can go no farther. He is done. He is shaken from his course and from his goal. He is excluded from further trial.

However, some get over this barrier and they get over it very easily, for the simple reason that they have been helped. It is easy to recognize that you know how that barrier is surmounted. We shall tell you later as we have told you before, but suffice it now to recognize that those who go on are a glorious company, not so many as before, but still a multitude. Now again the going seems smooth. All are happy, bright and joyful as they pursue the goal. A sense of triumph is enjoyed because of the great hurdle which has been passed and the ease with which it was taken. If you want to witness pure pleasure you will find nothing like that which exists among a group of new converts to Christianity. They delight in their Bible reading, in their testimony concerning what Christ has done for them, in their winning of others, in their meeting together for mutual consultation, and altogether they are as happy as larks. The world for them seems to be a pleasant place and they are moving rapidly on toward their goal.

But these believers are suddenly brought to their second stop with a jolt. Now they are faced by a greater fence, more formidable and insurmountable than the first one. Suddenly they discover that evil is present with them, just as much as the desire to be pure is present with them. Unquestionably they have a will to go on, an intention to be free from sins, but something hindered them. Suddenly they were caught in sin. Now every effort is made by diligent prayer, by more assiduous Bible reading, by more faithful attendance at worship, by engaging in doing good, by mortification of desires, by formulation of resolutions, but all of these things fail. Sin is still present. Evil is still grasping them and causing them to sin. Now this fence or obstacle is called sin, not sins. It actually refers to our sinful self, to a second personality different from the new creature which has been created in Christ. That second self is always with us, dogging our heels. He turns our personality into an arena of conflict between Dr. Jekyl and Mr. Hyde. Do what we please, we can not be free from this vile and hideous monster who is present in our lives.

This second self is the old Adam, the fallen man. It is sin. Paul described it by saying, "If, then, I do that which I would not, it is no more I that do it, but sin that dwelleth in me." He made a distinction between himself, as born again and desiring to do right, and sin, which dwelt in him, compelling him to do wrong and from which he longed for deliverance. We must simply recognize that as children of the fallen Adam we are bad in source and stock. We may set ourselves to keep the Ten Commandments, we may try to walk in the footsteps of Jesus, and we may attempt to carry out the instructions given in the epistles, but the result is failure and the more we struggle the more we fail. This dread experience of wrestling with one's sin nature shakes and unsettles numerous people who as believers have passed the first great hurdle of the guilt of their sins.

But there is a way past even this great obstacle and many have discovered it to their joy. The blessing of entering the place of victory over sin is quite comparable to the great joy of receiving the forgiveness of sin. Paul cried out, "Who shall deliver me?" and then as deliverance came, "I thank God Jesus Christ." With some people the passing of the second hurdle brings much greater joy and contentment than the first. Yet we are not to think that all is now to be smooth in this Christian course. There is still another terrible hurdle that remains. It is called suffering. We live today in a world of suffering. We see the brutality of war, with what seems to be unequaled suffering. We witness the ravages of disease, and we know something of the frustration of disappointed hopes, until we think that the suffering of our little day surpasses that of all others, but it has always been thus. Suffering has always been in the world. But for some, worse than suffering in general is the suffering of the righteous. To see a good man innocently suffering under the cruelty and barbarousness of modern evil is unsettling to many. Even to see the trials through which believers in enlightened places like America must sometimes undergo is a test. Some, seeing this, grow bitter and accuse God, because of the problem of suffering. Usually, however, the ones who do the suffering are not the ones who are embittered, especially if they are Christians. Usually God gives them sufficient grace to meet their suffering. It is not my purpose at this point to answer the problem of suffering. Perhaps no sufficient answer can be given, but only sufficient grace to endure it. We have already recently made the suggestion that much of the suffering of the righteous is caused by the authority and the attack of Satan against them in his role of the accuser of the brethren. Another suggestion is that suffering is the cosmic result of evil in the world in which the righteous and the evil suffer alike. At least we are sure that our bodies are not yet redeemed and we, together with all the creation, wait and groan together for the redemption of the human body. What a tragedy it is for any one to be stopped at this hurdle in his movement toward glory! If one passes the barrier of sins and the great obstacle of sin itself, let him take care not to be defeated by suffering.

But Paul describes in this great epistle one more thing which is a great barrier and which is the final barrier to our becoming like Christ. This is the satanic scheme of things called the world and worldliness. The practical part of the epistle is based upon the truth that we are living in a world which is ascribed to Satan's control, over which he is the god and the ruler. Therefore John said, "Love not the world, neither the things that are in the world. If any man love the world, the love of the Father is not in him, for all that is in the world, the lust of the flesh, and the lust of the eyes, and the pride of life; it is not of the Father, but is of the world." Again James says, "Friendship of the world is enmity with God." This conformity to the satanic system is the last hurdle to be taken by the believer. We are not talking about clothes or food or laws or externals. The separation and divorce between the Christian and the world must be in a heart attitude, not in externals alone. A true child of God is not of this world and, like his Lord, he may be actually hated by it. This world system is manifested in property, government, actions and relationships. In the midst of them the Christian is to recognize himself as a pilgrim in a foreign land, bearing the stamp of the image of Christ and moving on to glory. If you can pass this hurdle and win victory over the world you are near the end of the race, you are being conformed unto His image, you are accomplishing that which is urged so often and summarized in the words, "Let us lay aside every weight, and the sin which doth so easily beset us, and let us run with patience the race that is set before us, looking unto Jesus the author and finisher of our faith."

III. That Which Will Establish Believers.

God has given a means for the believer to take each hurdle in this course of the Christian life. That instrument is the person of the Lord Jesus Christ. For sins we have the propitiation of the Cross of Christ, for sin we have union with the burial and resurrection of Christ, for suffering we have identification with Christ, and for Satan's system, worldliness, we have the transforming of our minds into the image of Christ. God establishes believers by the preaching of Jesus Christ.

Remember the first great barrier was constituted by our sins and before these sins and their guilt many have been stopped. Some have tried repentance, reformation, prayers, the taking of the sacraments and various good works, but none of these things have ever taken the past away. They are effectively stopped. By their own efforts they are impotent to cross the barrier.

Paul no sooner tells us of this great barrier than he announces the means of overcoming it. "Being justified freely by His grace, through the redemption that is in Christ Jesus." Here Paul reveals that only God can take us over the barrier. First there is grace which is nothing else than the boundless love of the heart of God going out to sinners and acting for their blessing though they deserve nothing but punishment. This grace is the source of a full and free discharge of the burden and guilt of sins. Next there is the redemption which is in Christ Jesus. Our holy and righteous God, even though He be a God of love, would not and could not clear away the guilt of our sins in an unrighteous way. He was unable to make light of the awful guilt of our sins. Hence a stupendous work was done by Jesus on the Cross to glorify God even in the forgiveness of sin and to enable believers to be utterly clear of all guilt. Thus God's grace reaches us through the redemption which is in Christ Jesus. We may be justified from every charge of the guilt of sins because of faith in the Person and work of Jesus.

By the Person of Jesus Christ we have passed the barrier. Identified with him we have easily gone over it, for He carried us. He took "our sins in His body on the tree." As soon as the sinner repents and confesses his sins, they are laid upon Christ and the guilt is taken away. His faith in the blood is counted unto Him for righteousness. The hurdle is passed and forward he goes toward the image of the Lord Jesus Christ.

For the second barrier we have the burial and the resurrection of Christ. Having examined this barrier and seen that it consisted of our old nature, constantly brought into evidence by attempting to force it into the mold of righteousness, we realize that every human effort fails. Now a second body of truth concerning Christ avails. In this epistle, Paul tells of the two federal representatives, Adam and Christ, two kingdoms, darkness and light, two results, death and life, and he makes it plain that by faith we are to reckon ourselves to have died, to have been buried with Christ, and to have risen with Him in the new life. Hence by faith we sever the old connections with Adam and we live as a new creation in Christ. This great fact is made real to us by our supplanting the law as a motive of obedience with the Spirit as the energizing power of God in our lives. Christ fulfilled the law so that we are under it no longer. The indwelling Spirit now brings the victory through grace. What God expects from us in holiness and righteousness is now fulfilled in the power of the Spirit. Not the terrific efforts of self-will ever can take this second barrier, but the power and strength of the indwelling Holy Spirit.

For the third barrier, that of suffering, we have as a means of crossing it identification with Christ in life. Paul said, "The Spirit beareth witness with our spirit that we are the children of God, and if children, then heirs of God, and joint heirs with Christ. If so be that we suffer with him, that we may be glorified together, for I reckon that the sufferings of this present time are not worthy to be compared with the glory which shall be revealed in us." Yes, our present sufferings work out for us a far more eternal weight of glory. Christ suffered on earth in a satanic system, which oppressed Him and rejected Him and ultimately crucified Him. He warned His disciples that the servant is not greater than his Lord. "If they have persecuted me, they will also persecute you . . . if they have hated me they will also hate you." But the Holy Spirit, who witnesses that we are God's children, and fellow heirs with Christ, also witnesses according to Paul that all things work together for good for them that love God, to them who are called according to His purpose. Yes, in this great hurdle of suffering we are joined with our Christ. The promises of Christ are ours.

Finally, in meeting this great obstacle of worldliness Paul said, "I beseech you therefore, brethren, by the mercies of God, that you present your bodies a living sacrifice, holy, acceptable unto God, which is your reasonable service. And be not conformed to this world, but be ye transformed, by the renewing of your mind, that ye may prove what is that good, and acceptable, and perfect will of God." The fight against worldliness and the satanic system will continue as long as we live in this world. Conformity to the world will ruin our testimony. Therefore this wonderful section (Rom. 12:1-15:13) of practical advice was given by Paul to describe the life of the believer in the world. The believer is not to think of himself more highly than he ought to think. The believer is to mind not high things but to condescend to men of low estate. The believer is not to be wise in his own conceits. The believer is to earnestly attempt to render good for evil in fulfillment of the Sermon on the Mount. The believer is to be subject to the higher authorities. The believer is to be awake and clothed in the armor of light. The believer is to take care lest he cause his brother to stumble. And the believer is to follow the example of the Lord Jesus Christ. Through the Holy Spirit, Christ is in us and by His power He will work out His will in us, conforming to His blessed image. "Now are we the sons of God, and it doth not yet appear what we shall be; but we know that, when he shall appear, we shall be like him: for we shall see him as he is."

To be thus established, immoveable and unshaken in grace will be the effect of this gospel of God in Christ when it is seriously obeyed. Now therefore, "to him that is of power to stablish you according to my gospel, and the preaching of Jesus Christ, according to the revelation of the mystery, which was kept secret since the world began, but now is manifest, and by the scriptures of the prophets, according to the commandment of the everlasting God, made known to all nations for the obedience of faith; to the only wise God, be glory through Jesus Christ, forever." Amen.

www.ingramcontent.com/pod-product-compliance
Lightning Source LLC
Chambersburg PA
CBHW050849230426
43667CB00012B/2214